The BabyName Personality Survey

by
Bruce Lansky
and
Barry Sinrod

Meadowbrook Press

Distributed by Simon & Schuster
New York

Library of Congress Cataloging-in-Publication Data

Lansky, Bruce and Barry Sinrod

   The Baby Name Personality Survey

1 Names, Personal—Psychological aspects—Dictionaries. 2. Names, Personal—United States—Dictionaries.

   I. Sinrod, Barry. II. Title.

   CS2377.L37 1990   929.4'4'0321   88-27142

ISBN 0-88166-164-3 (pbk.)

Editorial Coordinator: Elizabeth Weiss
Cover Photo Collage: Anne Marie Hoppe
Text Design: Jennifer Nelson
Production Manager: Patsey Kahmann

Simon & Schuster Ordering #: 0-671-68382-9

Copyright © 1990 by Meadowbrook Press

Published by Meadowbrook Press, 18318 Minnetonka Boulevard, Deephaven, MN 55391.

BOOK TRADE DISTRIBUTION by Simon & Schuster, a division of Simon & Schuster, Inc., 1230 Avenue of the Americas, New York, NY 10020.

93 92 91   5 4 3 2

Printed in the United States of America.

Dedication:

To Doug and Dana, who like their names, I'm happy to say, even though I hadn't studied 75,000 survey responses before naming them.

Bruce Lansky

To but a few of the GREAT NAMES in my life . . .

Dr. Alan, Andy, Barbara, Bill, Blake, David, Eta, Fanny, Gail, Gene, Hal, Harry, Hillary, Irene, Jodey, Linda, Lenny, Marlo, Mel, Nat, Robin, Shelly, and Alexander Harry, our first grandchild.

With Love,

Barry M. Sinrod

CONTENTS

INTRODUCTION

This may be the most helpful book ever written for parents who want to select a name that will give their child a head start in life.

It is based on the fact that our first impressions of others are often influenced by their names. Because we are exposed to many of the same movies, TV shows, books, magazines, newspaper headlines, comic strips, and other forms of mass culture, we share many of the same images and stereotypes about names. For example, most people would match the personality traits and names listed below the same way

Personality Traits	Girls' Names	Boys' Names
dumb	Vanna	Elmer
intelligent	Agatha	Adlai
funny	Lucy	Dudley
elegant	Jacqueline	Alastair

Most of us associate the names listed above with real and fictional people whose images have shaped our perceptions of those names: Vanna ("Wheel of Fortune") White and Elmer ("Looney Tunes") Fudd; Agatha Christie and Adlai Stevenson; Lucille ("I Love Lucy") Ball and Dudley (*Arthur*) Moore; Jacqueline Kennedy Onassis and Alastair ("Masterpiece Theater") Cooke.

It is almost impossible to think of some uncommon names like Adolph or Elvis without thinking of their most famous namesakes: Adolph Hitler and Elvis Presley. Other uncommon names that bring to mind very clear mental pictures that most of us share are Madonna, Roseanne, Laverne, Elton, Gomer, and Rocky.

However, you are probably not thinking of naming your child Madonna or Gomer. You remember how cruel teasing can be during childhood — often because of an uncommon name. You would like your child to be accepted by his or her peers and have a good self image. It could help to give your child a name that is perceived positively. As you consider a number of different names, you will realize that you do not have as clear an image of John, for example, as you do of Rocky. And, unfortunately, you do not really know how others perceive the names you like best.

For example, as you think about the name Elizabeth you might picture Great Britain's Queen Elizabeth, Elizabeth Taylor, Elizabeth ("Bewitched") Montgomery, or Elizabeth Barrett ("How do I love thee?") Browning. You might think of Elizabeth as regal, glamorous, magical, or romantic. How do others think of Elizabeth?

This book is designed to help you answer that question for many common, popular, and even unusual names. It is organized into two main sections to make it both easy and fun to select an appropriate name for your baby.

The first section contains a list of adjectives describing physical, personality, life style, and other attributes (for example, freckled, funny, French, and flighty). Under each adjective, you will find the boys' and girls' names people most often associate with it. You can use this list as follows:

I. Ask yourself what traits you admire. Look up those traits and see what names are associated with them.

2. Scan the lists. You will find other traits that appeal to you. See what names are associated with them.

3. Finally, make a list of the names that reflect the traits that appeal to you. These are names worth considering further.

Then, turn to the second section of the book, which contains an alphabetical list of over 1400 boys' and girls' names complete with derivation, literal meaning, and famous namesakes. Most important, each listing also contains a composite image or personality profile based on what a sample of about 50 people had to say about the image associated with each name. This unique information gives you a more complete picture of each name — particularly of how other people view it. Use this list in the following way:

I. Look up the names you selected when reading the first section of this book to gain a better picture of the image associated with each name.

2. Think about your own impression of the names you are considering, your spouse's impression, and other peoples' impressions.

3. List the pros and cons of each name your are considering.

4. Finally, pick the names that sound good, look good, feel good, and make sense as a "label" that will last a lifetime.

If you have possible names for your baby already picked out, go straight to the Personality Profile section, which includes many more names than are listed under First Impressions.

I hope that the process of naming your baby is a pleasure for you. I hope you will agree that by considering the impression that names make on people you will be able to make a wise choice.

Bruce Lansky

ABOUT THE RESEARCH

When Bruce Lansky approached me with the idea of developing a research project to discover the images, associations, and stereotypes evoked by many well-known, popular, and even unusual names, my first thought was that it would be a massive undertaking. Most research of this type starts with a limited number of personality traits, such as intelligence, attractiveness, and athleticism, and asks people to match names and traits. From the start, Bruce ruled out that approach. He wanted me to find out the actual words people themselves used to describe the physical, psychological, ethnic, and behavioral traits associated with each name.

To accomplish this objective, we sent out 150,000 questionnaires to a nationally representative sample of men and women of all ages from urban, suburban, and rural locations in all 50 states. We used such a huge sample in order to capture a collective portrait of the personal characteristics associated with each name.

We asked four questions:

1. What image association comes to mind when you hear the name?

2. What kind of personality would a person with this name have?

3. What would a person with this name look like?

4. What well-known people share this name?

In our pretests, we had discovered that there was a limit to the number of names a respondent could handle. Therefore, we sent only ten names to each respondent, who on average sent back reactions to over half of the names. However, we discovered that some names did not evoke a clear image or association for many people. Therefore, we sent these names to more people in order to get enough responses to form a clear image of each of them. We sought to obtain at least 30 responses for each name, as it was extremely difficult to detect a pattern for names with less data. We dropped any names for which there were less than 30 responses or for which no clear image emerged.

Altogether, we received responses from over 75,000 people, making this the biggest survey of name images and stereotypes ever conducted, to the best of my knowledge. What I passed on to Bruce were between 30 to 150 responses — 50 on average — for each name in the book. It was his job to turn this data into clear and accurate composite descriptions of what people would expect someone with a particular name to be like. Believe me, reconstructing a consensus portrait from 30 to 150 pieces of data is not an easy task! As a professional researcher, I know that turning such data into coherent descriptions involves a certain amount of intuition and subjective judgement. For the most part, however, the descriptions in this book reflect actual language used by respondents with a minimum of editorializing.

A word of warning: Please do not jump to the conclusion that we are calling all Berthas fat or all Ivans terrible. As you read this book, bear in mind that we are simply revealing a consensus of opinion evident in the data. We hope you will find this information useful and informative, whether you are trying to name your baby or are just curious to find out what image your name or your friends' and relatives' names evoke.

Barry Sinrod

FIRST IMPRESSIONS OF GIRLS' NAMES

ACTIVE
Sonia
Stacy

ADVENTUROUS
Amelia

AGGRESSIVE
Lucinda
Oprah

AIRHEAD
Aurora
Fifi
Lacie
Suzanne
Trixie

ALL-AMERICAN
Sue

ALOOF
Sasha

AMBITIOUS
Eleanor
Kelly
Leigh

ANGELIC
Gabrielle

ANIMAL (name for)
Bessie
Elsie
Fifi
Kiki
Queenie

ARTISTIC
Marie
Zoë

ASIAN
Yoko

ATHLETIC
Chris
Colleen
Dena
Jessie
Jody
Katie
Lindsay
Martina
Steffi

ATTRACTIVE
Antonia
Caroline
Charlene
Jackie
Lucinda
Margo

AVERAGE
Doreen
Jean
Marsha
Ruth

BEAUTIFUL
Amanda
Ava
Blair
Candace
Celeste
Christina
Cinderella
Crystal
Desirée
Ebony
Elise
Elizabeth
Gloria
Lily
Linda
Morgan
Raquel
Rhonda
Shauna
Tara

BIBLICAL
Delilah
Jezebel

BIG
Anna
Aretha
Flo
Freda
Janine
Matilda
Tanya

BLACK
Alma
Aretha
Cassandra
Coretta
Deandra
Dionne
Eartha
Ebony
Kendra
Leona
Mahalia
Mamie
Oprah
Ruby
Simone
Sophie
Willa
Winona

BLACK HAIR
Abby
Yvonne

BLONDE
Bambi
Barbie
Brigitte
Bunny
Candy
Charlene
Christy
Cynthia

BLONDE (cont.)
Daisy
Dolly
Doreen
Doris
Faith
Farrah
Heather
Heidi
Inga
Jillian
Lara
Linda
Lorelei
Lorna
Madonna
Marcia
Marilyn
Marnie
Olivia
Randi
Rhonda
Sally
Shannon
Sheila
Tracy
Tricia
Trixie
Vanna

BLUE EYES
Cynthia
Linda

BOSSY
Joyce
Matilda
Myrna

BOUNCY
Suzie

BRIGHT
Alana
Courtney
June

BROWN EYES
Mallory

BUBBLY
Barb

BUSINESSLIKE
Alberta
Lorraine
Sylvia

BUXOM
Dolly
Lurleen

CALM
Amy
Hope

CAPABLE
Jean

CAREFREE
Isabel
Lottie

CARING
Vicki

CASUAL
Billie

CATHOLIC
Annamaria

CHEERFUL
Doris
Florence
Happy
Jody
Merry
Mitzi
Polly

CHILDLIKE
Annie
Barbie

Heidi
Sissy
Tabitha

CHUBBY
Mirabel

CHUNKY
Courtney
Patti

CLASSY
Jillian
Kay
Marjorie
Marlo

COLD
Chloris
Kay

**COLLEGE
GRADUATE**
Cassie

COMMON NAME
Jennifer

CONCEITED
Blair

CONFIDENT
Rosalie

COOL
Marlena

COUNTRY
Clementine
Dottie
Jenny
Jocelyn
Jolene
Patsy
Sadie
Tess
Willa

CURLY HAIR
Marlena
Shirley

CUTE
Annie
Becca
Bobbie
Caitlin
Cassie
Cheryl
Christy
Corey
Deanna
Debbie
Dee Dee
Denise
Dodie
Emily
Jennifer
Jody
Kari
Kate
Kim
Kitty
Kristi
Lacie
Lana
Leah
Mallory
Mandy
Marcie
Marlo
Megan
Mindy
Nanette
Peggy
Randi
Serena
Shannon
Shirley
Stacy
Steffi
Suzie
Tammy
Trudy

DARK
Gabrielle
Lainie
Lena
Lisa
Lucinda
Margo
Natalie
Natasha

DARK EYES
Marisa

DARK HAIR
Ali
Darlene
Haley
Liza
Marisa
Teresa

DELICATE
Iris

DELIGHTFUL
Joy

DETERMINED
Sandra

DOMINEERING
Alexandra
Esther

DOPEY
Dodie
Twyla

DOWDY
Hazel
Hilda

DOWN-HOME
Carly
Sissy

DREAMER
Ava
Gigi

DUMB
Bambi
Bunny
Candy
Daisy
Daphne
Honey
Kiki
Mallory
Vanna

DUMPY
Irma

EARTHY
Becky
Eartha

EDUCATED
Amy
Monica

ELEGANT
Catherine
Dionne
Jacqueline
Simone
Victoria

ELITE
Valerie

ENERGETIC
Cathy
Nikki
Rosie

ENGLISH
Chelsea

ENTHUSIASTIC
Roxanne

EUROPEAN
Anastasia
Francesca

EXCITING
Francesca
Shauna

EXOTIC
Nina
Nyssa
Sabra
Xaviera
Zola

EXTRAVAGANT
Tammy
Zsa Zsa

FAMILY-ORIENTED
Annamaria
Carol
Kathleen

FASHIONABLE
Jackie

FAT
Bertha
Beryl
Denise
Hilda
Henrietta
Lottie
Lulu
Olga

FEMININE
Alisha
Marina
Roxanne

FLIGHTY
Hilary
Lorraine

FLIRT
Bunny
Lurleen

Melanie
Priscilla
Trixie

FOREIGN
Alana
Bianca
Frederica
Nyssa
Sasha
Sonia
Zena
Zola

FRAIL
Emily
Lillian

FRECKLED
Belinda
Lydia
Maggie
Patricia
Sissy

FREE-SPIRITED
Alice
April
Dena
Steffi

FRENCH
Colette
Danielle
Dominique
Françoise
Gabrielle
Gigi
Giselle
Mimi
Simone
Yvette

FRIEND
Adelaide
Elaine
Janice
Joyce
Karen

FRIENDLY
Bernadette
Bobbie
Bonnie
Carol
Christy
Dorothy
Elaine
Georgia
Gwen
Joy
Julianne
Kathy
Kim
Lila
Marcie
Millie
Nancy
Nikki
Opal
Patricia
Rhoda
Rose
Ruby
Sandy
Vivian
Wendy

FRIVOLOUS
Tiffany

FUN
Anita
Bridget
Debbie
Gillian
Jenny
Maggie
Melinda
Mickie
Sally
Tina

FUN-LOVING
Dixie
Gerri
Imogene
Joyce
Liza

FUN-LOVING (cont.)
Marie
Marsha
Sandy

FUNNY
Erma
Gilda
Lucille
Lucy
Vivian

GENTLE
Beth
Hope

GERMAN
Freda
Heidi
Hildegarde
Greta
Gretchen
Olga

GIRL-NEXT-DOOR
Jenny
Nancy
Sally
Sheryl

GIRLISH
Stacy

GLAMOROUS
Eva

GLASSES
Dolores
Moira
Sheryl

GOOD COOK
Beatrice

GOOD-LOOKING
Julia

GORGEOUS
Gina
Rita

GOSSIP
Hedda
Ida
Rona

GRACEFUL
Giselle
Ursula

GRANDMA
Adelaide
Bea
Dora
Ella

HAPPY
Becky
Cassie
Eloise
Fanny
Gay
Happy
Joy
Marge
Rosie
Sunny

HARD WORKER
Ada
Eleanor
Ida
Ingrid
Louise
Marie
Margaret
Marjorie

HARSH
Agnes

HEAVY
Barbara
Bea
Beatrice
Fanny
Mahalia
Marsha
Mavis
Pearl

HELPFUL
Eloise
Heloise

HIGH-CLASS
Caresse

HISPANIC
Antonia
Lolita
Maria
Miranda
Marisa

HOMELY
Edna
Glenda
Imogene
Lulu

HOMEBODY
Ada
June
Millie

HORRIBLE
Henrietta

HUSKY VOICE
Marlena

INDEPENDENT
Carla
Lori
Maggie
Meredith
Paige
Pat

INTELLIGENT
Agatha
Barbara
Daria
Diana
Marcella
Vanessa

INTERESTING
Robin

IRISH
Bonnie
Colleen
Erin
Kelly
Maggie

ITALIAN
Annamaria
Antonia
Gina
Talia

JEWISH
Golda
Myra
Rhoda
Yetta

JOLLY
Merry

KIND
Arlene
Louise
Yetta

LARGE
Bella
Ella
Lane
Marjorie
Maud

LATIN
Lola
Xaviera

LEADER
Ruth

LIKABLE
Ella
Mary Beth
Mallory

LIVELY
Edie
Randi

LONG HAIR
Celia
Cher
Lori
Yvonne

LOUD
Dorothy
Dottie
Edna
Eunice
Marsha
Roseanne
Val
Verna
Zelda

LOVING
Eve
Frances
Janice
June

LOYAL
Trudy

LUSTY
Maureen

MAGIC
Minerva
Samantha

MAID
Alma
Hazel
Hilda

MATRONLY
Hildegarde
Mabel

MEAN
Velma

MIDDLE CLASS
Ann
Julia
Samantha

MISCHIEVOUS
Courtney
Missy
Sabrina
Suzanne

MOTHERLY
Charlotte
Katherine

MYSTERIOUS
Alana
Jacqueline
Lara
Lorelei
Miranda
Natasha

NASTY
Alexis
Olga

NATURAL-LOOKING
Lois

NICE
Bea
Deidre
Donna
Geraldine
Ginny
Irene
Janice
Jill
Judy
Kendra
Lila
Mary Lou
Norma
Reba
Sandy
Val

NOSY
Madge

OLD, OLDER
Ada
Alma
Aretha
Arlene
Augusta
Bea
Beatrice
Belle
Claire
Clara
Dolores
Golda
Ida
Lila
Lillian
Lois
Matilda
Maud
Mildred
Millicent
Millie
Minnie
Miriam
Mona
Myra
Myrna
Nora
Opal
Regina
Ruby
Selma
Thelma
Theodora
Violet
Wilma
Zelda

OLD-FASHIONED
Abigail
Adelaide
Adeline
Adelle
Alma
Amanda

Anna
Bea
Charlotte
Clementine
Cora
Diana
Dinah
Edith
Elsie
Emily
Emma
Esther
Eugenia
Frannie
Hattie
Henrietta
Hester
Ida
Katherine
Louise
Maggie
Mamie
Martha
Mary Ellen
Matilda
Mildred
Nellie
Nettie
Nora
Prudence
Rosalie
Thelma
Verna
Wilma

OPINIONATED
Rhea
Maud

ORDINARY
Mary

ORGANIZED
Julianne

OUTDOOR TYPE
Corey
Jo

OUTGOING
Carla
Cathy
Dolly
Ivy
Jenny
Jolene
Kate
Kerry
Kimberly
Kristi
Laverne
Lindsay
Pam
Sunny

OUTRAGEOUS
Xenia

OUTSPOKEN
Rebecca
Roz

OVERWEIGHT
Bev
Dolores
Martha
Sheila
Wynne

PERKY
Alana
Mindy
Molly

PETITE
Aileen
Brittany
Christin
Christina
Cynthia
Dixie
Kayla
Nicole

PIOUS
Hope

PLAIN
Ann
Blanche
Cara
Edith
Ginny
Jane
Joanna
Josephine
Karen
Leona
Mary Ellen
Mona
Sally
Willa

PLAYFUL
Tallulah

PLUMP
Bernadette
Charlotte
Estelle
Miriam

POPULAR
Cassie
Demi
Julianne
Mallory

PREPPY
Shelley

PRETTY
Adrienne
Aileen
Alissa
Ariel
Aurora
Bella
Belle
Bonnie
Brooke
Carmen
Cassandra
Catherine
Christin

Danielle
Dawn
Diana
Dionne
Eileen
Eve
Farrah
Fawn
Genevieve
Georgia
Greta
Gwen
Holly
Jasmine
Jewel
Jocelyn
Kendra
Kimberly
Kirsten
Lara
Laura
Lauren
Leigh
Lydia
Maria
Marie
Marisa
Naomi
Natalie
Nicole
Noreen
Roxanne
Sabrina
Samantha
Sarah
Scarlett
Simone
Stephanie
Tamara
Tanya
Tessa
Whitney

PRIM
Camille
Francine
Mildred

PRISSY
Alissa
Diana
Greta

PROMISCUOUS
Lolita

PROPER
Alissa
Annabel
Antoinette
Camille
Celeste
Constance
Francine
Judith
Regina

PRUDISH
Adeline
Harriet
Phoebe

PURE
Chastity

QUIET
Bernice
Beth
Cathleen
Chloe
Christin
Deanna
Diana
Donna
Doria
Faith
Fawn
Fay
Fern
Grace
Jocelyn
Kari
Leona
Lisa
Lori

QUIET (cont.)
Lorna
Lydia
Mary
Mia
Moira
Nina
Sheryl
Teresa
Tessa
Ursula
Violet
Yoko

QUIRKY
Tuesday

REDHEAD
Amber
Arlene
Bonnie
Ginger
Kitty
Maureen
Megan

REGAL
Alexandra
Antoinette
Elizabeth

RELIGIOUS
Agnes
Faith
Moira
Teresa

RESERVED
Moira

RICH, WEALTHY
Alexis
Amanda
Blair
Chastity
Chelsea
Christina
Crystal

Deandra
Meredith
Tiffany
Tricia
Zsa Zsa

ROMANTIC
Lily

RUSSIAN
Bella
Natasha

SCANDINAVIAN
Elke
Heidi
Helga
Inga
Kirsten
Ursula

SELF-ASSURED
Inga

SELF-CENTERED
Christa
Merry

SELF-CONFIDENT
Aileen

SELFISH
Erin

SENSIBLE
Val

SERIOUS
Catherine
Nora
Shannon
Trudy

SEXY
Alana
Bambi
Brigitte
Brooke

Honey
Jillian
Lola
Marilyn
Marlena
Marlo
Sabrina
Simone
Ursula
Zsa Zsa

SHALLOW
Merry

SHORT
Judy
Marsha
Mary Lou
Nettie
Rhea

SHY
Ariel
Fawn
Julianne
Tess

SILLY
Dee Dee
Gilda
Lulu
Myrna
Wynne

SIMPLE
Norma
Wynne

SKINNY
Talia

SLEAZY
Lola

SLENDER
Sheena

SMALL
Abby
Betty
Charity
Gilda
Kathy
Lacie
Lena
Lindsay
Martina
Mia
Nadia

SMART
Abigail
Ariel
Eleanor
Frederica
Helen
Janine
Lisa
Meredith
Rebecca
Yvonne

SMOKER
Vicki

SNOBBY
Eloise
Frederica
Kim
Kirsten
Michelle
Mindy

SNOOTY
Dominique

SOFT-SPOKEN
Ellen

SOPHISTICATED
Adrienne
Audrey
Leigh
Lane
Marlena

Mercedes
Paige
Victoria

SOUTHERN
Annabel
Belle
Charlotte
Clementine
Dixie
Ellie
Georgeanne
Georgia
Jolene
Luella
Lurleen
Mirabel
Rosalind
Tara
Winona

SPOILED
Jewel
Melinda
Melissa
Nellie

SPUNKY
Haley
Maureen

STERN
Etta

STOCKY
Wilma

STODGY
Augusta

STRANGE
Twyla
Yoko

STRICT
Josephine
Olga
Penelope
Phyllis

STRONG
Coretta
Lynn
Martha
Rhoda
Tyne

STRONG-WILLED
Erica
Felicia
Jezebel
Marlo

STUBBORN
Evelyn

STUCK-UP
Adeline
Darlene
Mimi
Nadine
Olivia
Pamela

STUDIOUS
Fern

STUFFY
Millicent

SWEET
Abby
Alissa
Angela
Bernice
Betsy
Candy
Cara
Cheryl
Cindy
Dana
Desirée
Elise
Ellie
Esther
Grace
Heather
Heidi

SWEET (cont.)
Honey
Kari
Kristi
Laura
Linda
Lori
Marian
Marie
Marjorie
Melinda
Melissa
Olivia
Pam
Peggy
Rose
Shauna
Sonia
Sue
Tammy
Teri
Wanda

TALKATIVE
Beryl
Madge
Sophie

TALENTED
Tina

TALL
Daria
Geraldine
Inga
Jill
Judith
Julie
Kim
Lynn

TEACHER
Trudy

TEMPTRESS
Jezebel

THIN
Amanda
Jill

TOMBOY
Alberta
Ali
Becky
Billie
Celia
Haley
Jo
Pat
Teri
Vicki

TOUGH
Alberta
Rhea
Roz

TRADITIONAL
Bernice
Joanna

TRENDY
Lane

TWO-FACED
Vera

UGLY
Hedda
Hester

UNATTRACTIVE
Chloris
Hortense
Lillian
Thelma

UNIQUE
Chelsea

UNISEX NAME
Bobbie
Charlie

Corey
Dana
Jody
Morgan
Noel
Ronni
Toni

UPPER-CLASS
Gwendolyn

UPTIGHT
Priscilla

VIBRANT
Carly

VIVACIOUS
Patti
Sadie

WARM
Estelle
Pat

WEIRD
Elvira
Opal

WELL-LIKED
Wanda

WELL-TRAVELED
Marina

WHINY
Wynne

WILD
Bobbie
Gypsy

WILLOWY
Blythe

YUPPIE
Diane

FIRST IMPRESSIONS
OF BOYS' NAMES

ACCOUNTANT
Hal
Myron

ADVENTUROUS
Rory

AFFLUENT
Clement

ALL-AMERICAN
Richard

ANGELIC
Gabriel

ANIMAL (name for)
Fritz
Rolf
Rusty
Siegfried

ARAB
Omar

ARISTOCRATIC
Armand
Barton
Conrad
Geoffrey
Montgomery

ARROGANT
Constantine
Gustave

ARTISTIC
Vincent

ASSERTIVE
Bart

ATHLETIC
Alex
Bart
Bjorn
Brett

Brian
Buck
Chuck
Connor
Cooper
Curt
Daniel
Derek
Jake
Jed
Jim
Jock
Kevin
Kirby
Marcus
Rod
Terry
Wes

ATTRACTIVE
Drew

AVERAGE
Artie
Bill
Bob
Dick
Doug
Graham
Jeffrey

AVERAGE INTELLIGENCE
Emmett

AWKWARD
Angus
Elmo

BALD/BALDING
Archibald
Ed
Edgar
Gavin
Mel
Solomon
Willard

BEARDED
Burl
Noah
Roland

BIBLICAL
Elijah
Ezekiel
Jeremiah
John
Saul
Zachary

BIG
Ace
Andrew
Ben
Bernard
Bruce
Bruno
Burl
Carleton
Clarence
Dallas
Rock
Wallace

BIG-BONED
Thad

BIG HANDS
Waldo

BLACK
Alphonse
Amos
Armand
Arnold
Cleon
Erasmus
Freeman
Isaiah
Jackson
Kareem
Lamar
Lamont
Leon

BLACK (cont.)
Leroy
Lionel
Muhammad
Otis
Percy
Rochester
Sanford
Terence
Theo
Tyrone

BLOND
Bjorn
Brett
Bud
Chick
Colin
Dane
Dennis
Derek
Dwayne
Eric
Josh
Keith
Kerry
Kipp
Kyle
Lars
Leif
Louis
Martin
Olaf
Sven
Tab
Van

BLUE-COLLAR
Arnie

BLUE-EYED
Sven
Toby

BOISTEROUS
Wallace

BOOKWORM
Clifford
Gaylord
Theo

BORING
Howard
Stu

BOYISH
Bobby
Donny
Jeffrey
Jimmy
Johnny
Timmy

BRAINY
Edwin
Elliott

BRAT
Dennis

BRITISH
Alastair
Byron
Clive
Chauncey
Earl
Emerson
Fairfax
Gardner
Jeremy
Nigel
Reginald
Roderick
Trevor

BULLY
Butch
Chuck

BUSINESSLIKE
Ted

BUSINESSMAN
Gregory

CAREFREE
Charlie

CASUAL
Artie
Dave

CHARMING
Dante
Victor

CHEERFUL
Bud

CHUBBY
Butch
Paddy
Rob

CLASSY
Geoffrey
DeWitt

CLEAN-CUT
Chet

CLOD
Claude

CLOWN
Ethan

CLUMSY
Clyde

COLLEGIATE
Stanford
Yale

COMIC
Alvin
Barney
Woody

CONTINENTAL
Yves

COOL
Dirk
Wade

COUNTRY
Chester
Elroy
Jess
Judd
Roy

COURAGEOUS
Noah

COWBOY
Calhoun
Cody
Cort
Dallas
Dusty
Dwayne
Roy
Shane
Travis

CRANKY
Ebenezer

CREATIVE
Elton

CRIMINAL
Leopold

CRUEL
Adolph

CUBAN
Ricardo

CUDDLY
Teddy

CURLY HAIR
Dorian
Dwayne
Russ

CUTE
Barry
Benjamin
Chick
Danny
Jon
Kipp
Linus
Louis
Matthew
Nicholas
René
Rory
Stevie
Timothy
Wade

DASHING
Errol

DARK
Alonzo
Anthony
Bart
Cain
Carlos
Chico
Cliff
Cosmo
Damien
Dmitri
Farley
Ferdinand
Gino
José
Juan
Marco
Rory

DARK HAIR
Ben
Claude
Curt
Earl
Jeffrey
Johnny
Jordan
Mario

Ray
Rick
Victor
Vinny

DEBONAIR
Errol

DECEITFUL
Oswald

DEPENDABLE
John

DESIGNER
Yves

DETECTIVE
Ephraim
Sherlock

DETERMINED
Christopher

DEVIL
Damon
Eli

DIGNIFIED
Earl

DISTINGUISHED
Averill
Bernard
Burke
Edmund

DOCTOR
Sigmund

DOMINEERING
Ivan

DRINKER
Ralph

DULL
Allen

DUMB
Abner
Elmer
Elmo
Jock

EASYGOING
Andy
Bing
Clay
Ron
Tim
Todd
Virgil
Ward

EGGHEAD
Adlai
Egbert
Engelbert

ELDERLY
Earl
Emmett
Omar
Wallace

ELEGANT
Alastair

ENGLISH
Cedric
Neville
Ogden
Winslow

ENTERTAINER
Conway

EUROPEAN
Caesar

EVIL
Damian
Damon

FARMER
Cyrus
Elmer

Emmett
Silas
Willard

FAT
Albert
Archibald
Arnold
Barney
Herbert
Hugo
Kermit
Norman
Orson
Tyler

FATHERLY
Ward

FIGHTER
Cassius

FIRM
Paul

FLIRT
Colin

FOREIGN
Armand
Herschel
Muhammad

FORMAL
Barton

FRECKLED
Elwood
Jody

FRIENDLY
Allen
Bing
Cal
Casper
Cole
Dan
Danny
Denny

Ed
Fred
Gary
Jeff
Jerry
Jim
Rob
Russ
Wally

FRENCH
André
Claude
Jacques
Marcel
Phillipe
Pierre
René

FUN-LOVING
Bradley
Chip
Denny
Jay
Jerry
Terry

FUNNY
Abbott
Allen
Archie
Artie
Carson
Chase
Dudley
Edsel
Fletcher
Grady
Jerome
Rochester
Roscoe
Sid
Tim
Vinny

FUSSY
Felix

GANGSTER
Vito

GENEROUS
Elvis

GENTLEMAN
Clive
Ramsey

GERMAN
Fritz
Ludwig
Otto
Rolf
Siegfried
Werner
Wolfgang

GLASSES
Clarence
Dexter
Edward
Gilbert
Les
Norbert
Vic

GOOD-LOOKING
Bobby
Boone
Cain
Curt
Daniel
Jeff
Jeremy
Jim
Ryan
Sean
Tyrone

GOOD-NATURED
Brad
Willie

GOOD PERSONALITY
Bud

GRAY-HAIRED
Spencer

GREEK
Constantine
Dmitri

HANDSOME
Adam
Alonzo
Bart
Beau
Blake
Burt
Christopher
Clint
Curtis
Damian
David
Dmitri
Don
Douglas
Engelbert
Grant
Humphrey
Joe
Jude
Keith
Kirk
Lorenzo
Lucas
Mitchell
Randolph
Rick
Rod
Vance
Vern
Victor

HAPPY
Alex
Patrick
Rudy

HARDHEADED
Rolf

HARDWORKING
Jake
Jed
Manuel
Ron
Todd

HE-MAN
Brian
Duke

HEAVY
Boris
Ron

HELPFUL
Elwood

HENPECKED
Wally

HICK
Clement

HILLBILLY
Clem
Cletus
Clyde
Jed
Zack
Zeke

HISPANIC
Alonzo
Carlos
Chico
Geraldo
Hector
Jesus
José
Luis
Manuel
Marco
Orlando
Pablo

HOMEBODY
Cyrus

HONEST
Abe
Abraham
Barnabas
Christian

HOTSHOT
Ace

INDEPENDENT
Drew

INTELLECTUAL
Brent
Creighton
Dag
Eugene

INTELLIGENT
Adlai
Alexander
Barton
Brock
Clifford
David
Edward
Jefferson
Jerome
John
Kenneth
Merlin
Ned
Nelson
Roderick
Samuel
Sebastian
Tim
Virgil

INVENTIVE
Benjamin
Eli

IRISH
Brian
Devin
Grady
Paddy
Pat
Patrick

ITALIAN
Angelo
Angus
Anthony
Carmine
Dominic
Gino
Marco
Mario
Roman
Romeo
Rudolph
Salvatore
Vinny
Vito

JERK
Ace

JEWISH
Micah
Sol

JOCK
Ace
Dirk

JOLLY
Andrew
Arnold
Nicholas

JOVIAL
Wally

KIND
Barnabas
Ed

KLUTZ
Clem

LANKY
Duane
Homer
Jan

LEADER
Alexander
Caesar

Dwight
Lance
Napoleon
Ulysses

LITTLE
Tommy

LONG-HAIRED
Kim

LOVABLE
Ben

LOVER
Rudolph

LOVING
Adrian
Alonzo

LOYAL
Rusty

MACHO
Carson
Jack

MAMA'S BOY
Virgil

MASCULINE
Brett
Derek
Hector
Mitchell

MEAN
Butch
Ebenezer

MEDIUM BUILD
Ted

MEEK
Cyril

MILD
Duncan

MILD-MANNERED
Wally

MINISTER
Deacon

MISCHIEVOUS
Billy
Bobby
Dennis

MISERLY
Ebenezer

MYSTERIOUS
Ellery

NARROW-MINDED
Duke

NEIGHBORLY
Waldo

NERD
Arnie
Clarence
Clifford
Creighton
Dexter
Egbert
Myron
Norman
Vern
Waldo

NERVOUS
Barney

NICE
Brendan
Burl
Cecil
Craig
Dale
Joe
Joel
Kenny

Kim
Rob
Todd

NITPICKER
Charles

NUT
Filbert

OLD, OLDER
Amos
Bertrand
Burl
Cy
Edwin
Erasmus
Ezekiel
Ezra
Grover
Harvey
Herbert
Herschel
Kermit
Lloyd
Sanford
Silas
Spencer
Stanley
Vic
Wilfred

OLD-FASHIONED
Abe
Erskine
Jerome

ORDINARY
Hal

ORIENTAL
Kim

OUTDOORSMAN
Abe
Boone
Buck

Chad
Erskine

OUTGOING
Arnie
Charlie
Dave

OVERWEIGHT
Alfred
Horton
Lanny

PLAYBOY
André
Colin
Dirk

PLUMP
Morris

POLITE
Austin

POLITICAL
Adlai

POPULAR
Eric
Joel
Kerry
Patrick
Rod

POWERFUL
Franklin
Sherwin

PREPPY
Brendan
Tyler
Yale

PROFESSOR
Neville

PROPER
Kenneth

QUIET
Aaron
Benedict
Curtis
Cy
Douglas
Gerald
Gideon
Jeremiah
Kyle
Robert
Robin

RABBI
Solomon

REDHEAD
Danny
René
Rusty
Virgil

RELIGIOUS
Barnabas
Calvin
Christian
Dominic
Emmanual
Gideon
Isaiah
Jacob
Jesus
Saul

RESERVED
Averill

RICH, WEALTHY
Bartholomew
Bradley
Brock
Burke
Cameron
Carlos
Chet

Clayborne
Clinton
Colin
Dane
Dante
Dillon
Frederick
Geoffrey
Hamilton
Harper
Jay
Jock
Jules
Kipp
Montgomery
Percy
Randolph
Roosevelt
Rupert
Sterling
Vance
Vaughn
Winslow
Winthrop
Yale

RIGHTEOUS
Deacon

RIGID
Mac
Rolf

ROMAN
Constantine

ROMANTIC
Juan
Phillipe
Pierre
Romeo

ROUGH
Dallas
Dirk

ROYALTY
Constantine

RUGGED
Clinton
Cort
Dirk
Dusty

RULER
Moses

RUSSIAN
Vladimir

RUTHLESS
Cain
Fidel

SCANDINAVIAN
Bjorn
Dane
Eric
Leif
Olaf
Sven

SCARY
Boris

SCHOLARLY
Archibald

SCOTTISH
Sean

SENSITIVE
Bradley
Joel

SERIOUS
Vincent
Vladimir

SEXY
Cliff
Dmitri
Don
Victor

SHORT
Arnold
Creighton
Dominic
Dudley
Dustin
Igor
Kermit
Kirby
Napoleon
Ralph
Solomon
Sonny
Stu
Willie

SHOW-OFF
Don

SHY
Casper
Dwayne
Joshua
Woody

SILENT TYPE
André
Morton

SINCERE
Delbert

SINGER
Elvis
Engelbert
Rick
Sonny

SINISTER
Barnabas
Boris

SISSY
Beau

SKINNY
Armand
Ebenezer
Willie

SLIM
Jay
Kim

SMALL
Danny
Joel

SMART
Abel
Adam
Allen
Benjamin
Charles
Erskine
Ethan
Jack
Miles
Norman
Walter
Wendell
Yale

SNEAKY
Vic

SNOBBY
Bradford
Percival
Prescott
Wesley

SOCIABLE
Cameron

SOFT
Jon

SOPHISTICATED
Clifton
Grant
Neville
Prescott
Vaughn

SOUTHERN
Creighton

SPOILED
Bradley
Clayborne
Devin
Timmy

SPORTS LOVER
Cy

SPORTS CAR DRIVER
Roland

SQUEAKY VOICE
Alvin

STATELY
Jefferson

STORMY
Gale

STRONG
Alphonse
Amos
Andrew
Ben
Benjamin
Brandon
Brock
Bronson
Bruce
Cain
Christopher
Cody
Coleman
Curtis
Delbert
Dillon
Dirk
Dorian
Douglas
Duke
Dwight
Eli
Hunter
Jed
Jordan

STRONG (cont.)
Kurt
Lawrence
Leo
Luke
Marcus
Max
Michael
Nate
Nathan
Nick
Nolan
Richard
Rocky
Roosevelt
Sampson
Samuel
Seth
Stefan
Thor
Ulysses
Wade

STUBBORN
Kenneth

STUDIOUS
Linus
Waldo

STUFFY
Archibald
Barton
Bernard
Cyril
Edwin
Gaylord
Horton
Percival

STUPID
Ace
Jethro

SUAVE
Vaughn

SWEDISH
Dag
Gustave
Knute

SWEET
Devin
Josh
Wesley

TALENTED
Dudley
Neil

TALKATIVE
Al
Hubert

TALL
Abraham
Armand
Bart
Blake
Brent
Caesar
Chuck
Clinton
Cooper
Dallas
Darrell
Deacon
Dean
Dick
Donald
Emerson
Israel
Jay
Jeff
Jefferson
Jerry
Jonathan
Jordan
Kareem
Keith
Kirk
Lane
Leif
Lincoln
Ned

Owen
Terence
Van
Walter

THIN
Jonathan
Tim

THOUGHTFUL
Adrian
Carl
Dante

TOUGH
Bronson
Bruno
Butch
Cassius
Clint
Geraldo
Hugh
Lucas
Mike
Rocky

TRAITOR
Benedict

TRIM
Drew

UNATTRACTIVE
Herschel

UNDERSTANDING
Vincent

UPPER-CLASS
Cyril
Ethan

WARM
Curt
Kerry

WEIRD
Cosmo
Vernon

WELL-EDUCATED
Herbert

WELL-GROOMED
John

WELL-MANNERED
Christian

WESTERN
Dillon
Jared

WHITE-HAIRED
Moses

WILD
Brett
Garrett
Wade

WIMP
Cecil
Darren

WISE
Dwight

WITHDRAWN
Samuel

WITTY
Connor
Jan
Ogden

WORLDLY
Stu

WRITER
Truman

YOUNG
Alonzo
Chip
Darren
Lucas
Rusty

YUPPIE
Brandon

PERSONALITY PROFILES OF GIRLS' NAMES

ABBY, Abbie short forms of Abigail

   Image: People think of Abby as a small, cute woman who is quiet, loving, and sweet.

   Famous Abbys: Abigail (Dear Abby) Van Buren; TV's Abby ("Knots Landing") Ewing, Abby ("L.A. Law") Perkins; activist Abbie Hoffman

ABIGAIL (Hebrew) "father of joy"

   Image: Abigail is pictured as an old-fashioned girl with a ponytail who is talkative, helpful, and smart.

   Famous Abigails: the biblical Abigail, wife of King David; First Lady Abigail Adams; Abigail (Dear Abby) Van Buren

ADA (Old English) "prosperous, happy"; a short form of Adelaide

   Image: Ada strikes people as a good name for an older homebody who is conservative and hardworking.

   Famous Adas: Vladimir Nabokov's novel *Ada*; actress Ada Neilson; Ada (*Tobacco Road*) Lester

ADELAIDE (Old German) "noble, kind"

   Image: People describe Adelaide as a perfect grandma — an old-fashioned older woman who is lots of fun and a good friend.

Famous Adelaide: Adelaide, Nathan Detroit's girlfriend in the musical *Guys and Dolls*

ADELINE an English form of Adelaide

   Image: Adeline is pictured as an old-fashioned, sour old maid who is prudish and stuck-up — a Puritan or Quaker, perhaps.

   Famous Adelines: the song "Sweet Adeline"; opera singer Adelina Patti

ADELLE a French form of Adelaide

   Image: Adelle is viewed as an old-fashioned, gray-haired, matronly homebody who is soft-spoken and sweet.

   Famous Adelles: Adele Astaire, Fred's sister; nutrition writer Adelle Davis

ADRIENNE, Adrian (Latin) "dark, rich"

   Image: People say Adrienne is a pretty woman who is sexy, sophisticated, and shapely.

   Famous Adriennes: cosmetics magnate Adrien Arpel; actress Adrienne ("Maude") Barbeau; Adrian *(Rocky)* Balboa

AGATHA (Greek) "good, kind"

   Image: Agatha Christie is the dominant image for this name. Agatha is pictured as a well-known mystery writer who is highly intelligent, imaginative, and rather proper.

   Famous Agathas: mystery writer Agatha Christie; Saint Agatha; Agatha on TV's "Magnum, P.I."

AGNES (Greek) "pure"

Image: Agnes is described as a highly religious older woman who is stuffy, harsh, and grouchy.

Famous Agneses: Saint Agnes, the virgin martyr; actress Agnes ("Bewitched") Moorhead; the movie *Agnes of God*; choreographer Agnes De Mille

AILEEN (Irish Gaelic) "light-bearer"; an Irish form of Helen (see also Eileen, Ilene)

Image: People say Aileen is a very pretty, petite older woman who is self-confident and strong willed, but a bit naive and flighty.

Famous Aileen: Aileen, a line of women's clothing

AIMEE see Amy

ALANA, Alanna (Irish Gaelic) "fair, beautiful"; feminine forms of Alan

Image: Alana is pictured as a foreign beauty who is sexy, bright, perky, and mysterious.

Famous Alana: Alana Hamilton Stewart, ex-wife of both George Hamilton and Rod Stewart

ALBERTA (Old English) "noble, brilliant"; a feminine form of Albert

Image: Alberta is described as a big, tough, talkative, and tomboyish girl who will grow up to be a successful businesswoman.

Famous Albertas: blues singer Alberta Hunter; the province of Alberta, Canada; Alberta peaches; "Alberta Clipper" storms

ALEXANDRA (Greek) "helper and defender of mankind"; a feminine form of Alexander

Image: The name Alexandra conveys the image of an Old World noblewoman who is haughty, regal, and quite domineering.

Famous Alexandras: Russian Czarina Alexandra Feodorovna; dancer Alexandra Danilova

ALEXIS a form of Alexandra

Image: Thanks to TV's "Dynasty," most people think of Alexis as a rich, beautiful woman who is smart, bossy, and downright nasty.

Famous Alexises: actress Alexis Smith; TV's Alexis ("Dynasty") Carrington Colby Rowan

ALI, Allie, Alley short forms of Alexandra, Alice, Allison

Image: The name Ali calls to mind a cute, dark-haired, possibly black, tomboy with dirty jeans who is perky, funny, and popular — a yo-yo or marbles champ, perhaps.

Famous Alis: actresses Ali (*Love Story*) MacGraw, Ally (*Breakfast Club*) Sheedy; boxer Muhammad Ali; the story of "Ali Baba and the Forty Thieves"; TV's "Kate and Allie"

ALICE (Greek) "truth"; (Old German) "noble"

Image: Most people think of Alice as "Alice in

Wonderland" — a young daydreamer who is gregarious and free spirited. Some, though, see her as a prissy old homebody.

Famous Alices: Lewis Carroll's children's story *Alice's Adventures in Wonderland*; rock singer Alice Cooper; actress Alice Faye; TV's Alice ("The Honeymooners") Kramden; Arlo Guthrie's song "Alice's Restaurant"

ALISHA an English form of Alice

Image: Alisha is envisioned as a young, dark-skinned girl who is friendly, sweet, and very feminine.

Famous Alicia: ballet dancer Alicia Markova

ALISSA, Alyssa forms of Allison

Image: Most people think of Alissa as a pretty, sweet, feminine woman who is either active and lots of fun or refined and rather prissy.

Famous Alyssa: actress Alyssa ("Who's the Boss?") Milano

ALLISON, Allyson (Irish Gaelic) "little, truthful"; (Old German) "famous among the gods"

Image: The name Allison evokes an image of a pretty, dainty woman who is bright, caring, and demure.

Famous Allisons: novelist Alison Lurie; actress June Allyson

ALMA (Arabic) "learned"; (Latin) "soul"

Image: People describe Alma as an old-fashioned, older black woman who might be a maid or a cook.

Famous Almas: opera singer Alma Gluck; actresses Alma Tell, Alma Kruger; Alma, wife of Gustav Mahler, Walter Gropius, and Franz Werfel

ALTHEA (Greek) "wholesome, healing"

Image: Some people picture Althea as a tall, intelligent, outspoken black athlete, like tennis star Althea Gibson. Others picture a Greek goddess or an old-fashioned, gentle blonde beauty.

Famous Altheas: the mythological Althea, wife of Oeneus; tennis's Althea Gibson

AMANDA (Latin) "worthy of love"

Image: Amanda is described as an old-fashioned, beautiful, and thin woman who is sweet and very rich.

Famous Amandas: actresses Amanda ("Gunsmoke") Blake, Amanda Pays, Amanda Plummer; TV's Amanda ("Dynasty") Carrington, Amanda ("Scarecrow and Mrs. King") King

AMBER (Old French) "amber"

Image: The name Amber calls to mind a tall, elegant redhead who is intelligent, sexy, strong willed, and snooty.

Famous Amber: Kathleen Winsor's novel *Forever Amber*

AMELIA (Old German) "hard working"; a form of Emily

Image: The name Amelia brings to mind two different images: a smart, strong-willed adventurer, like Amelia Earhart, or a delicate, sickly introvert.

Famous Amelias: aviator Amelia Earhart; feminist Amelia Jenks Bloomer; Henry Fielding's novel *Amelia*; Amelia (*Vanity Fair*) Sedley

AMY, Aimee (Latin) "beloved"

Image: People picture Amy as a small, slender woman who is quiet, calm, educated, and refined.

Famous Amys: Amy Carter, President Carter's daughter; actress Amy (*Crossing Delancey*) Irving; Ray Bolger's theme "Once in Love with Amy"; singer Amy Grant; etiquette expert Amy Vanderbilt

ANASTASIA (Greek) "of the Resurrection, of springtime"

Image: Most people think of Anastasia as a European of royal birth — an exotic woman who is formal, dramatic, and mysterious. Some, though, think Anastasia is an ugly, wicked stepsister.

Famous Anastasias: Anastasia Romanov, Russian czar Nicholas's daughter; Anastasia, Cinderella's stepsister

ANDREA (Latin) "womanly"

Image: Andrea is pictured as a large, sturdy woman who may be bright or dull, soft-spoken or stern, but is considered average in most respects.

Famous Andreas: tennis's Andrea Jeager; the ship *Andrea Doria*; actress Andrea (*Annie*) McArdle

ANGELA (Greek) "angel, messenger"

Image: Angela is described as a pretty, dainty woman who is either sweet and gentle or spirited and sassy.

Famous Angelas: Saint Angela Merici; actresses Angela ("Murder, She Wrote") Lansbury, Angela ("Make Room for Daddy") Cartwright; TV's Angela ("Who's the Boss?") Bower

ANITA a Spanish form of Ann

Image: Anita strikes people as a good name for a small, beautiful, middle-class woman with a lovely personality who is bright, pleasant, and lots of fun.

Famous Anitas: actresses Anita Bryant, Anita Ekberg, Anita (*Moonstruck*) Gillette; novelists Anita (*Gentleman Prefer Blondes*) Loos, Anita (*Clear Light of Day*) Desai; singer Anita Baker

ANN, Anne (Hebrew) "graceful"; English forms of Hannah

Image: The name Ann calls to mind a plain, middle-class woman who is kind, practical, industrious, and dull.

Famous Anns: Anne Boleyn, wife of King Henry VIII; actresses Ann Jillian, Anne (*Fatal Attraction*) Archer; dancer Ann Miller; entertainer Ann-Margret; L. M. Montgomery's novel *Anne of Green*

Gables; Anne (*Diary of a Young Girl*) Frank; novelist Anne (*The Accidental Tourist*) Tyler; advice columnist Ann Landers; Raggedy Ann

ANNA a form of Ann

Image: Most people think of Anna as a big, old-fashioned woman who is quiet and sweet but also strong and determined — a perfect combination for a pioneer.

Famous Annas: Leo Tolstoy's novel *Anna Karenina*; Russia's Empress Anna Ivanovna; dancer Anna Pavlova; children's story writer Anna (*Black Beauty*) Sewell; opera singer Anna Moffo; Anna (*The King and I*) Leonowens

ANNABEL, Annabelle combinations of Anna and Belle

Image: Annabel is described as a southern belle — a proper, polite, high-society type from a small town who might be a librarian.

Famous Annabels: Edgar Allan Poe's poem "Annabel Lee"; actress Annabella

ANNAMARIA, Anna Maria combinations of Anna and Maria

Image: Annamaria is considered a good name for a dark, Catholic Italian woman who is fun and family oriented.

Famous Annamaria: singer Anna Maria Alberghetti

ANNETTE a form of Ann

Image: People say Annette is a pretty, dark-haired girl who is bouncy and fun, though perhaps a bit shallow, and

who will grow up to be a happy, wholesome mom.

Famous Annettes: actresses Annette Funicello, Annette (*Superman III*) O'Toole

ANNIE a form of Ann

Image: Like Little Orphan Annie, Annie is pictured as a cute little girl who is silly but smart; and friendly but tough.

Famous Annies: "Little Orphan Annie" comics; the Wild West's Annie Oakley; the movie *Annie Hall*; actress Annie ("Designing Women") Potts; singer Annie Lennox of the Eurythmics

ANTOINETTE (Latin) "priceless"; a feminine form of Anthony

Image: The name Antoinette calls to mind Marie Antoinette — a proper, regal, upper-class woman who is rich, vain, and egotistical.

Famous Antoinette: France's Queen Marie Antoinette

ANTONIA a form of Antoinette

Image: Antonia is pictured as an attractive dark-haired Italian or Hispanic woman who has a great body and a quiet, friendly nature.

Famous Antonias: novelists Lady Antonia Fraser, Antonia White; Willa Cather's novel *My Ántonia*

APRIL (Latin) "opening"

Image: When people hear the name April, they imagine a dainty young girl who is sweet, social, and free spirited.

Famous Aprils: TV's April ("Dallas") Stevens, April ("The Girl from U.N.C.L.E.") Dancer

ARETHA (Greek) "best"

Image: People describe Aretha as an older black woman who is big and very talented, like Aretha Franklin.

Famous Aretha: singer Aretha Franklin

ARIEL (Hebrew) "lioness of God"

Image: A lioness of God? Hardly! Ariel has a more ethereal image as a slim, pretty, princesslike girl who is smart and shy.

Famous Ariels: Ariel in Shakespeare's play *The Tempest*; Sylvia Plath's poem "Ariel"; the planet Uranus's moon Ariel

ARLENE (Irish Gaelic) "pledge"

Image: Arlene is pictured as an older redhead who is either friendly and kind or mouthy, flashy, and stuck-up.

Famous Arlenes: actresses Arlene Dahl, Arlene Francis

ASHLEY (Old English) "from the ash tree meadow"

Image: Ashley is described as a very beautiful professional woman who is shy but friendly with good values and taste. Ashley may play the piano, enjoy the company of an exquisite cat or schnauzer, and wear long, flowing dresses designed by Laura Ashley.

Famous Ashleys: fashion designer Laura Ashley; Ashley (*Gone with the Wind*) Wilkes;

Lady Brett (*The Sun Also Rises*) Ashley; anthropologist Sir Francis Ashley Montagu

AUDREY (Old English) "noble strength"

Image: Two very different pictures of Audrey emerge: a petite woman with sophistication, style, self-assurance, and humor, like Audrey Hepburn, or a domineering nag, like Audrey Meadows's character on TV's "The Honeymooners."

Famous Audreys: actresses Audrey Hepburn, Audrey Meadows

AUGUSTA (Latin) "majestic"

Image: Majestic? You bet! Augusta is considered a good name for an older mother or grandmother of striking proportions who rules the roost with an old-fashioned, stodgy, and commanding style.

Famous Augustas: the cities of Augusta, Georgia, and Augusta, Maine; Irish dramatist Lady Augusta Gregory

AURORA (Latin) "dawn"

Image: Aurora is regarded as a pretty, ethereal woman who may be artsy but is definitely an airhead.

Famous Auroras: aurora borealis, the northern lights; the mythological Aurora, Roman goddess of the dawn; Aurora in the movie *Terms of Endearment*; the cities of Aurora, Colorado, and Aurora, Illinois

AVA (Latin) "birdlike"

Image: Ava calls to mind two different images: an exotic, beautiful woman who is a seductive, eccentric dreamer or an older woman who is vain, rude, and bossy.

Famous Ava: actress Ava Gardner

BAMBI (Italian) "child"

Image: People say Bambi is a *Playboy* centerfold — a small, sexy, buxom blonde who is quiet, immature, and downright dumb.

Famous Bambi: Walt Disney's movie *Bambi*

BARB a short form of Barbara

Image: Most people think of Barb as a grown-up Barbie — sweet, friendly, and bubbly — whose figure is now sturdy.

BARBARA, Barbra (Latin) "stranger"

Image: The name Barbara has two different images: a heavy, plain older woman who is nice, boring, and thoroughly average or a small, pretty career woman who is very intelligent and a bit snobbish.

Famous Barbaras: First Lady Barbara Bush; singers Barbara Mandrell, Barbra ("People") Streisand; actresses Barbara ("Leave It to Beaver")

Billingsley, Barbara ("I Dream of Jeannie") Eden, Barbara ("Dallas") Bel Geddes; interviewer Barbara Walters; former congresswoman Barbara Jordan

BARBIE, Barbi short forms of Barbara

Image: For most people the name Barbie calls to mind Barbie dolls. People say Barbie is a cutesy, childlike girl who is blonde, spacy, and plastic.

Famous Barbies: Mattel's Barbie doll; actress Barbi Benton

BEA a short form of Beatrice

Image: Aunt Bea is the dominant image for this name — a big, heavy, old-fashioned grandma who is simple and very nice.

Famous Beas: actress Bea ("The Golden Girls") Arthur; Aunt Bea on TV's "The Andy Griffith Show"

BEATRICE, Beatrix (Latin) "bringer of joy"

Image: Beatrice is pictured as a big, heavy older woman who is a spinster and a great cook.

Famous Beatrices: actress Beatrice Lillie; Britain's Princess Beatrice; children's story writer/illustrator Beatrix (*Peter Rabbit*) Potter; Beatrice, Dante's beloved; Beatrice in Shakespeare's play *Much Ado About Nothing*

BECCA a short form of Rebecca

Image: The name Becca calls to mind a cute, dark-haired little girl who is a sweet, huggable, bouncy bundle of joy.

Famous Beccas: TV's Becca ("Life Goes On") Thatcher

BECKY a short form of Rebecca

Image: Becky is described as a cute young tomboy who is earthy, quiet, and happy.

Famous Beckys: Becky (*The Adventures of Tom Sawyer*) Thatcher; Becky (*Vanity Fair*) Sharp

BELINDA (Spanish) "beautiful"

Image: People say Belinda is a freckled redhead who is shy and simple.

Famous Belindas: Belinda in Alexander Pope's long poem *The Rape of the Lock*; pop singer Belinda Carlisle; the movie *Johnny Belinda*

BELLA a form of Belle

Image: When people think of Bella, they imagine a large, tall Russian woman who is pretty and nice.

Famous Bella: politician Bella Abzug

BELLE (French) "beautiful"

Image: Belle calls to mind an older, pretty, graceful southern belle with a pleasant disposition and hospitable ways.

Famous Belles: outlaw Belle Starr; Belle (*Gone with the Wind*) Watling; suffragist Belle Sherwin

BERNADETTE a form of Bernadine

Image: Bernadette is pictured as a plump, average-looking woman who is sweet and friendly.

Famous Bernadettes: actress Bernadette Peters; Saint Bernadette of Lourdes; Franz Werfel's novel *Song of Bernadette*

BERNADINE (French) "brave as a bear"; a feminine form of Bernard

Image: Bernadine is pictured in two ways: an old-fashioned elderly woman who is religious and likes to stay home all day and cook or a freckle-faced redhead with a boyish figure and a good head on her shoulders.

BERNICE (Greek) "bringer of victory"

Image: Bernice is described as a traditional middle-aged woman who is either sweet and quiet or talkative and nagging.

Famous Bernices: Edgar Allan Poe's short story "Berenice"; TV's Bernice ("Barney Miller") Fish

BERTHA (Old German) "shining"

Image: Most people picture Bertha as a fat older woman wearing a tent dress to hide her shape. Bertha might be quiet and shy; or goofy and awkward.

Famous Berthas: A.A. Fair's detective Bertha Cool; World War I's "Big Bertha" cannon; Bertha, Saxon Queen of Kent

BERYL (Greek) "beryl, a sea-green jewel"

Image: Most people say Beryl is a fat, talkative woman who is level headed, unrefined, and funny. Some people, though, see Beryl as snobby and reserved.

Famous Beryl: writer Beryl
(*West With the Night*) Markham

BESSIE a short form of Elizabeth

Image: Bessie is a name that
calls to mind an elderly, gray-
haired, old-fashioned farm
woman. The name Bessie
also seems to fit a cow.

Famous Bessies: blues singer
Bessie Smith; Bessie (*Tobacco
Road*) Rice; artist Bessie
Persse; actress Bess (*High
Road to China*) Armstrong

BETH a short form of Elizabeth

Image: Beth is pictured as
a sweet and innocent girl
right out of the pages of *Little
Women* — a petite blonde
who is quiet, gentle, and
honest.

Famous Beths: model/actress
Beth Henley; Beth (*Little
Women*) March

BETSY a short form of Elizabeth

Image: Betsy is described as a
cute young girl with braids, a
ponytail, or lots of curls — a
sweet, intelligent country girl
with a cheerful disposition and
a sparkle in her eye.

Famous Betsys: flag-maker
Betsy Ross; fashion designer
Betsey Johnson; actress Betsy
(*Marty*) Palmer

BETTE a short form of Elizabeth

Image: Most people picture
Bette as Bette Midler —
headstrong, funny, and nice.
Some, though, say she is sultry
and scary, like Bette Davis.

Famous Bettes: actress Bette
Davis; entertainer Bette Midler

BETTY a short form of Elizabeth

Image: The name Betty
conjures up an image of a
small young blonde who is
silly, lovable, and lots of fun.

Famous Bettys: First Lady
Betty Ford; "Betty Boop"
cartoons; actresses Betty
Grable, Betty ("The Golden
Girls") White, Betty ("Eight Is
Enough") Buckley; consumer
advisor Betty Furness; feminist
writer Betty Friedan; Betty
Crocker foods

BEV a short form of Beverly

Image: Bev is pictured as
either an overweight, straitlaced teacher, a kindhearted
nurse, or an outgoing waitress.

BEVERLY (Old English) "from
the beaver-meadow"

Image: People say Beverly is
a name from the fifties that
calls to mind a tall, active
redhead who is easygoing,
well mannered, and kind.

Famous Beverlys: opera
singer Beverly Sills; actresses
Beverly (*National Lampoon's
Vacation*) D'Angelo, Beverly
("My Three Sons") Garland;
children's story writer Beverly
Cleary

BIANCA an Italian form of
Blanche

Image: Bianca is described as
a real jet-setter — a beautiful
foreign sophisticate who is
intriguing, ritzy, sexy, and wild.

Famous Biancas: Bianca,
Mick Jagger's ex-wife; Bianca
in Shakespeare's play *The
Taming of the Shrew*

BILLIE (Old English) "strong-willed"; a short form of Wilhelmina

Image: Billie is regarded as the stereotypical tomboy — a casual kid who is perky, athletic, and irresponsible.

Famous Billies: tennis's Billie Jean King; TV's Billie ("Lou Grant") Newman, Billie Jo ("Petticoat Junction") Bradley; blues singer Billie Holliday; actress Billie (*The Wizard of Oz*) Burke

BLAIR (Scottish Gaelic) "dweller on the plain"

Image: Blair strikes people as a good name for a rich, beautiful sophisticate who is snobby and conceited.

Famous Blairs: TV's Blair ("Facts of Life") Warner; actresses Linda (*The Exorcist*) Blair, Blair ("The Days and Nights of Molly Dodd") Brown

BLANCHE (Old French) "white, fair"

Image: People picture Blanche as either pretty and athletic or plain and mousy.

Famous Blanches: Blanche (*A Streetcar Named Desire*) Dubois; Blanche (*Jane Eyre*) Ingram; Blanch (*Bonnie and Clyde*) Barrow; suffragist/artist Blanche Ames; TV's Blanche ("The Golden Girls") Devereaux

BLYTHE (Old English) "joyous"

Image: Most people picture Blythe as having a willowy frame, wispy blonde hair, blue eyes, and a high-spirited and likeable manner. Some, though, picture Blythe as a quiet bookworm.

Famous Blythes: actresses Blythe Danner, Ann Blyth

BOBBIE, Bobbi short forms of Roberta

Image: Bobbie is a popular unisex name. A female Bobbie is pictured as an all-American teenager — a cute athletic girl who is friendly, carefree, and wild.

Famous Bobbies: singer Bobbie Gentry; TV's Bobbie Jo ("Petticoat Junction") Bradley

BONNIE (Scottish-English) "beautiful, pretty"

Image: The name Bonnie calls to mind a pretty, redheaded Irish country girl who is cheerful, friendly, and sweet.

Famous Bonnies: actresses Bonnie ("One Day at a Time") Franklin, Bonnie (*Die Hard*) Bedelia; Bonnie Parker of Bonnie and Clyde; blues singer Bonnie Raitt; rock singer Bonnie Tyler

BRENDA (Old English) "firebrand"; a feminine form of Brandon, Brendan

Image: Brenda is pictured as either a pretty, young, blonde or black southern woman with a pleasant personality, or a businesslike career girl in a suit.

Famous Brendas: singer Brenda ("I'm Sorry") Lee; "Brenda Starr" comics

BRIDGET, Bridgett, Brigid (Irish Gaelic) "resolute strength"

Image: Bridget is described as a short, cute, athletic Irish lass with red hair and freckles who is outgoing, energetic, fun, and a good organizer.

Famous Brigids: Saint Brigid, patron saint of Ireland; Irish novelist Brigid Brophy

BRIGITTE a French form of Bridget

Image: Brigitte is pictured as a sexy blonde who is either French and flirty, like Brigitte Bardot, or tall and self-assured, like Brigitte Nielsen.

Famous Brigittes: actresses Brigitte Bardot, Brigitte (*Red Sonja*) Nielsen

BRITTANY (Latin) "from England"

Image: People say Brittany is a trendy name that reminds them of a pretty, petite aristocrat who is nice, slightly spoiled, and self-assured.

Famous Brittanys: actress Morgan Brittany; TV's Brittany ("thirtysomething") Weston

BROOKE (Old English) "from the brook"; a feminine form of Brook

Image: Brooke is described as a pretty girl with thick eyebrows, like Brooke Shields. She is also described as a rich, sexy sophisticate who is superficial and stuck-up.

Famous Brookes: model/actress Brooke (*The Blue Lagoon*) Shields; singer Brooke Benton

BUNNY (English) "little rabbit"

Image: Thanks to Playboy bunnies, Bunny is pictured as a stereotypical dumb

blonde — a silly, beautiful airhead who is flirty and affectionate.

Famous Bunnys: Playboy bunnies; "Bugs Bunny" cartoons; musician Bunny ("I Can't Get Started") Berrigan

CAITLIN an Irish form of Catherine

Image: Caitlin is pictured as a cute, slender woman of Irish descent who might be either a trendy, ambitious yuppie or a friendly, charming country woman.

Famous Caitlins: Caitlin on TV's "Airwolf", Caitlin on TV's "Miami Vice"

CAMILLE (Latin) "young ceremonial attendant"

Image: Camille is described as a quiet woman who is as beautiful as a flower, prim and proper, and very trustworthy.

Famous Camilles: Camille in Alexandre Dumas's play *La Dame aux camélias*; Camille in Puccini's opera *La Bohème*; composer Camille Saint-Saëns

CANDACE, Candice (Greek) "glittering, flowing white"

Image: The name Candace calls to mind actress Candice Bergen — tall, flawlessly beautiful, outgoing, forthright, independent, and sweet.

Famous Candaces: Candace, the historical name and title of the queens of ancient Ethiopia; actresses Candice ("Murphy Brown") Bergen, Candace ("Full House") Cameron; textile designer Candace Wheeler

CANDY a short form of Candace, Candida

Image: Candy is described as a stereotypical dumb blonde — a tall, sexy girl who is free and easy and sweet.

Famous Candys: actress Candy Clark; comic actor John Candy

CARA, Kara (Irish Gaelic) "friend"; (Latin) "dear"

Image: When people think of Cara, they imagine a petite, plain woman who has a sweet disposition.

Famous Caras: singer Irene ("Fame") Cara; Kara, Supergirl's name on Krypton

CARESSE (French) "beloved"

Image: Most people think of Caresse as a long-haired, elegant jet-setter — a high-class beauty who is a bit of a snob.

Famous Caresse: Caresse soap

CARISSA (Greek) "loving"

Image: Carissa is described as a beautiful, dainty, or fragile woman who is sweet and shy.

CARLA a form of Caroline; a feminine form of Carl, Charles

Image: The name Carla calls to mind a strong, good-looking

woman who is bright, independent, outgoing, and tough.

Famous Carlas: TV's Carla ("Cheers") Lebec; public official Carla Hills

CARLY a short form of Caroline

Image: Carly is regarded as a boyish but pretty woman who is vibrant and sweet with a real down-home style.

Famous Carly: singer Carly ("Anticipation") Simon

CARMEN (Latin) "song"; (Spanish) "from Mount Carmel"

Image: Carmen's image comes straight from the opera. Carmen is pictured as a pretty, dark-skinned, brown-eyed Spanish girl who is tough and very attractive to men.

Famous Carmens: Bizet's opera *Carmen*; Santa Maria del Carmen; "Mary at Mount Carmen"; entertainers Carmen Miranda, Carmen McRae

CAROL, Carole (Latin) "strong, womanly"; (Old French) "song of joy"; feminine forms of Carl, Charles

Image: Carol Burnett is the dominant image for this name. Carol is imagined as a friendly, family-oriented extrovert who is lots of fun.

Famous Carols: actresses Carol Burnett, Carol (*Hello, Dolly!*) Channing, Carole Lombard; singer Carole ("You've Got a Friend") King; skater Carol Heiss

CAROLINE, Carolyn (Latin) "little and womanly"; forms of Carol; feminine forms of Carl, Charles

Image: Most people think of Caroline as an attractive, dark-haired woman who is rich, spoiled, and either sweet and shy or loud and ornery.

Famous Carolines: Caroline, President Kennedy's daughter; TV's Caroline ("Little House on the Prairie") Ingalls; Princess Caroline of Monaco

CARRIE a short form of Carol, Caroline (see also Kerry)

Image: Carrie is described as a cute, intelligent young blonde who might be either a fun-loving extrovert or a quiet loner.

Famous Carries: actress Carrie (*Star Wars*) Fisher; temperance crusader Carrie Nation; feminist Carrie Chapman Catt; Theodore Dreiser's novel *Sister Carrie*; Stephen King's novel *Carrie*

CASSANDRA (Greek) "helper of men, disbelieved by men"

Image: The name Cassandra calls to mind a pretty, feminine black woman who is cunning but not bright.

Famous Cassandras: the mythological Greek prophet Cassandra; Cassandra (Elvira, Mistress of the Dark) Peterson

CASSIE a short form of Cassandra, Catherine

Image: Cassie is expected to be a cute, popular college graduate who is happy and sweet.

Famous Cassie: Cassie on TV's "One Life to Live"

CATHERINE (Greek) "pure"; an English form of Katherine (see also Katherine)

Image: People have two different images of the name Catherine: a pretty, elegant, upper-class sophisticate who is formal, serious, and proper or a large, common woman who is friendly, popular, and nice.

Famous Catherines: Russia's Czarinas Catherine I, II; actresses Catherine ("The Dukes of Hazard") Bach; Catherine Deneuve

CATHLEEN a form of Catherine (see also Kathleen)

Image: Cathleen is pictured as a pretty and delicate Irish woman who may be either wealthy, sophisticated, and proper or sweet, gentle, and quiet.

CATHY a short form of Catherine (see also Kathy)

Image: Cathy is pictured as a cute young blonde who is energetic, outgoing, fun, and nice, like Cathy Rigby. Some, though, think of Cathy as spoiled and self-centered.

Famous Cathys: gymnast Cathy Rigby; actress Cathy Lee Crosby; cartoonist Cathy ("Cathy") Guisewite; Chatty Cathy doll

CAYLA a form of Catherine (see also Kayla)

Image: Cayla is perceived as an interesting contemporary name that fits a pretty, wealthy, vivacious young woman who is quite unique — an artist or hippie, perhaps.

CECILIA (Latin) "blind"; a feminine form of Cecil

Image: There are two images of the name Cecilia: a pretty, feminine jet-setter who is sexy and vain or an average, plain woman who is down-to-earth and kind.

Famous Cecilias: Saint Cecilia of Rome; Simon and Garfunkel's song "Cecilia"

CELESTE (Latin) "heavenly"

Image: Celeste is described as a proper, beautiful woman who may be either sweet or brash.

Famous Celestes: actress Celeste Holm; the musical instrument celesta

CELIA a short form of Cecilia

Image: Celia is pictured as either a long-haired, tomboyish city girl who is cold and nasty or a wealthy, willowy woman who is vulnerable and lonely.

Famous Celia: actress Celia Johnson

CHARITY (Latin) "charity, brotherly love"

Image: When people hear the name Charity, they imagine a very small, feminine woman who is spoiled and insecure.

Famous Charitys: the musical *Sweet Charity*; Charity, one of the seven virtues

CHARLENE, Sharlene forms of Caroline, Charlotte

Image: To most people Charlene is a short, attractive blonde, like Charlene Tilton of TV's "Dallas." But to others, Charlene is a tall, fun-loving girl-next-door.

Famous Charlenes: actress Charlene Tilton; TV's Charlene ("Designing Women") Frazier

CHARLIE a feminine form of Charles

Image: The advertising campaign for Charlie perfume gave this traditionally masculine name a feminine twist. A girl with this name is pictured as either an energetic tomboy or a gorgeous blonde who is outgoing and carefree.

Famous Charlies: Charlie perfume; actor Charlie (*Modern Times*) Chaplin

CHARLOTTE (French) "little and womanly"; a short form of Carol; a feminine form of Charles

Image: Charlotte is regarded as a good name for a plump, old-fashioned southern woman who is friendly, fun, and motherly.

Famous Charlottes: actress Charlotte ("Facts of Life") Rae; French political assassin Charlotte Corday; the movie *Hush...Hush Sweet Charlotte*; novelist Charlotte (*Jane Eyre*) Brontë; E. B. White's children's story *Charlotte's Web*

CHASTITY (Latin) "purity"

Image: Chastity has two different images: a rich, upper-class socialite or a pure, quaint, and unpopular woman.

Famous Chastitys: Chastity Bono, Sonny and Cher's daughter; chastity belts

CHELSEA (Old English) "a port of ships"

>**Image:** The name Chelsea calls to mind a rich English-woman with a unique character.

>**Famous Chelseas:** Chelsea, a section of London, England; actress Chelsea ("Major Dad") Herford

CHER (French) "beloved"

>**Image:** When people think of the name Cher, they think of the incomparable singer/actress. They envision a woman with this name as a slinky singer with long, dark hair — a one-of-a-kind woman who will try anything.

>**Famous Cher:** entertainer Cher ("I Got You Babe"; *Moonstruck*)

CHERYL a form of Charlotte (see also Sheryl)

>**Image:** Most people think of Cheryl as cute, petite, sweet, and friendly, though some picture her as fat.

>**Famous Cheryls:** model Cheryl Tiegs; actress Cheryl ("Charlie's Angels") Ladd

CHIQUITA (Spanish) "little girl"

>**Image:** The name Chiquita calls to mind a Spanish woman with long, straight, dark hair and a dark complexion who has a bubbly, outgoing personality. This name also makes people think of Chiquita bananas.

>**Famous Chiquita:** Chiquita bananas

CHLOE (Greek) "young grass"

>**Image:** Chloe has two different images: a wealthy aristocrat who is quiet and sensitive or an airhead who is popular and fun loving.

>**Famous Chloes:** the mytho-logical Chloe, Greek goddess of green grain; lovers Daphnis and Chloë; the perfume Chloe; Chloe in the movie *The Big Chill*

CHLORIS, Cloris (Greek) "pale"

>**Image:** Chloris is described as a talented but unattractive woman who is uptight, pushy, and cold.

>**Famous Chlorises:** the mythological Chloris, Niobe's daughter; actress Cloris ("Phyllis") Leachman

CHRIS, Kris short forms of Christine, Kristine

>**Image:** Chris is a unisex name that most people connect with Chris Evert. People picture Chris as a tomboy or an ath-letic woman with lots of confi-dence, a ready smile, and an outgoing, energetic style.

>**Famous Chris:** tennis's Chris Evert

CHRISTA a form of Christine (see also Krista)

>**Image:** Astronaut Christa McAuliffe brought this name to prominence, but it does not have a very clear-cut image. There is some agreement, however, that Christa is likely to be smart, peppy, arrogant, and self-centered.

Famous Christa: *Challenger* astronaut/teacher Christa McAuliffe

CHRISTIN, Kristen forms of Christine

> **Image:** People picture Christin as a pretty, petite, quiet blonde mama's girl with a headstrong streak.

CHRISTINA, Kristina forms of Christine

> **Image:** What a beauty! Christina is described as a beautiful, petite lady with wealth, brains, and sophistication.

> **Famous Christinas:** millionaire Christina Onassis; actress Christina ("St. Elsewhere") Pickles; Andrew Wyeth's painting *Christina's World*; poet Christina Rossetti

CHRISTINE, Kristine (Greek) "Christian; annointed"

> **Image:** The name Christine calls to mind either a slender, beautiful brunette with an angelic face and sweet manner or a tall, striking, athletic woman who is rather dull.

> **Famous Christines:** Stephen King's novel *Christine*; British call girl Christine Keeler; sex-change groundbreaker Christine Jorgensen

CHRISTY, Christie short forms of Christine (see also Kristi)

> **Image:** Christie Brinkley provides the dominant image for this name — a cute, young, friendly blonde who is bubbly, fun, and popular.

Famous Christys: model Christie Brinkley; actress Julie (*Dr. Zhivago*) Christie; Catherine Marshall's novel *Christy*

CICELY an English form of Cecilia

> **Image:** Most people describe Cicely as Cicely Tyson — a strong, dynamic black woman who is a talented actress. Some, though, see Cicely as a wealthy, prudish Englishwoman.

> **Famous Cicely:** actress Cicely Tyson

CINDERELLA (French) "little one of the ashes"

> **Image:** People picture Cinderella as a beautiful, sweet, hardworking girl from a rags-to-riches fairy tale.

> **Famous Cinderellas:** the fairy tale *Cinderella*; the movie *Cinderella Liberty*

CINDY, Cyndi short forms of Cinderella, Cynthia, Lucinda

> **Image:** Cindy is described as an all-American teen queen — a sweet, attractive blonde who is peppy and wholesome but not too bright.

> **Famous Cindys:** singer Cyndi Lauper; actress Cindy ("Laverne and Shirley") Williams; Cindy Bear, Yogi's girlfriend

CLAIRE a French form of Clara (see also Clare)

> **Image:** Claire is described as an attractive older woman who is strong, assertive, and nice.

Famous Claires: actresses Claire Bloom, Claire Trevor; TV's Claire ("The Cosby Show") Huxtable; Debussy's composition "Claire de Lune"

CLARA (Greek) "clear, bright"

Image: The name Clara reminds people of a favorite aunt or grandmother — a little old woman who is sweet and kind.

Famous Claras: nurse Clara Barton; actress Clara Bow; Clara in Tchaikovsky's ballet *The Nutcracker*; promoter Clara ("Where's the beef?") Peller

CLARE a form of Clara (see also Claire)

Image: Clare is pictured as a fat, sickly, homely older woman who is well educated and quiet.

Famous Clares: diplomat Clare Boothe Luce; Saint Clare of Assisi

CLAUDIA (Latin) "lame"; a feminine form of Claude

Image: Claudia is pictured as a tall blonde southerner who could be a bespectacled, intelligent eavesdropper; a slender, graceful sweetie; or a brawny klutz.

Famous Claudias: actress Claudia Cardinale; First Lady Claudia (Lady Bird) Johnson

CLEMENTINE (Greek) "mercy"

Image: Clementine is regarded as an old-fashioned name suitable for an older southern country gal who is sweet, homely, and uneducated.

Famous Clementines: Lady Clementine Churchill; the song "Oh, My Darling Clementine"

CLORIS see Chloris

COLETTE, Collette (Greek-French) "victorious in battle"; forms of Nicole

Image: The name Colette calls to mind a daring, vivacious Frenchwoman who is sophisticated and snobby.

Famous Colette: French novelist Colette

COLLEEN (Irish Gaelic) "girl"

Image: Colleen is pictured as a cute, athletic Irish girl who is either funny and gregarious or sweet and shy.

Famous Colleens: actresses Colleen Dewhurst, Colleen Gray, Colleen Moore; novelist Colleen (*The Thorn Birds*) McCullough

CONNIE a short form of Constance

Image: People think of Connie in one of two ways: a dainty, petite, pretty woman who is peppy, silly, and popular or a tall, hardworking, frumpy mom.

Famous Connies: singers Connie Francis, Connie Stevens; actress Connie ("Hotel") Sellecca; newscaster Connie Chung; Connie (*Lady Chatterley's Lover*) Chatterley

CONSTANCE (Latin) "constancy, firmness"

Image: Constance is described as a plain, old-fashioned woman who is prim, proper, patient, and reliable.

Famous Constances:
Constance (*Lady Chatterley's Lover*) Chatterley; actress Constance Moore

CORA (Greek) "maiden"

Image: Cora is an old-fashioned name that seems appropriate for a plain, dark-haired, elderly spinster who is smart and friendly.

Famous Coras: Cora (*The Last of the Mohicans*) Munro; Cora ("Blondie") Dithers

CORETTA a form of Cora

Image: People describe Coretta as an attractive, professional, black or Hispanic woman who, like Coretta Scott King, is strong and fair minded.

Famous Coretta: Coretta Scott King, Dr. Martin Luther King Jr.'s widow

COREY (Irish Gaelic) "from the hollow"

Image: Corey is a name that is used mostly for boys, so it is not surprising that people think of a girl named Corey as a tomboy who is cute, blonde, rugged, and energetic — definitely the outdoor type. They imagine Corey climbing trees and getting into mischief.

Famous Corey: Canadian singer Corey ("Never Surrender") Hart; actor Corey (*Stand By Me*) Feldman

COURTNEY (Old English) "from the court"

Image: Courtney is pictured as a cute girl who is either petite or chunky. Courtney is described as either bright

and mischievous or snobby, stuck-up, and spoiled.

Famous Courtneys: Courtney Gibbs, Miss USA 1988; actress Courtney ("Family Ties") Cox

CRYSTAL (Latin) "clear as crystal" (see also Krystle)

Image: Crystal is pictured as a rich, tall, beautiful woman who is talented but pretentious.

Famous Crystals: singer Crystal Gayle

CYBIL see Sybil

CYNTHIA (Greek) "moon"

Image: Cynthia is pictured as a petite, attractive, blue-eyed blonde who is sweet, quiet, and perhaps a bit spoiled.

Famous Cynthia: novelist Cynthia Freeman

DAISY (Old English) "eye of the day, daisy flower"

Image: Thanks to "Li'l Abner," people picture Daisy as Daisy Mae Yokum; the prototypical "dumb blonde" hillbilly who is feminine, cheerful, and sweet.

Famous Daisys: Daisy (*The Great Gatsby*) Buchanan; Henry James's novella *Daisy Miller*; Daisy Mae ("Li'l Abner") Yokum; Daisy Duck, Donald Duck's girlfriend; TV's Daisy ("Dukes of Hazzard") Duke;

Daisy, Dagwood and Blondie Bumstead's dog; the movie *Driving Miss Daisy*

DANA (Scandinavian) "from Denmark"

Image: Dana is growing more popular as a name for both girls and boys. A girl with this name is pictured as either a tall, sweet, willowy, statuesque dancer or a bratty tomboy.

Famous Danas: actors Dana Andrews, Dana Elcar; actress Dana ("China Beach") Delaney; comic actor Dana ("Saturday Night Live") Carvey

DANIELLE (Hebrew) "judged by God"; a feminine form of Daniel

Image: Danielle is pictured as a pretty, exotic Frenchwoman who is intelligent, well-bred, and reserved.

Famous Danielles: novelist Danielle Steele; Romanian gymnast Daniela Silivas

DAPHNE (Greek) "laurel tree"

Image: People describe Daphne as a rich older woman who may be a spry, dumb blonde or a demure brunette.

Famous Daphnes: novelist Daphne (*Rebecca*) Du Maurier; Daphne on TV's "Scooby Doo"

DARA (Hebrew) "compassion"

Image: Some people describe Dara as a dowdy, boring intellectual; others picture her as a giggly, stupid child; most say Dara is her mother's darling.

DARCY (Irish Gaelic) "dark"

Image: Darcy is described as a chubby and bubbly girl-next-door. Some, though, say Darcy is a cheerleader or the kind of girl who enjoys a rowdy time at a bar after the game.

DARIA (Greek) "queenly"; a feminine form of Darius

Image: Daria is described as a tall, friendly, highly intelligent woman who loves to travel through foreign lands.

DARLENE (Old French) "little darling"

Image: People picture Darlene as a dark-haired, bratty, stuck-up woman who is wealthy but not overly bright.

Famous Darlenes: TV's Darlene ("Head of the Class") Merriman, Darlene the Mouse-keteer, Darlene ("Roseanne") Conner

DAWN (Old English) "dawn"

Image: People think of Dawn as a pretty, smart, quiet innocent who wants to make the world a better place.

Famous Dawns: the song "Delta Dawn"; singers Tony Orlando and Dawn; actress Dawnn ("A Different World") Lewis

DEANDRA (Latin) "divine"; a form of Diana

Image: Deandra is considered an unusual name that fits an upper-class French or black woman who is extremely wealthy.

DEANNA a form of Dena, Diana; a feminine form of Dean

Image: Most people think of Deanna as a cute, big-boned girl who is very quiet but wants to be noticed.

Famous Deannas: actress Deanna Durbin; TV's Deanna ("Star Trek: The Next Generation") Troi

DEBBIE a short form of Deborah, Debra

Image: Debbie is pictured as a cute, healthy kid who is chatty, vibrant, and lots of fun.

Famous Debbies: actresses Debbie Allen, Debbie (*Singing in the Rain*) Reynolds; singers Debbie ("You Light Up My Life") Boone, Debbie Gibson; Little Debbie snack cakes

DEBORAH, Debra (Hebrew) "bee"

Image: Most people agree that Deborah is a good name for a willowy beauty who is dependable and intelligent. Some, though, think of Deborah as theatrical or even wild.

Famous Deborahs: the biblical Deborah, prophet and judge; actresses Debra (*Terms of Endearment*) Winger, Deborah (*The King and I*) Kerr, Deborah Raffin; TV host Deborah ("The Today Show") Norville; singer Deborah Harry of Blondie

DEE (Welsh) "black, dark"; a short form of Deirdre, Delia, Diana

Image: Dee is described as a cute, lively woman who might not have money but dresses neatly, works hard, and uses her wits.

Famous Dees: actresses Dee (*E.T. — The Extra-Terrestrial*) Wallace, Sandra (*Gidget*) Dee; Sandra Dee in the musical *Grease*

DEE DEE, Didi forms of Dee

Image: Most people picture Dee Dee as a fifties cheerleader type — cute, bouncy, and silly. Some, though, see Dee Dee as quiet, prissy, and dull.

Famous Dee Dees: TV's Dee Dee ("Hunter") McCall; actress Didi ("Benson") Conn

DEIDRE (Irish Gaelic) "sorrow, complete wanderer"

Image: The name Diedre has two different images: a simple blonde who is quiet and very nice or a rich French go-getter who is elegant and snobbish.

Famous Deidres: actress Deidre ("Our House") Hall; Deidre, heroine of Irish legend

DELIA (Greek) "visible, from Delos"; a short form of Cordelia

Image: People seem to have mixed images of this name. Delia is described as either wicked and sly, scatterbrained and helpless, or calm and serene.

Famous Delias: Delia in Virgil's "Bucolics poetry"; Delia in Alexander Pope's satires

DELILAH (Hebrew) "brooding"

Image: Most people picture Delilah as a pretty, seductive, dark-haired woman who cannot be trusted, like the biblical Delilah.

Famous Delilahs: the biblical Delilah, Samson's Philistine betrayer; Tom Jones's song "Delilah"

DELLA a form of Adelaide, Delia

Image: The name Della calls to mind a strong, overweight, middle-aged black woman with a jovial personality and a loud voice — a singer like Della Reese, perhaps.

Famous Dellas: singer Della Reese; TV's Della ("Perry Mason") Street

DEMI (French) "half or small"

Image: Demi Moore is the dominant image for this name. Demi is considered a trendy name appropriate for a smart, pretty, popular girl who likes to have fun.

Famous Demis: actress Demi (*St. Elmo's Fire*) Moore; Demi in Louisa May Alcott's novel *Little Men*

DENA, Dina (Hebrew) "vindicated"; (Old English) "from the valley"; feminine forms of Dean

Image: Most people think of Dena as a high-energy athlete who is perky, bubbly, free spirited, and wholesome.

Famous Dina: actress Dina Merrill

DENISE (French) "adherent of Dionysus (god of wine)"; a feminine form of Dennis

Image: Denise is pictured as cute, fat, funny, and friendly — the kind of fun-loving girl who does not ever want to grow up. Some, though, think of Denise as stuck-up and moody.

Famous Denises: singer Deniece Williams; TV's Denise ("The Cosby Show") Huxtable

DESIRÉE (French) "longed-for"

Image: The name Desirée calls to mind an extremely beautiful, exotic woman (possibly French) who is strong willed, self-centered, and sexy. She is considered sweet but not very smart.

Famous Desirées: Neil Diamond's song "Desirée"; Desirée, Napoleon's mistress

DIANA (Latin) "divine"

Image: Most people see Diana as a pretty, upper-class blonde who is old-fashioned, prissy, quiet, and intelligent. Some, though, see Diana as opportunistic.

Famous Dianas: the mythological Diana, Roman goddess of the moon, fertility, and the hunt; Britain's Princess Diana; singer Diana Ross; actress Diana ("The Avengers") Rigg; swimmer Diana Nyad

DIANE a form of Diana (see also Dyan)

Image: Diane is pictured as a good-looking, energetic, blonde yuppie who is smart, tough, and too self-assured.

Famous Dianes: newscaster Diane Sawyer; actresses Diahann ("Dynasty") Carroll, Diane (*Baby Boom*) Keaton; TV's Diane ("Cheers") Chambers

DIDI see Dee Dee

DINA see Dena

DINAH (Hebrew) "vindicated"

Image: The name Dinah calls to mind an old-fashioned, middle-aged or older woman with a sunny disposition and an energetic, hardworking, outgoing style.

Famous Dinahs: the biblical Dinah, daughter of Jacob and Leah; singers Dinah Shore, Dinah Washington; the song "Someone's in the Kitchen with Dinah"; actress Dinah ("Empty Nest") Manoff

DIONNE (Greek) "divine queen"

Image: Dionne Warwick is the dominant image for this name — a pretty, elegant black woman who is musical and dependable.

Famous Dionnes: the mythological Dione, Aphrodite's mother; singers Dionne Warwick, Dion and the Belmonts; the Dionne quintuplets

DIXIE (French) "ten, tenth"

Image: People describe Dixie as a real southern belle — a cute, petite woman with a bubbly, kind, fun-loving personality.

Famous Dixies: actress Dixie ("Designing Women") Carter; film critic Dixie Watley

DODIE, Dody (Hebrew) "beloved"; short forms of Dora, Dorothy

Image: People think of Dodie as a cute little old lady with a screw or two loose who is friendly but decidedly dopey and scatterbrained.

Famous Dody: actress Dody ("Mary Hartman, Mary Hartman") Goodman

DOLLY a short form of Dorothy

Image: Thanks to Dolly Parton, people picture Dolly as a doll-like buxom blonde with a bubbly, outgoing personality.

Famous Dollys: singer Dolly Parton; First Lady Dolley Madison; the musical *Hello, Dolly!*

DOLORES (Spanish) "sorrows"

Image: People say Dolores is an overweight, bespectacled older woman who is a slow but steady worker.

Famous Doloreses: Santa Maria de los Dolores (Saint Mary of the Sorrows); actresses Dolores Del Rio, Dolores (*Kismet*) Gray; TV's Dolores ("Kukla, Fran, and Ollie") Dragon

DOMINIQUE (French-Latin) "belonging to God"; a feminine form of Dominic

Image: Dominique is pictured as a Frenchwoman with dark eyes and dark hair who is either rich, snooty, and strong willed or quiet, kind, and religious.

Famous Dominique: TV's Dominique ("Dynasty") Deveraux

DONNA (Latin-Italian) "lady"

Image: Donna is considered a good name for a lovely, motherly woman who is quiet, friendly, and nice.

Famous Donnas: actresses Donna ("The Beverly Hill-billies") Douglas, Donna (*It's a Wonderful Life*) Reed, Donna ("Knots Landing") Mills; Donna Rice, former senator Gary Hart's friend; singer Donna ("Bad Girls") Summers

DORA (Greek) "gift"

Image: Most people picture Dora as a dowdy, fussy grandmother. Some, though, say she is a swinging "dumb Dora."

Famous Doras: Dora in John Steinbeck's novel *Cannery Row;* Dora (*David Copperfield*) Spenlow; TV's "I Married Dora"

DOREEN (Irish Gaelic) "sullen"; an Irish form of Dora

Image: People picture Doreen as an average small-town blonde homemaker who enjoys a night out at the bowling alley.

Famous Doreen: TV's Doreen the Mouseketeer

DORIA (Greek) a feminine form of Dorian

Image: Doria strikes most people as an old-fashioned name befitting a large woman who is quiet and shy. Some, though, picture Doria as spirited, sophisticated, and snobby.

Famous Doria: the ill-fated ship *Andrea Doria*

DORIS (Greek) "from the sea"

Image: Doris is described as a clean-cut, cheerful blonde who is talkative and pleasant, like Doris Day.

Famous Dorises: the mythological Doris, mother of the Nereids sea nymphs; actress Doris (*Pillow Talk*) Day; author Doris Lessing

DOROTHY (Greek) "gift of God"

Image: Dorothy has two radically different images: a loud, friendly, fun-loving adventurer or a large, mousy wallflower who is shy, dull, and methodical.

Famous Dorothys: skater Dorothy Hamill; actress Dorothy Lamour; Dorothy in the movie *The Wizard of Oz*; social worker Dorothy Day; Dorothy (*Tootsie*) Michaels

DORY a short form of Dora, Doria, Doris, Dorothy

Image: Dory is pictured as a small woman who grew up in the country. However, there are several different views of her personality: kind and generous, selfish and phony, energetic and giggly, or quiet and demure.

DOTTIE, Dotty short forms of Dorothy

Image: People say Dottie is a cute, chubby, old-fashioned country girl who is scatterbrained, chatty, and loud.

Famous Dotties: country-western singer Dottie West; TV's Dotty ("Scarecrow and Mrs. King") West

DYAN a form of Diana (see also Diane)

Image: This name brings actress Dyan Cannon to

mind — a thin, buxom California blonde who is flashy, self-assured, and smart.

Famous Dyan: actress Dyan Cannon

EARTHA (Old English) "of the earth"

Image: People describe Eartha as a big black woman who is sensual, natural, earthy, and a bit odd, like Eartha Kitt.

Famous Eartha: singer/actress Eartha Kitt

EBONY (Greek) "a hard, dark wood"

Image: Ebony is pictured as a beautiful black woman who is sleek and savvy with an air of mystery about her.

Famous Ebonys: *Ebony* magazine; the song "Ebony and Ivory"

EDIE a short form of Edith

Image: Edie is described as an attractive woman who is lively, outgoing, fun loving, and full of life.

Famous Edies: singers Edie Adams, Eydie Gorme; Andy Warhol protégé Edie Sedgwick; TV's Edie ("Peter Gunn") Hart, Edie ("The Mary Tyler Moore Show") Grant

EDITH (Old English) "rich gift"

Image: To most people Edith is a plain, old-fashioned frump, who is loving, gullible, and dull, like TV's Edith Bunker. Some see Edith as a disapproving teacher.

Famous Ediths: TV's Edith ("All in the Family") Bunker; costume designer Edith Head; nurse Edith Cavell; novelist Edith (*Ethan Frome*) Wharton; authors Dame Edith Sitwell, Edith Hamilton

EDNA (Hebrew) "rejuvenation"

Image: Edna is pictured as a tall, homely, old-fashioned family woman who is pleasant, caring, loud, and fastidious.

Famous Ednas: the apocryphal Edna, Enoch's wife; novelist Edna (*Show Boat*) Ferber; poet Edna St. Vincent Millay; TV's Edna ("Facts of Life") Garrett; actress Edna Mae Oliver

EILEEN an Irish form of Helen (see also Aileen, Ilene)

Image: When people hear the name Eileen, they picture a very pretty woman who is witty and easygoing — an entertainer, perhaps.

Famous Eileens: actress Eileen (*Private Benjamin*) Brennan; modeling magnate Eileen Ford

ELAINE a French form of Helen

Image: Elaine is described as an attractive blonde — a smart, business-minded trend-setter who is not only friendly but also a good friend.

Famous Elaines: actress/ writer Elaine May; the Elaines of Arthurian legend, who both loved Lancelot; Elaine's, a literary restaurant in New York City; TV's Elaine ("Soap") Lefkowitz

ELEANOR a form of Helen

Image: Eleanor is pictured as a pretty, statuesque woman who is ambitious, hardworking, serious, and smart.

Famous Eleanors: First Lady Eleanor Roosevelt; actresses Eleanor Powell, Eleanor Parker, Elinor ("Father Knows Best") Donahue; the Beatles' song "Eleanor Rigby"

ELISE a French form of Alice, Elizabeth

Image: When people think of Elise, they picture a beautiful, feminine, family-oriented mother who is patient and sweet.

Famous Elises: TV's Elyse ("Family Ties") Keaton; Beethoven's composition "Für Elise"

ELIZA a short form of Elizabeth

Image: Eliza is described as a quiet, fragile, dull-witted old-fashioned woman — a nun or teacher, perhaps.

Famous Elizas: Eliza (*My Fair Lady*) Doolittle; Eliza in Harriet Beecher Stowe's novel *Uncle Tom's Cabin*

ELIZABETH, Elisabeth
(Hebrew) "oath of God"

Image: The name Elizabeth has two different images: a beautiful, regal woman who is spoiled, proper, and very much in control or a pretty, old-fashioned woman who is friendly and nice.

Famous Elizabeths: the biblical Elizabeth, mother of John the Baptist; actresses Elizabeth ("Bewitched") Montgomery, Elizabeth Taylor, Elisabeth Schue; Britain's Queens Elizabeth I, II; poet Elizabeth ("How Do I Love Thee?") Barrett Browning; suffragist Elizabeth Cady Stanton

ELKE a form of Alice, Alexandra

Image: Elke is pictured as a tall and graceful Scandinavian blonde who is very sexy.

Famous Elke: actress Elke Sommers

ELLA (Old English) "elf, beautiful fairy woman"

Image: People say Ella is a large, heavy black woman — an old-fashioned grandma who is happy, likeable, and friendly, like singer Ella Fitzgerald.

Famous Ellas: singer Ella Fitzgerald; actress Ella Raines; former Connecticut governor Ella Grasso

ELLEN an English form of Helen

Image: Ellen is described as a real sweetie — a pretty, pleasant, soft-spoken woman who enjoys helping others.

Famous Ellens: actress Ellen (*Same Time Next Year*) Burstyn; English political leader Ellen Wilkinson; columnist Ellen Goodman

ELLIE, Elly short forms of Eleanor, Ella, Ellen

Image: People picture Ellie as a cute, southern, old-fashioned country girl who is innocent, loving, and sweet.

Famous Ellies: TV's Elly May ("Beverly Hillbillies") Clampett, Miss Ellie ("Dallas") Ewing; Ellie in George Bernard Shaw's play *Heartbreak House*

ELOISE a French form of Louise

Image: Most people think of Eloise as happy, quiet, and very helpful. To some, though, Eloise is smart and snobby.

ELSA, Ilsa (Old German) "noble"; forms of Elizabeth

Image: The name Elsa calls to mind an actress or affluent European woman who is proud, happy, and outgoing.

Famous Elsas: actress Elsa (*Bride of Frankenstein*) Lanchester; Ilsa (*Casablanca*) Lund; Elsa, the *Born Free* lioness; couturiere Elsa Schiaparelli

ELSIE a form of Elsa, Elizabeth

Image: People picture Elsie as a pleasant, capable, old-fashioned mother. They also picture a cow.

Famous Elsies: Elsie, the "Borden's Milk" cow; interior decorator Elsie De Wolf; Martha Finley's novel *Elsie Dinsmore*

ELVIRA (German-Spanish) "elf-counsel, excelling"

Image: Elvira's image comes straight from TV's horror hostess. People imagine Elvira as a tramp who is weird, spooky, and sexy.

Famous Elviras: TV's Elvira, Mistress of the Dark; the movie *Elvira Madigan*; the Oak Ridge Boys' song "Elvira"

EMILY (German) "industrious"; (Latin) "flatterer"; a form of Amelia; a feminine form of Emil

Image: Most people picture Emily as a cute, small, quiet old-fashioned woman who is intelligent, frail, loving, and a bit prissy.

Famous Emilys: etiquette expert Emily Post; poet Emily Dickinson; novelist Emily (*Wuthering Heights*) Brontë; playwright Emily Mann

EMMA (Old German) "universal, nurse"; a short form of Emily

Image: The name Emma has a down-home image. Emma is seen as a plump, plain, elderly homebody who is happy, quiet, well mannered, and dependable.

Famous Emmas: actress Emma ("Dynasty") Samms; TV's Emma ("The Avengers") Peel; Jane Austen's novel *Emma*; poet Emma Lazarus; anarchist Emma Goldman

ENID (Welsh) "purity, woodlark"

Image: Some people think of Enid as an upper-class spinster who is stuffy and studious, but others see Enid as a vivacious party-goer.

Famous Enids: English writers Enid Bagnold, Enid Blyton; Enid of Arthurian legend

ERICA (Old Norse) "ever powerful"; a feminine form of Eric

Image: Ever powerful? You bet! Erica is regarded as a strong-willed, sultry blonde who is rich, spoiled, and always on the go.

Famous Ericas: novelist Erica (*Fear of Flying*) Jong; Erica on TV's "All My Children"

ERIN (Irish Gaelic) "peace"

Image: Most people picture Erin as a cute, fair-skinned Irish woman who is a snobby, self-centered troublemaker. To some, though, Erin is a sweet, plain, family-oriented woman.

Famous Erins: Erin, another name for Ireland; actresses Erin ("Happy Days") Moran, Erin ("Silver Spoons") Gray

ERMA (Latin) "noble" (see also Irma)

Image: Most people think of Erma as a simple, hard-working, funny woman with a happy disposition, like Erma Bombeck.

Famous Erma: humorist Erma Bombeck

ERNESTINE (Old English) "earnest"; a feminine form of Ernest

Image: When most people think of Ernestine, they picture a homely, lower-class woman who is hardworking and slow. Some also picture Lily Tomlin's funny, loudmouthed telephone operator.

Famous Ernestine: Lily Tomlin's character Ernestine

ESTELLE (Old French) "star"

Image: The name Estelle calls to mind a plump, pleasant woman who is witty and warm.

Famous Estelles: actresses Estelle ("The Golden Girls") Getty, Estelle Parsons; Estella in Charles Dickens's novel *Great Expectations*

ESTHER (Persian) "star"

Image: Two different images of Esther come to mind: a matronly homebody who is domineering and old-fashioned or a pretty woman who is sweet and serene.

Famous Esthers: the biblical Queen Esther; swimmer Esther Williams; actress Esther ("Good Times") Rolle; Henry Adams's novel *Esther*; novelist Esther Forbes; Esther P. (Ann Landers) Lederer

ETHEL (Old English) "noble"

Image: Ethel is pictured as an exuberant, warm, and friendly woman, though some also see her as matronly and grand.

Famous Ethels: entertainer Ethel Merman; actresses Ethel (*Member of the Wedding*) Waters, Ethel Barrymore; TV's Ethel ("I Love Lucy") Mertz; Ethel, Robert Kennedy's widow

ETTA (Old German) "little"; a short form of Henrietta

Image: Etta strikes people as a good name for a dumpy, older homebody who is stern and prim.

Famous Etta: blues singer Etta James

EUGENIA (Greek) "well born"

Image: Eugenia is considered an old-fashioned name befitting an awkward, unattractive woman.

Famous Eugenias: Saint Eugenia; musician Eugenia Zuckerman; France's Empress Eugenie, Napoleon's consort

EUNICE (Greek) "happy victory"

Image: Most people picture Eunice as the Carol Burnett character — loud and silly. Some, though, think Eunice is quiet, simple, and gracious.

Famous Eunices: the biblical Eunice, mother of Timothy; Eunice on TV's "The Carol Burnett Show"; Eunice Shriver, President Kennedy's sister

EVA a short form of Evangeline; a form of Eve

Image: To most people Eva is an elegant, glamorous temptress who is strong willed and devious. Some, though, think Eva is kind and sweet.

Famous Evas: actresses Eva ("Green Acres") Gabor, Eva La Gallienne, Eva-Marie Saint; Argentina's leader Eva Perón; Eva Braun, Hitler's mistress; Little Eva in Harriet Beecher Stowe's novel *Uncle Tom's Cabin*

EVE (Hebrew) "life"

Image: Eve is usually viewed as a pretty, gentle woman who is quiet and lovely. To some, though, Eve is a sexy, elegant schemer.

Famous Eves: the biblical Eve, first woman; actresses Eve ("Our Miss Brooks") Arden, Eve ("The Brady Bunch") Plumb; the movies *The Two Faces of Eve*, *All About Eve*

EVELYN (Latin) "hazel nut"

Image: The name Evelyn has two very different images: small, soft-spoken, sensitive, and mousy or large, pushy, stubborn, and strong.

Famous Evelyns: Evelyn Wood reading school; novelist Evelyn Waugh; runner Evelyn Ashford

EVITA a form of Eve

Image: The name Evita calls to mind a wild, daring, and strong Spanish woman.

Famous Evita: the musical *Evita*

EVONNE see Yvonne

FAITH (Middle English) "fidelity"

Image: People picture Faith as a petite, blonde, highly religious woman who is trustworthy, gentle, shy, and quiet.

Famous Faiths: novelist Faith Baldwin; artist Faith Ringgold; futurist Faith Popcorn

FANNY, Fannie forms of Frances

Image: Fanny is described as a dark-haired, heavy woman who is happy, funny, and so lively that she is sometimes considered impertinent or rambunctious.

Famous Fannys: entertainer Fanny (*Funny Girl*) Brice; Fannie Farmer candies; writer Fannie Hurst; actress Fannie Flagg

FARRAH (Middle English) "beautiful; pleasant"

Image: The name Farrah calls to mind actress Farrah Fawcett. Farrah is described as a pretty blonde who is sweet, flighty, and dumb.

Famous Farrah: actress Farrah ("Charlie's Angels") Fawcett

FAWN (Old French) "young deer"

Image: Fawn is pictured as a sensitive, quiet, pretty, and shy brunnette.

Famous Fawn: Oliver North's secretary, Fawn Hall

FAY, Faye (Old French) "fairy elf"

Image: Fay is described as an attractive, middle-class brunette who is loving, pleasant, and quiet.

Famous Fays: actresses Fay (*King Kong*) Wray, Faye (*Bonnie and Clyde*) Dunaway, Faye Emerson; TV's Fay ("Hill Street Blues") Furillo; reproductive rights campaigner Faye Wattleton

FELICIA, Phylicia (Latin) "happy"; feminine forms of Felix

Image: Most people think Felicia is a dark-skinned or black woman who is strong willed, intelligent, rich, and

proper. To some, though, Felicia is pouty and sickly.

Famous Felicias: actresses Phylicia ("The Cosby Show") Rashad, Felicia Farr; poet Felicia Hemans

FERN (Old English) "fern"

Image: Most people view Fern as a small, unattractive homebody who is studious and quiet. Some, though, see Fern as unpleasant and demanding.

Famous Fern: Fern in *Charlotte's Web*

FIFI a French form of Josephine

Image: The name Fifi calls to mind the expression "all looks and no brains." She is thought of as a cute but scatterbrained airhead with a French accent and curly hair. Fifi is also considered a great name for a poodle.

FLO a short form of Florence

Image: Flo is pictured as a big woman who is either fun loving and sassy or dumpy, oldfashioned, and dependable.

Famous Flos: TV's Flo ("Alice") Castleberry; Flo in "Andy Capp" comics; producer Flo Ziegfeld; runner Florence (Flo-Jo) Griffith-Joyner

FLORENCE (Latin) "blooming, prosperous"

Image: The name Florence has two different images: a vivacious woman who is cheerful and charming or a prudish, quiet old maid.

Famous Florences: actress Florence ("The Brady Bunch")

Henderson; nurse Florence Nightingale; Florence on TV's "The Jeffersons"; runner Florence Griffith-Joyner; the city of Florence, Italy

FRAN a short form of Frances

Image: Fran is pictured as a strong, tall, skinny woman who is a fun-loving smart aleck.

Famous Frans: Fran on TV's "Kukla, Fran, and Ollie"; actress Mary ("Newhart") Frann

FRANCES (Latin) "free, from France"; a feminine form of Francis

Image: Most people picture Frances as a slight, old-fashioned woman who is nice, loving, and rather staid.

Famous Franceses: former secretary of labor Frances Perkins; author Frances Trollope; children's story writer Frances Hodges (*The Secret Garden*) Burnett; magazine publisher Frances Lear

FRANCESCA a form of Frances

Image: The name Francesca has a decidedly European flavor. People say Francesca is a pretty, upper-class sophisticate who is quiet, yet sultry, and very exciting.

Famous Francescas: actress Francesca Annis; Francesca de Remini in Dante's *Inferno*; Mother Francesca Cabrini, first American saint

FRANCINE a French form of Frances

Image: When people think of the name Francine, they imagine a dainty woman who is prim, proper, and quiet — a high-class model, perhaps.

Famous Francines: TV's Francine ("Scarecrow and Mrs. King") Desmond, Francine ("One Day at a Time") Webster

FRANÇOISE a French form of Frances

Image: Françoise is described as a Frenchwoman who speaks with a decided accent, has a dark complexion and curly hair, and maintains a happy-go-lucky attitude.

FRANNIE, Franny short forms of Frances

Image: Most people picture Frannie as a plain-looking, older woman who is old-fashioned, down-to-earth, and caring. To some, though, Frannie is a pretty redhead who is mischievous and outgoing.

Famous Frannies: J. D. Salinger's novella *Franny and Zooey*; Franny in John Irving's novel *Hotel New Hampshire*

FREDA, Frieda (Old German) "peaceful"; short forms of Frederica

Image: Freda is pictured as a big, plain, old-fashioned German spinster who could be jovial, gentle, or even pushy.

Famous Fredas: singer Freda ("Band of Gold") Payne; Frieda von Richthofen Lawrence, wife of D. H. Lawrence; psychoanalyst Frieda Fromm-Reichmann

FREDERICA, Frederika
(Old German) "peaceful ruler"; feminine forms of Frederick

Image: The name Frederica calls to mind an older foreign woman who is smart, capable, and snobby

Famous Frederika: Queen Frederika of the Netherlands

GABRIELLE
(Hebrew) "God is my strength"; a feminine form of Gabriel

Image: Gabrielle is pictured as a dark, angelic Frenchwoman with quiet strength.

Famous Gabrielles: designer Gabrielle (Coco) Chanel; tennis's Gabriela Sabatini

GAIL, Gayle
(Old English) "gay, lively"; short forms of Abigail; forms of Gay

Image: The name Gail evokes an image of a short, average-looking woman whose pleasant personality is either gentle, quiet, and serene or joyous and bubbly.

Famous Gails: country singers Gail Davies, Crystal Gayle; actress Gale ("My Little Margie") Storm; novelist Gail Godwin

GAY
(Old French) "merry"; a form of Gail, Gayle

Image: People picture Gay as either lively, happy, and fun loving or quiet, peaceful, and shy.

Famous Gays: novelist Gay Talese; singer Marvin ("I Heard It Through the Grapevine") Gaye; golfer Gay Brewer, Jr.

GENEVIEVE
(Old German-French) "white wave"; a form of ˙Guinevere

Image: Genevieve is described as a very pretty woman with long, dark hair who is an outgoing organizer.

Famous Genevieves: Saint Genevieve, patron saint of Paris; actress Genevieve (*Anne of the Thousand Days*) Bujold

GEORGEANNE, Georgiana
forms of Georgia

Image: Georgeanne is imagined as a southern farm girl who may be either self-conscious and shy or talkative and scatterbrained.

Famous Georgiana: Georgiana Darcy in Jane Austen's novel *Pride and Prejudice*

GEORGIA
(Latin) "farmer"; a feminine form of George

Image: People think Georgia is a good name for a pretty southern belle who is a friendly social butterfly.

Famous Georgias: the songs "Sweet Georgia Brown," "Georgia on My Mind"; the state of Georgia; American painter Georgia O'Keeffe

GERALDINE (Old German-French) a feminine form of Gerald

> **Image:** Most people picture Geraldine as a tall woman who is talented, strong, and nice.

> **Famous Geraldines:** politician Geraldine Ferraro; actresses Geraldine Fitzgerald, Geraldine (*The Trip to Bountiful*) Page; Flip Wilson's character Geraldine

GERRI, Jerry short forms of Geraldine; feminine forms of Gerald

> **Image:** Gerri is described as a friendly, fun-loving brunette who enjoys being the life of the party.

> **Famous Jerry:** model/actress Jerry Hall

GERTRUDE (Old German) "spear strength, warrior woman"

> **Image:** The name Gertrude has two different images: a somber, introverted little old lady or an overbearing, busy, buxom woman.

> **Famous Gertrudes:** Saint Gertrude, patron saint of travelers; writer Gertrude Stein; comic actresses Gertrude ("The Goldbergs") Berg, Gertrude Lawrence; Gertrude in Shakespeare's play *Hamlet*; novelist Gertrude Atherton; swimmer Gertrude Ederle; blues singer Gertrude (Ma) Rainey

GIGI (Old German) a short form of Gilberte

> **Image:** Gigi's image comes straight from the musical of the same name. People say Gigi is a cute, playful French girl who is a bit of a dreamer.

> **Famous Gigi:** the musical *Gigi*

GILDA (Old English) "covered with gold"

> **Image:** Gilda Radner is the dominant image for this name. Gilda is pictured as a small, silly, funny show-off.

> **Famous Gildas:** comic actress Gilda ("Saturday Night Live") Radner; Gilda in Verdi's opera *Rigoletto*

GILLIAN a form of Jillian (see also Jillian)

> **Image:** Gillian is considered a good name for a cute, thin, dark-haired southern belle who is rich, popular, and lots of fun.

GINA, Geena, Jena short forms of Angelina, Regina

> **Image:** The name Gina has two very different images: a petite, gorgeous, dark-haired Italian woman who is a spoiled brat or a plain, chubby woman who is lots of fun.

> **Famous Ginas:** actresses Gina Lollobrigida, Gena Rowlands, Geena (*The Accidental Tourist*) Davis

GINGER (Latin) "ginger (the flower or spice)"; a short form of Virginia

> **Image:** People picture Ginger as a thin, cute, redheaded dancer who is witty, lively, and perhaps a bit short tempered.

> **Famous Gingers:** dancer Ginger Rogers; Ginger on TV's "Gilligan's Island"

GINNY a short form of Virginia

> **Image:** Most people regard Ginny as a thin, plain, nice hometown girl who is either quiet and shy or talkative.
>
> **Famous Ginny:** Ginny Mae, a nickname for the Government National Mortgage Association

GISELLE (Old German) "pledge, hostage"

> **Image:** Most people picture Giselle as a pretty, dark-haired French dancer who is graceful and serene. To some, though, Giselle is a big, dowdy old gossip.
>
> **Famous Giselles:** the ballet *Giselle*; singer Gisele MacKenzie

GLADYS (Celtic) "princess"; (Latin) "small sword, gladiolus flower"; a Welsh form of Claudia

> **Image:** People picture Gladys as a heavyset, dowdy older woman with thick glasses. Gladys may come across as old-fashioned and friendly; or boozy and loudmouthed.
>
> **Famous Gladyses:** singer Gladys Knight; TV's Gladys ("Bewitched") Kravitz; English painter Gladys Cooper; musician Gladys Bentley

GLENDA (Irish Gaelic) "from the valley or glen"; a form of Glenna; a feminine form of Glenn

> **Image:** Glenda is described as an energetic woman with a sparkling personality and a rather homely appearance.
>
> **Famous Glendas:** actresses Glenda Jackson, Glenda Farrell

GLORIA (Latin) "glory"

> **Image:** To most people Gloria is a beautiful, blonde glamour girl who has been spoiled rotten. To some, though, Gloria is a quiet, happy, middle-class homemaker.
>
> **Famous Glorias:** singer Gloria Estefan from The Miami Sound Machine; actresses Gloria DeHaven, Gloria Swanson, Gloria Grahame; feminist Gloria (*Ms.*) Steinem; designer Gloria Vanderbilt

GOLDA (Old English) "gold"

> **Image:** The name Golda brings Golda Meir to mind. People picture Golda as an older Jewish woman who is highly intelligent, staunch, and upright.
>
> **Famous Goldas:** Israel's former prime minister Golda Meir; Golde, Tevye's wife in the musical *Fiddler on the Roof*

GRACE (Latin) "graceful"

> **Image:** When people think of Grace, they imagine an old woman who is quiet, sweet, and witty.
>
> **Famous Graces:** actresses Gracie Allen, Grace (Princess Grace of Monaco) Kelly; singer/actress Grace Jones; singer Grace Slick from The Jefferson Airplane; TV's Grace ("L.A. Law") Van Owen

GRETA a German short form of Margaret

> **Image:** Most people picture Greta as a sexy blonde actress of Swedish or German descent with great legs. To some,

though, Greta is a studious, hardworking, and prissy woman.

Famous Greta: actress Greta Garbo

GRETCHEN a German form of Margaret

Image: People describe Gretchen as a blonde of German or Swedish descent who is either a friendly, old-fashioned country girl or a bright, ambitious go-getter.

Famous Gretchens: TV's Gretchen ("Benson") Kraus; Gretchen Carlson, Miss America 1989; Gretchen in Johann Goethe's play *Faust*

GWEN, Gwyn short forms of Guinevere, Gwendolyn

Image: People picture Gwen as a pretty woman who is either quiet, sweet, and gentle or friendly and vivacious.

Famous Gwens: actresses Gwen (*Damn Yankees*) Verdon, Nell Gwyn

GWENDOLYN (Welsh) "white, white-browed"

Image: Gwendolyn is described as an upper-class sophisticate who is restrained and proper.

Famous Gwendolyns: poet Gwendolyn Brooks; Gwendolyn, wife of Merlin the Magician; Gwendolen (*The Importance of Being Earnest*) Fairfax

GYPSY (Old English) "wanderer"

Image: The name Gypsy reminds people of either a stripper or a dark-haired, wild, and free-spirited vagabond.

Famous Gypsys: entertainer Gypsy Rose Lee; Europe's Gypsy people

HALEY, Hayley (Scandinavian) "hero"

Image: Haley is a contemporary-sounding name that calls to mind a dark-haired tomboy who is smart, spunky, bubbly, and perhaps a bit of a rascal.

Famous Haleys: actress Hayley (*The Parent Trap*) Mills; novelist Alex (*Roots*) Haley; singer Bill Haley of Bill Haley and the Comets; Halley's comet

HANNAH, Hanna (Hebrew) "graceful"; Hebrew forms of Ann

Image: People think the name Hannah has an old-fashioned or old-world flavor that might suit a big, sickly woman, a black singer, or a rich snob.

Famous Hannahs: the movie *Hannah and Her Sisters*; tennis's Hana Mandlikova; the biblical Hannah, Samuel's mother; Hanna-Barbera cartoons; political philosopher Hannah Arendt

HAPPY (English) "happy"

Image: Not surprisingly, this name evokes an image of a

smiling, cheerful woman who is full of fun and just as happy as her name suggests.

Famous Happys: Happy Rockefeller, former governor Nelson Rockefeller's wife; Happy (*Death of a Salesman*) Loman; Xaviera Hollander's book *The Happy Hooker*; Happy, one of the seven dwarves

HARRIET (Old French) "ruler of the home"

Image: This name calls to mind a number of different images: a plain-looking, dull, stodgy hardworker; a smiling, outgoing scatterbrain; or a spoiled, rich prude.

Famous Harriets: TV's Harriet ("Ozzie and Harriet") Nelson, Harriet ("Little House on the Prairie") Oleson; novelist/abolitionist Harriet Beecher (*Uncle Tom's Cabin*) Stowe; abolitionist Harriet Tubman

HATTIE a short form of Harriet, Henrietta

Image: Hattie is pictured as a chubby, motherly, old-fashioned black woman who is sweet and lovable.

Famous Hatties: actress Hattie (*Gone with the Wind*) McDaniel; entertainer Hilo Hattie; designer Hattie Carnegie

HAZEL (Old English) "hazelnut tree, commanding authority"

Image: TV's Hazel the maid is the dominant image for this name — a stout, dowdy older woman who is hardworking, nice, and nutty.

Famous Hazels: TV's "Hazel"; pianist Hazel Scott; Hazel in John Steinbeck's novel *Cannery Row*

HEATHER (Middle English) "flowering heather"

Image: People say Heather is a very sweet blonde who is carefree, outgoing, and fun but not very bright.

Famous Heathers: actresses Heather ("Dynasty") Locklear, Heather ("The Fall Guy") Thomas, Heather (*Poltergeist*) O'Rourke; the movie *Heathers*

HEDDA (Old German) "strife"

Image: Strife? You bet! Hedda is described as an ugly old gossip and a tough, nosy busybody.

Famous Heddas: Henrik Ibsen's play *Hedda Gabler*; columnist Hedda Hopper

HEIDI a short form of Adalheid, Adelaide

Image: People picture Heidi as the childlike character in the book or movie — a pretty, quiet, sweet Germanic or Scandinavian girl with braided blonde hair.

Famous Heidi: Johanna Spyri's children's story *Heidi*

HELEN (Greek) "light"

Image: People picture Helen as a pretty upper-class woman with dark hair and dark eyes who is graceful, smart, and well educated.

Famous Helens: actresses Helen Hayes, Helen (*Ruthless People*) Slater, Helen Hunt;

Helen Keller; singer Helen
("Delta Dawn") Reddy;
legendary beauty Helen of
Troy; *Cosmopolitan* editor
Helen Gurley Brown

HELGA (Old German) "pious";
a form of Olga

Image: Helga strikes people as
a good name for a big, strong,
pigtailed Scandinavian blonde
who is loud and bossy.

Famous Helgas: Helga,
Andrew Wyeth's model; Helga
in "Hagar the Horrible" comics

HELOISE a French form of
Eloise

Image: Heloise is inseparably
linked with household hints.
People say Heloise is smart,
helpful, and informative.

Famous Heloises: columnist
Heloise; Heloise, beloved of
Paul Abelard

HENRIETTA (French) "mistress
of the household"; a feminine form
of Henry

Image: Henrietta is described
as fat, fussy, old-fashioned,
and downright horrible.

Famous Henriettas: Zionist
leader Henrietta Szold; Phineas
Fogg's ship *Henrietta*; TV's
Henrietta ("The New Zoo
Review") Hippo; American
financier Henrietta Green

HESTER (Greek) "star"; a Dutch
form of Esther

Image: Hester is described as
an ugly, old-fashioned,
straitlaced old farm woman —
a teacher or grandmother,
perhaps.

Famous Hester: Hester
(*The Scarlet Letter*) Prynne

HILARY, Hillary (Greek)
"cheerful, merry"

Image: Hilary is pictured as
a pretty woman, possibly
English, who is a flighty,
sophisticated snob.

Famous Hillary: climber Sir
Edmund Hillary

HILDA (Old German) "woman
warrior"; a short form of
Hildegarde

Image: Hilda strikes people
as a good name for a fat,
unattractive older woman with
a hairnet — a dowdy maid or
farmer, perhaps.

Famous Hildas: poet/writer
Hilda Doolittle; "Broom Hilda"
comics; Hilda, one of the
Valkyrie of Norse mythology

HILDEGARDE (Old German)
"fortress"

Image: A fortress, indeed!
People say Hildegarde is a
large, stocky German woman
who may be an opera singer,
gym teacher, matron, or witch.

Famous Hildegardes: actress
Hildegarde (*The Snows of
Kilimanjaro*) Neff; Hildegarde
in Wagner's opera *The
Nibelungen Ring*; Saint
Hildegarde, eleventh-century
abbess

HOLLY (Old English) "holly tree"

Image: Most people think of
Holly as a pretty, dark-haired
girl who is bright, cheerful,
vivacious, and sweet. To some,
though, Holly is homely and
shy.

Famous Hollys: actress Holly (*Broadcast News*) Hunter; Holly (*Breakfast at Tiffany's*) Golightly

HONEY, Honi (Old English) "sweet"

Image: Honey is regarded as a stereotypical dumb blonde — a pretty, blue-eyed, sexy woman with a sweet disposition, a raspy voice, and no brains.

Famous Honeys: TV's "Honey West;" Bobby Goldsboro's song "Honey"; Honey in the movie *Who's Afraid of Virginia Woolf?*; Honi in "Hagar the Horrible" and "Doonesbury" comics

HOPE (Old English) "hope"

Image: When people think of Hope, they picture a pious, calm, angelic woman who is quiet, gentle, and demure.

Famous Hopes: actress Hope Lange; comic actor Bob Hope; TV's Hope ("thirtysomething") Steadman

HORTENSE (Latin) "gardener"

Image: People picture Hortense as an unattractive, awkward older woman who is old-fashioned and strange.

Famous Hortenses: novelist Hortense Calisher; anthropologist Hortense Powdermaker

IDA (Old English) "prosperous"; (Old German) "hardworking"

Image: People think of Ida as an old gossip who is old-fashioned, hardworking, and stern.

Famous Idas: actress Ida (*High Sierra*) Lupino; Mount Ida; singer Ida Cox

ILENE a form of Aileen (see also Aileen, Eileen)

Image: The name Ilene has two different images: a quiet, pure, and gentle woman or a loud, buxom bimbo.

ILSA see Elsa

IMOGENE (Latin) "image"

Image: The name Imogene reminds people of Imogene Coca. They say Imogene is homely, fun loving, and zany.

Famous Imogenes: comedienne Imogene Coca; Imogen in Shakespeare's play *Cymbeline*

INEZ a Spanish form of Agnes

Image: The name Inez calls to mind an elderly Spanish matron who is either loud and hot tempered or carefree and nice.

Famous Inezes: suffragist/writer Inez Haynes Gillmore Irwin; Donna Inez, mother of Don Juan in Lord Byron's poem "Don Juan"

INGA, Inge (Scandinavian) "Inge, an old Germanic hero"; forms of Ingrid

Image: People picture Inga as a tall Scandinavian blonde who is strong willed and self-assured.

Famous Ingas: actress Inga ("Benson") Swenson; dramatic soprano Inge Borkh

INGRID (Scandinavian) "hero's daughter"

Image: People picture Ingrid as a Scandinavian blonde who is intelligent, enthusiastic, and hardworking. Inga is pictured as either beautiful, like Ingrid Bergman, or as a big, strong, older woman.

Famous Ingrid: actress Ingrid (*Casablanca*) Bergman

IRENE (Greek) "peace"

Image: Irene strikes people as a good name for a quiet, middle-aged Irishwoman who is nice, funny, and light on her feet.

Famous Irenes: the mythological Irene, Greek goddess of peace; singer Irene ("Fame") Cara; dancer Irene Castle; the song "Good Night, Irene"; Irene Adler, who bested Sherlock Holmes; actress Irene ("Beverly Hillbillies") Ryan; Irene (*Life with Father*) Powell; Irene (*Penny Serenade*) Dunne

IRIS (Greek) "rainbow"

Image: People picture Iris as tall, slender, delicate, and prissy.

Famous Irises: Iris, Greek goddess of the rainbow; novelist Iris Murdoch; film critic Iris Barry

IRMA (Latin) "noble" (see also Erma)

Image: Irma reminds people of Irma La Douce, the hardworking, dumpy French prostitute played by Shirley MacLaine in the movie of the same name.

Famous Irma: Broadway musical/movie *Irma La Douce*

ISABEL, Isabella (Old Spanish) "consecrated to God"; a Spanish form of Elizabeth

Image: Isabel is pictured by some as a carefree, fun-loving, sultry beauty and by others as an old-fashioned, demanding, wealthy woman.

Famous Isabels: Queen Isabella I of Spain; actresses Isabel ("The Jeffersons") Sanford, Isabella (*Blue Velvet*) Rossellini; explorer Isabella Bird

ISADORA (Latin) "gift of Isis"; a feminine form of Isador

Image: Some people picture Isadora as an ugly witch or cruel stepmother from a fairy tale. Others, though, picture a wild, crazy, and avant-garde woman, like Isadora Duncan.

Famous Isadoras: dancer Isadora Duncan; Saint Isadore of Seville; Isadora (*Fear of Flying*) Wing

IVETTE see Yvette

IVY (Old English) "ivy tree"

Image: The name Ivy has two different images: an outdated, motherly woman who is staid and sedate or a southern belle who is outgoing and quick witted.

Famous Ivys: U. S. Treasurer Ivy Baker Priest; novelist Ivy Compton-Burnett

JACKIE a short form of Jacoba, Jacqueline

Image: People picture Jackie as an attractive jet-setter who is fashionable, stylish, sophisticated, and self-centered.

Famous Jackies: First Lady Jackie Kennedy Onassis; comic actors Jackie Cooper, Jackie Gleason; athlete Jackie Joyner-Kersee; Little Jackie ("Puff, the Magic Dragon") Paper

JACQUELINE, Jaclyn

(Hebrew) "supplanter"; (Old French) "little Jacques"; feminine forms of Jacob (through Jacques)

Image: Thanks to the First Lady, Jacqueline is described as dark, slender, beautiful, and mysterious — a rich, elegant sophisticate who is loaded with charm but is not above throwing a tantrum now and then.

Famous Jacquelines: First Lady Jacqueline Kennedy Onassis; actresses Jacqueline (*The Deep*) Bissett, Jaclyn ("Charlie's Angels") Smith;

aviator Jacqueline Cochran; novelist Jacqueline (*Once Is Not Enough*) Susann

JAIME, Jamie (French) "I love"; feminine forms of James

Image: Jaime is a popular unisex name. A girl with this name is pictured as cute, sensual, and mischievous.

Famous Jamies: actor Jamie ("M*A*S*H") Farr; actress Jamie Lee ("Anything But Love") Curtis

JANA (Arabic) "a harvest of fruit"; a form of Johanna

Image: People say Jana is an attractive woman who is hardworking and strong, yet warm and gentle.

JANE (Hebrew) "God is gracious"; a feminine form of John

Image: No surprise! People think of Jane as plain. The name calls to mind the common, dependable, garden-variety girl-next-door to whom some people refer as "Jane Doe."

Famous Janes: Charlotte Brontë's novel *Jane Eyre*; actresses Jane Fonda, Jane Russell, Jane Wyman, Jane Curtin; TV host Jane Pauley; generic Jane Doe; frontierswoman Calamity Jane

JANET a form of Jane

Image: Janet is seen as a bright, lively, and social woman who is likely to be a reliable hardworker.

Famous Janets: novelist Janet Dailey; actresses Janet (*A Star*

Is Born) Gaynor, Janet
(*Psycho*) Leigh; swimmer Janet
Evans; pop singer Janet
Jackson

JANICE a form of Jane
(see also Janis)

Image: Unlike the brassy Janis,
Janice is perceived as a nice,
loving friend.

JANINE a form of Jane

Image: Janine is considered
a suitable name for a big, solid
woman who is sweet and
smart.

JANIS a form of Jane
(see also Janice)

Image: Janis is pictured as a
tall, willowy woman with bright
green eyes who expresses her
emotions freely and may step
on a few toes once in a while.

Famous Janises: singers
Janis ("Me and Bobby
McGee") Joplin, Janis
("At Seventeen") Ian

JASMINE (Persian) "jasmine
flower"

Image: The name Jasmine
evokes an image of delicate
flowers and the fragrance of
perfume. A woman named
Jasmine is perceived as a
pretty and gentle free spirit.

Famous Jasmines: the flower
jasmine; actress Jasmine
("A Different World") Guy

JEAN, Jeanne Scottish forms
of Jane, Joan

Image: Jean is a common
name that seems appropriate
for a capable, reliable woman
who might be either cute and

feminine or plain and
tomboyish.

Famous Jeans: diplomat
Jeane Kirkpatrick; actress Jean
("All in the Family") Stapleton;
TV's "I Dream of Jeannie"

JENNIFER (Welsh) "white, fair";
a form of Guinevere

Image: Recently Jennifer has
become a popular name (some
say too popular). People think
Jennifer is a perfect name for a
cute, blonde cheerleader who
is popular and sweet.

Famous Jennifers: actresses
Jennifer Warren, Jennifer
(*Flashdance*) Beals, Jennifer
Jones, Jennifer (*Summer of
'42*) O'Neill, Jennifer (*Dirty
Dancing*) Grey

JENNY, Jennie short forms
of Jane, Jennifer

Image: Jenny is described as
a fun, outgoing girl-next-door
with a country-western style.
Some people, though, see
Jenny as a frumpy homemaker
or grandmother.

Famous Jennys: singer Jenny
(The Swedish Nightingale)
Lind; Jenny (*The World
According to Garp*) Fields;
Theodore Dreiser's novel
Jennie Gerhardt; the song
"A Portrait of Jenny"

JERRY see Gerri

JESSICA (Hebrew) "wealthy";
a feminine form of Jesse

Image: Most people see
Jessica as a sweet, pretty,
popular girl; some see her as
a dainty, spoiled, rich girl;
others are reminded of a
hardy pioneer woman.

Famous Jessicas: actresses Jessica (*Tootsie*) Lange, Jessica (*Driving Miss Daisy*) Tandy, Jessica (*Play Misty for Me*) Walters; newscaster Jessica Savitch; TV's Jessica ("Murder, She Wrote") Fletcher; Jessica Hahn, Jim Bakker's friend; Jessica (*Who Framed Roger Rabbit*) Rabbit

JESSIE a short form of Jasmine, Jessica; a Scottish form of Janet

Image: Jessie is a unisex name that calls to mind a big, cute, athletic tomboy who is fun, friendly, and smart.

Famous Jessies: singer Jessye Norman; Carly Simon's song "Jesse"

JEWEL (Old French) "precious gem"

Image: Precious gem? You bet! Jewel has a reputation as a real daddy's girl who is very pretty, popular, and spoiled.

JEZEBEL (Hebrew) "unexalted, impure"

Image: Jezebel's main image is straight from the Bible — a sultry temptress who is strong willed and faithless. To some, though, Jezebel is an over-weight, old-fashioned black nanny.

Famous Jezebels: the biblical Jezebel, wife of King Ahab; the movie *Jezebel*

JILL a short form of Jillian

Image: People think that Jill is a good name for a tall, thin young girl who is plain, quiet, and very nice.

Famous Jills: actresses Jill (*Diamonds Are Forever*) St. John, Jill (*An Unmarried Woman*) Clayburgh, Jill (*Death Wish II*) Ireland; the nursery rhyme "Jack and Jill"

JILLIAN (Latin) "young, downy-haired child" (see also Gillian)

Image: Ann Jillian provides the dominant image for this name. People describe Jillian as a sexy blonde who is classy and vivacious.

Famous Jillian: actress Ann Jillian

JO short form of Joan, Joanna, Josephine

Image: When people think of Jo, they imagine a real tomboy who is outdoorsy, down-to-earth, and caring.

Famous Jos: skater Jo-Jo Starbuck; Jo (*Little Women*) March; actress Jo (*East of Eden*) Van Fleet

JOAN (Hebrew) "God is gracious"; a form of Jane; a feminine form of John

Image: To most people Joan is plain, serious, boring, and kind. To some, though, Joan is obnoxious, brassy, and loud.

Famous Joans: Saint Joan of Arc; actresses Joan ("Dynasty") Collins, Joan (*Mildred Pierce*) Crawford, Joan (*Rebecca*) Fontaine, Joan ("Knots Landing") Van Ark; novelist Joan Didion; come-dienne Joan Rivers; TV host Joan Lunden; singers Joan ("I Love Rock and Roll") Jett, Joan Armatrading; opera singer Joan Sutherland

JOANNA a form of Jane; a feminine form of John

Image: Joanna is considered a good name for a plain, traditional, family-oriented woman — a secretary or nurse, perhaps.

Famous Joannas: Spain's Queen, Joanna the Mad; actress Joanna ("Growing Pains") Kerns; TV's Joanna ("Newhart") Loudon

JOCELYN (Latin) "merry"; (Old English) "just"

Image: Jocelyn is pictured as a very pretty country girl who is quiet, playful, and sweet.

JODY, Jodie forms of Joan, Judith

Image: Jody is a unisex name that calls to mind a cute, athletic, freckle-faced girl with a cheerful disposition and a high level of energy. Girls named Jody tend to be regarded as tomboys.

Famous Jodys: actress Jodie (*The Accused*) Foster; public official Jody Powell; singer Jody Watley; Jody (*The Yearling*) Baxter

JOLENE (Middle English) "he will increase"

Image: The jury is split on the name Jolene. She is pictured as either a spoiled, snotty southern belle or an outgoing, boisterous country girl.

Famous Jolene: Dolly Parton's song "Jolene"

JOLIE (French) "pretty"

Image: Contrary to the original French meaning of the name, Jolie is often pictured as a short, dark, mousy older woman.

JOSEPHINE (Hebrew) "he shall increase"; a feminine form of Joseph

Image: Josephine is described as a plain, big, dark-haired older woman who is proper and strict.

Famous Josephines: Josephine de Beauharnais, Napoleon's empress; novelist Josephine Tey; actresses Josephine (*Arsenic and Old Lace*) Hull, Josephine Baker; the song "Come, Josephine, in My Flying Machine"

JOY (Latin) "joy"

Image: Joy's image lives up to her name as a delightful woman who is happy, friendly, and a joy to be with. To some, Joy is slightly kooky; to others, she is serious and hard-working.

Famous Joys: author Joy (*Born Free: A Lioness of Two Worlds*) Adamson; scientist Joy Williams

JOYCE (Latin) "joyous"

Image: Most people think of Joyce as a peppy, fun-loving, loyal friend. Some, though, think of Joyce as bright but bossy.

Famous Joyces: psychologist Dr. Joyce Brothers; TV's Joyce ("Hill Street Blues") Davenport; novelists Joyce Carol Oates, James Joyce

JUANITA a Spanish form of Joan

Image: Juanita is described as a Mexican woman who is either fat, homely, and quiet or pretty, flirty, and fun.

Famous Juanitas: former secretary of commerce Juanita Kreps; actress Juanita Hall; the song "Juanita"

JUDITH (Hebrew) "of Judah"

Image: People think Judith is a stodgy name suitable for someone tall, introspective, well organized, and very proper — a writer, perhaps.

Famous Judiths: the apocryphal Judith, slayer of Holofernes; actresses Dame Judith Anderson, Judith ("Who's the Boss?") Light; novelists Judith (*Ordinary People*) Guest, Judith (*Princess Daisy*) Krantz; humor writer Judith Viorst

JUDY a short form of Judith

Image: Judy is regarded as a little pixie who is short, cute, and very nice.

Famous Judys: actresses Judy (*The Wizard of Oz*) Garland, Judy (*Born Yesterday*) Holliday; children's story writer Judy Blume; TV's "Punch and Judy" shows

JULIA (Latin) "youthful"; a feminine form of Julius

Image: People think of Julia as a good-looking brunette who is kind, lively, and thoroughly middle class.

Famous Julias: chef Julia Child; Lillian Hellman's story "Julia"; actresses Julia

("Newhart") Duffy, Julia (*Steel Magnolias*) Roberts; reformer Julia Ward Howe; the Beatles' song "Julia"

JULIANNE, Juliana forms of Julia

Image: People picture Julianne as either studious, well organized, and shy or friendly, popular, and outgoing.

Famous Juliannes: model Julianne Phillips; Queen Juliana of the Netherlands

JULIE a form of Julia

Image: The name Julie calls to mind a tall, quiet woman who is pleasant and average.

Famous Julies: singer/actress Julie (*Mary Poppins*) Andrews; singer Julie London; actresses Julie (*Doctor Zhivago*) Christie, Julie (*East of Eden*) Harris; Julie Nixon Eisenhower, President Nixon's daughter

JUNE (Latin) "June"

Image: Most people think of June as the girl-next-door — a bright, loving homebody with medium coloring and a medium build. Some, though, see June as plain, tacky, and dull.

Famous Junes: singer June Carter Cash; actresses June (*Little Women*) Allyson, June ("Lassie") Lockhart; TV's June ("Leave It to Beaver") Cleaver; the June Taylor dancers

JUSTINE (Latin) "just"; a feminine form of Justin

Image: Justine is pictured as a tall, dark, and pretty woman who may be French. Justine is also perceived as snobby or even secretive due to her regal, sophisticated bearing.

Famous Justines: actress Justine ("Family Ties") Bateman; the Marquis de Sade's novel *Justine*; Lawrence Durrell's novel *Justine*; Judge Justine Wise Polier

KARA see Cara

KAREN a Danish form of Katherine

> **Image:** People think of Karen as a plain, brown-haired woman who is dependable, fun, and a good friend.

> **Famous Karens:** singer Karen ("We've Only Just Begun") Carpenter; actresses Karen (*Animal House*) Allen, Karen (*Five Easy Pieces*) Black, Karen ("Room 222") Valentine; novelist Baroness Karen (*Out of Africa*) Blixen; right-to-die patient Karen Ann Quinlan

KARI a short form of Katherine

> **Image:** To most people Kari is a small, cute girl who is smart, fun loving, friendly, and sweet. To some, though, Kari is sickly and quiet.

KATE a short form of Katherine

> **Image:** The name Kate calls to mind a cute, outgoing, energetic, and down-to-earth woman.

Famous Kates: singers Kate ("God Bless America") Smith, Kate Bush, Kate Wolf; actress Kate ("Charlie's Angels") Jackson; the musical *Kiss Me, Kate*

KATHERINE (Greek) "pure" (see also Catherine)

> **Image:** Katherine is pictured as an old-fashioned, motherly woman who is very nice.

> **Famous Katherines:** Katherina in Shakespeare's play *The Taming of the Shrew*; actresses Katharine (*The African Queen*) Hepburn; novelists Katherine Mansfield, Katherine Anne Porter

KATHLEEN (Greek) "pure"; an Irish form of Katherine (see also Cathleen)

> **Image:** Kathleen is thought of as an old-fashioned, family-oriented Irishwoman who is overweight but cute and a real sweetheart.

> **Famous Kathleens:** actress Kathleen (*Romancing the Stone*) Turner; TV host Kathleen ("CBS This Morning") Sullivan; the song "I'll Take You Home Again, Kathleen"

KATHY, Kathie short forms of Katherine, Kathleen (see also Cathy)

> **Image:** Kathy is described as a small dark-haired woman who is quiet, friendly, and very kind.

> **Famous Kathys:** TV host Kathie Lee Gifford; TV's Kathy ("Father Knows Best") Anderson

KATIE, Katy short forms of Katherine

Image: Katie is pictured as a cute, blonde, petite athlete with an entertaining style.

Famous Katies: the movie *The Sons of Katie Elder;* Steely Dan's song "Katy Lied"; the song "K-K-K Katie, Beautiful Katie"

KAY, Kaye short forms of Katherine

Image: Kay is said to be an overweight but classy woman who is friendly and sweet on the surface and calculating and cold underneath.

Famous Kays: jazz band-leader Kay Kaiser; actresses Kaye ("The Mothers-in-Law") Ballard, Kay (*White Line Fever*) Lenz; actor Danny (*White Christmas*) Kaye; short story writer/poet Kay Boyle; Sir Kay of Arthurian legend

KAYLA a form of Kay, Katherine (see also Cayla)

Image: The name Kayla evokes an image of a petite, pretty girl who is well behaved and has a sunny, sweet disposition.

Famous Kayla: TV's Kayla ("Days of Our Lives") Johnson

KELLY (Irish Gaelic) "warrior"

Image: Two different images of Kelly come to mind: a cute, redheaded Irish girl who is charming and fun or a heavy, ambitious bigmouth who is bossy and obnoxious.

Famous Kellys: actress Kelly (*Witness*) McGillis; actor/

dancer Gene (*An American in Paris*) Kelly; comedian Kelly Monteith; clown Emmett Kelly

KENDRA (Old English) "knowledgeable"

Image: Kendra is described as a very pretty black woman who is smart, reserved, and nice.

KERRY (Irish Gaelic) "dark, dark-haired" (see also Carrie)

Image: Kerry is a unisex name that seems appropriate for a freckle-faced tomboy who is friendly and outgoing. Some, though, think of Kerry as rich and spoiled.

Famous Kerrys: Senator John Kerry; Kerry county in Ireland

KIKI (American) a short form of names beginning with *K*

Image: Kiki is pictured as cute, exotic, happy, kooky, and rather dumb. People think Kiki is a fine name for a rock star or the family pet.

Famous Kikis: singer Kiki ("Don't Go Breaking My Heart") Dee; basketball's Kiki Vandeweghe; baseball's Kiki Cuyler; French model/singer Kiki de Montparnasse

KIM (Old English) "chief, ruler"; a short form of Kimberly

Image: Kim is pictured as a tall cute blonde who is either friendly and nice or cool and snobby.

Famous Kims: actresses Kim (*Vertigo*) Novak, Kim (*True Grit*) Darby, Kim (*Planet of the Apes*) Hunter, Kim (*Batman*) Basinger; Rudyard Kipling's novel *Kim*

KIMBERLY (Old English) "from the royal fortress meadow"

> **Image:** Kimberly is thought to be a pretty, outgoing woman who is kind, considerate, and down-to-earth.
>
> **Famous Kimberly:** Kimberly-Clark products

KIRA, Kiri (Persian) "sun"; feminine forms of Cyrus

> **Image:** The name Kira has an exotic flavor, though people are not sure of its origin. Kira is imagined as attractive, energetic, nice, and refined.
>
> **Famous Kiri:** opera singer Kiri Te Kanawa

KIRSTEN a Scandinavian form of Christine

> **Image:** People picture Kirsten as a pretty Scandinavian blonde who may be either wealthy and snobby, intellectual and quiet, or fun and easy to talk to.
>
> **Famous Kirsten:** soprano Kirsten Flagstad

KITTY a short form of Katherine

> **Image:** When people hear the name Kitty, they imagine a cute redhead who is sexy, fun loving, and strong.
>
> **Famous Kittys:** actress Kitty Carlisle; TV's Miss Kitty ("Gunsmoke") Russell; Kitty Dukakis, wife of Massachusetts Governor Michael Dukakis; the city of Kitty Hawk, North Carolina

KRIS see Chris

KRISTA a form of Kristen, Kristine (see also Christa)

> **Image:** To some, Krista is a fun-loving, personable, sexy woman with short dark hair. Others think Krista is a quiet, heavy, girl-next-door type.

KRISTI, Kristie, Kristy short forms of Kristen, Kristine (see also Christy)

> **Image:** People are prepared to like someone named Kristi. They think of Kristi as a cute brunette who is helpful, friendly, outgoing, and lots of fun.
>
> **Famous Kristy:** actress Kristy ("Empty Nest") McNichol

KRISTEN see Christin

KRISTINA see Christina

KRISTINE see Christine

KRYSTLE, Kristle forms of Crystal (see also Crystal)

> **Image:** The name Krystle brings to mind Krystle Carrington on TV's "Dynasty." People think of Krystle as beautiful and rich.
>
> **Famous Krystle:** TV's Krystle ("Dynasty") Carrington

LACIE, Lacey, Lacy (Greek) "cheerful"; forms of Larissa

> **Image:** Lacie is pictured as a small, cute woman who is an airhead but is tough enough to do things her own way.

Famous Lacies: country singer Lacy J. Dalton; Lacey Davenport of "Doonesbury" comics; TV's "Cagney and Lacey"

LANA an English form of Helen; a short form of Alana

Image: Lana is pictured as a cute, teenaged tomboy who will grow up into an elegant beauty.

Famous Lanas: actresses Lana Turner, Lana Wood; singer Lana Cantrell; Lana Lang, Superboy's girlfriend

LANE (Middle English) "from the narrow road"

Image: People have two images of Lane: a large, tall woman who is funny and easygoing or a trendy social climber who is posh and sophisticated.

Famous Lanes: Lane Bryant clothing stores; Lois (*Superman*) Lane

LAINIE a short form of Elaine, Lane

Image: The name Lainie evokes an image of a pretty, dark, unique woman who may be zany, artistic, or sweet.

Famous Lainie: singer/actress Lainie Kazan

LARA (Latin) "shining, famous"

Image: People imagine Lara as a very pretty blonde who is unusual and mysterious.

Famous Lara: "Lara's Theme" from the movie *Doctor Zhivago*

LARAINE see Lorraine

LAURA (Latin) "crown of laurel leaves"; a feminine form of Lawrence

Image: People say Laura is a pretty, blue-eyed blonde with a traditional style and a sweet disposition.

Famous Lauras: designer Laura Ashley; novelist Laura (*Little House on the Prairie*) Ingalls Wilder; TV's Laura ("Remington Steele") Holt; Laura in Tennessee Williams's play *The Glass Menagerie*

LAURIE see Lori

LAUREN an English form of Laura

Image: Lauren is described as a tall, thin, pretty, and smart woman who is either friendly and sweet or sophisticated and snobbish.

Famous Laurens: actresses Lauren (*To Have and Have Not*) Bacall, Lauren (*American Gigolo*) Hutton; Lauren perfume; designer Ralph Lauren

LAVERNE (Old French) "from the grove of alder trees"; (Latin) "springlike"

Image: People picture Laverne as the character on TV's "Laverne and Shirley." They say Laverne is an outgoing, fun-loving, homely working-class woman who is extremely scatterbrained.

Famous Lavernes: TV's Laverne ("Laverne and Shirley") DeFazio; singer LaVerne Andrews

LEAH, Lea (Hebrew) "weary"

Image: People do not have a very clear image of Leah but they generally imagine her as dark haired and cute.

Famous Leahs: the biblical Leah, Rachel's sister; Princess (*Star Wars*) Leia; actress Lea (*Back to the Future*) Thompson

LEIGH, Lee (Old English) "from the meadow"; forms of Leah

Image: People think of Leigh as a pretty woman who is wealthy, sophisticated, contemporary, and ambitious.

Famous Leighs: actresses Vivien (*Gone with the Wind*) Leigh, Janet (*Psycho*) Leigh, Leigh (*The Horseman*) Taylor-Young, Lee ("Barnaby Jones") Meriwether, Lee Remick

LENA (Latin) "temptress"; a short form of names ending in "leen," "lena," "lina," "line"

Image: Lena has two very different images: a small, dark, vivacious singer or a sturdy, older Norwegian woman with a husband named Ole.

Famous Lenas: singer Lena ("Stormy Weather") Horne; Lena the Hyena in "Li'l Abner" comics; Lena Grove in William Faulkner's novel *Light in August;* Ole and Lena jokes

LENORE a Russian form of Eleanor

Image: Two different portraits of Lenore come to mind: a homely, quiet, unambitious girl-next-door or an intelligent, strong-willed busybody.

Famous Lenores: actress Lenore (*Camille*) Ulric; Lenore in Edgar Allan Poe's poem "The Raven"

LEONA (Latin) "lion"; a feminine form of Leo

Image: Leona is pictured as a plain, older black woman who is a quiet, middle-class or wealthy homemaker.

Famous Leonas: hotel magnate Leona Helmsley; social worker Leona Boyd

LESLIE, Lesley (Scottish Gaelic) "from the gray fortress"

Image: Leslie is a popular unisex name. Leslie is pictured as small, pretty, sexy, and athletic and is thought to be smart, self-involved, sophisticated, and fun. People say Leslie is likely to be a professional or to run her own business.

Famous Leslies: actresses Lesley Ann (*Cinderella*) Warren, Leslie-Anne (*The Great Train Robbery*) Down, Leslie (*Roots*) Uggams, Leslie (*Gigi*) Caron; newscaster Lesley Stahl

LIBBY a short form of Elizabeth

Image: People picture Libby as a cute and chubby woman who is warm, friendly, homespun, and very talkative.

Famous Libbys: Libby's canned foods; actress Libby Holman

LILA a short form of Delilah, Lillian

Image: Lila is described as a white-haired old woman who is old-fashioned, friendly, and nice.

LILLIAN (Latin) "lily flower"

Image: The name Lillian calls to mind a frail, unattractive, wealthy older woman with glasses — a librarian, perhaps. Some think of Lillian as nice, while others think she is uppity and mouthy.

Famous Lillians: actress Lillian (*The Birth of a Nation*) Gish; Miss Lillian, President Carter's mother; playwright/author Lillian (*The Little Foxes*) Hellman; writer Lillian Smith; singer Lillian Russell

LILY, Lillie short forms of Lillian

Image: Lily has a reputation as a beautiful blonde who is romantic and shy. Some, though, think of Lily as unusual and funny, like Lily Tomlin.

Famous Lilys: actresses Lily (*All of Me*) Tomlin, Lillie (The Jersey Lily) Langtry; singer Lily Pons

LINDA (Spanish) "pretty"

Image: Pretty? You bet! People expect Linda to be a blue-eyed blonde who is sweet and quiet.

Famous Lindas: actresses Linda ("Dynasty") Evans, Lynda ("Wonder Woman") Carter, Linda ("Lou Grant") Kelsey, Linda ("Alice") Lavin, Linda ("Dallas") Gray; singer Linda ("You're No Good") Ronstadt

LINDSAY, Lindsey (Old English) "from the linden tree island"

Image: When people think of Lindsay, they imagine a small, cute athlete who is popular and outgoing.

Famous Lindsays: banking executive Lindsay Taylor; actress Lindsay ("The Bionic Woman") Wagner; sportscaster Lindsey Nelson

LINETTE, Lynette (Celtic) "graceful"; (Old French) "linnet (bird)"

Image: Most people describe Linette as a small, graceful blonde who is sheltered, sweet, and shy. To some, though, Linette is sophisticated, outspoken, and bossy.

Famous Lynettes: The "Family's" Lynette (Squeaky) Fromme; Lynette of Arthurian legend

LISA a form of Elizabeth

Image: Lisa is pictured as a pretty, dark girl who is smart, quiet, and kind. Some people also think Lisa is fun loving and friendly.

Famous Lisas: actresses Lisa ("The Cosby Show") Bonet, Lisa ("Tabitha") Hartman, Lisa ("Facts of Life") Whelchel, Lisa (*Cutter's Way*) Eichhorn, Lisa (*The Winds of War*) Eilbacher; Leonardo da Vinci's painting Mona Lisa

LIZ, Lizzie short forms of Elizabeth

Image: People picture Liz as a beautiful, tall, energetic woman with short brown hair and big brown eyes. Liz's bold, outspoken behavior may at times be earthy, brassy, snobby, or just plain crabby.

Famous Lizes: actress Liz Taylor; designer Liz Claiborne; alleged ax-murderer Lizzie Borden

LIZA a short form of Elizabeth

Image: The name Liza brings Liza Minnelli to mind. People imagine Liza as dark-haired, flashy, outgoing, popular, and fun loving.

Famous Liza: entertainer Liza Minnelli

LOIS a form of Louise

Image: People think of Lois as a lively little old lady who is intelligent, natural-looking, and nice.

Famous Loises: Lois (*Superman*) Lane; "Hi and Lois" comics

LOLA a form of Dolores, Louise

Image: Lola is described as a sexy Latin woman who is pleasant but sleazy.

Famous Lolas: actresses Lola Falana, Lola Albright; Lola in the musical *Damn Yankees*; the Kinks' song "Lola"; dancer Lola Montez

LOLITA a Spanish form of Lola

Image: People picture Lolita as an exotic, black or Hispanic, dark-haired young girl who is pretty, flamboyant, seductive, and promiscuous — a singer or dancer, perhaps.

Famous Lolita: Vladimir Nabokov's novel *Lolita*

LORELEI (German) "alluring"

Image: Lorelei is described as a blonde who is either a graceful, mysterious siren or a buxom, unintelligent prostitute.

Famous Lorelei: Lorelei (*Gentlemen Prefer Blondes*) Lee

LORETTA a form of Laura

Image: The name Loretta calls to mind two different images: an unattractive, domineering woman with a foul mouth or an old-fashioned woman who is pleasant, dependable, and proper.

Famous Lorettas: country singer Loretta ("Coal Miner's Daughter") Lynn; actresses Loretta ("M*A*S*H") Swit, Loretta (*The Farmer's Daughter*) Young; Loretta in "The Lockhorns" comics

LORI, Laurie forms of Laura

Image: Lori is pictured as a petite woman with long straight hair who is independent, smart, quiet, and sweet.

Famous Lori: actress Lori (*Footloose*) Singer

LORNA a form of Laura

Image: People describe Lorna as a pretty blonde who is quiet and subdued, maybe even depressed.

Famous Lornas: Richard Blackmore's novel *Lorna Doone*; Lorna Doone cookies; actress Lorna Luft, Judy Garland's daughter

LORRAINE, Laraine (French) "from Lorraine"

Image: To most people Lorraine is an average-looking woman with curly hair who is businesslike, steady, and quiet, like Laraine Day. Some, though, picture Lorraine as a skinny-minny, like Laraine Newman, who is flighty, funny, and possibly angry.

Famous Lorraines: actresses Laraine ("Saturday Night Live") Newman, Laraine (Amana TV commercials) Day; playwright Lorraine Hansberry

LOTTIE, Lotte short forms of Charlotte

Image: Lottie is described as an old-fashioned "hick from the sticks" — a cute, fat, carefree older woman whose mental acuity is described by most as childlike, silly, or ignorant.

Famous Lotte: actress Lotte (*The Threepenny Opera*) Lenya

LOUELLA see Luella

LOUISE (Old German) "famous woman warrior"; a feminine form of Louis

Image: Louise is described as very old-fashioned — a homey, kind, hardworking woman who might be a bit pompous.

Famous Louises: country singer Louise Mandrell; actresses Louise ("Mary Hartman, Mary Hartman") Lasser, Louise (*One Flew over the Cuckoo's Nest*) Fletcher, Tina ("Gilligan's Island") Louise; TV's Louise ("The Jeffersons") Jefferson; novelist Louise (*Love Medicine*) Erdrich; artist Louise Nevelson

LUCILLE a form of Lucy

Image: The name Lucille brings the image of Lucille Ball

to mind — a funny, vivacious woman with a nonstop mouth.

Famous Lucilles: comic actress Lucille ("I Love Lucy") Ball; fitness businesswoman Lucille Roberts; Little Richard's song "Lucille"; B. B. King's guitar "Lucille"; Kenny Rogers's song "You Picked a Fine Time to Leave Me, Lucille"

LUCINDA a form of Lucy

Image: Lucinda is described as a dark, attractive, classy woman who is an aggressive go-getter with a reputation for arrogance.

Famous Lucindas: Lucinda in plays by Molière; singer Lucinda Williams

LUCY, Lucie (Latin) "light; light-bringer"; feminine forms of Lucius, Luke

Image: Thanks to Lucille Ball, people think of Lucy as a very funny redhead who is bouncy, zany, loud, and lovable.

Famous Lucys: TV's "I Love Lucy"; Saint Lucy, patron saint of the blind; Lucy Baines Nugent, President Lyndon Johnson's daughter; Lucy ("Peanuts") Van Pelt; Lucy (*A Room with a View*) Honeychurch; feminist/abolitionist Lucy Stone

LUELLA, Louella (Old English) "elf"

Image: Luella is pictured as an old-fashioned southern grandmother — a plump, talkative, older woman who does not often get out and about.

Famous Louella: gossip columnist Louella Parsons

LULU a short form of Louise, Luella

> **Image:** People describe Lulu as a homely, old-fashioned woman who is silly, scatter-brained, fat, and sweet.
>
> **Famous Lulus:** "Little Lulu" comics; sixties singer Lulu; Zona Gale's novel *Miss Lulu Bett*

LURLEEN a form of Lorelei

> **Image:** The name Lurleen has a definite southern flavor but an unflattering image. People picture Lurleen as a buxom, blonde southern belle who is a scatterbrained flirt.
>
> **Famous Lurleen:** former Alabama governor Lurleen Wallace

LYDIA (Greek) "from Lydia"

> **Image:** Lydia strikes people as a good name for a pretty, old-fashioned woman who is quiet, friendly, and loaded with freckles.
>
> **Famous Lydias:** Lydia, an ancient land ruled by Midas; the song "Lydia, the Tattooed Lady"; Hawaii's Queen Lydia Liliuokalani; Lydia in the movie *Beetlejuice*

LYNN, Lynne (Old English) "waterfall, pool below a fall"; short forms of names containing "lin," "line," "lyn"

> **Image:** Lynn is pictured as a tall, thin, strong young woman who is dependable and friendly.

Famous Lynns: actresses Lynn (*Georgy Girl*) Redgrave, Lynn Fontanne; country singer Lynn ("I Never Promised You a Rose Garden") Anderson; cartoonist Lynn ("For Better or For Worse") Johnston

LYNETTE see Linette

MABEL (Latin) "lovable"

> **Image:** Mabel strikes people as a good name for a matronly, overweight older woman — a dowdy teacher or farmer, perhaps.
>
> **Famous Mabels:** author Mabel Dodge Luhan; silent screen actress Mabel Normand; composer Mabel Wheeler Daniels

MADELINE (Greek) "Magdalene, woman from Magdala"

> **Image:** Madeline is pictured as a pretty blonde who is rich, classy, friendly, and happy.
>
> **Famous Madelines:** actresses Madeline (*Young Frankenstein*) Kahn, Madolyn (*Urban Cowboy*) Smith; novelist/children's story writer Madeleine L'Engle

MADGE a short form of Madeline, Margaret

> **Image:** The name Madge reminds people of the nosy

gossip who promotes Palmolive dishwashing liquid on TV commercials — a down-to-earth, old-fashioned woman who does not know how to stop talking.

Famous Madge: Madge the manicurist in Palmolive commercials

MADONNA (Latin) "my lady"

Image: Interestingly, most people think of Madonna as a wild, sexy, dumb blonde rock singer rather than as the pure and holy mother of Jesus.

Famous Madonnas: the biblical Madonna, mother of Christ; singer/actress Madonna ("Like a Virgin") Ciccone; Leonardo da Vinci's painting Madonna of the Rocks; the Beatles' song "Lady Madonna"

MAGGIE a short form of Margaret

Image: Maggie is thought to be an old-fashioned, heavyset, freckle-faced Irishwoman who is friendly, fun, flamboyant, independent, and loud.

Famous Maggies: Maggie in Tennessee Williams's play *Cat on a Hot Tin Roof;* actress Maggie (*A Room with a View*) Smith; Maggie, Jigg's wife in "Bringing Up Father" comics; Stephen Crane's novel *Maggie: A Girl of the Streets*; Rod Stewart's song "Maggie May"

MAHALIA (Hebrew) "affection"

Image: The name Mahalia reminds most people of a heavyset black gospel singer, like Mahalia Jackson. Some people, though, connect the name with a beautiful Hawaiian princess.

Famous Mahalia: singer Mahalia Jackson

MALLORY (French) "the mailed"

Image: People think of Mallory as a cute girl with big brown eyes who is popular, likable, and downright dumb.

Famous Mallorys: TV's Mallory ("Family Ties") Keaton; model/actress Carole Mallory

MAMIE a short form of Margaret

Image: Mamie is described as an old-fashioned black woman who is outgoing and perhaps even rude.

Famous Mamies: First Lady Mamie Eisenhower; actress Mamie (*Teacher's Pet*) Van Doren

MANDY a short form of Amanda, Manda, Melinda

Image: People picture Mandy as a young, cute, energetic girl who is outgoing and fun.

Famous Mandys: Barry Manilow's song "Mandy"; British call girl Mandy Rice-Davies; model Mandy Smith

MARCELLA (Latin) "belonging to Mars, warlike"; a feminine form of Mark

Image: Though this name lacks a clear image, people tend to describe Marcella as an intelligent, refined European woman who is sweet and generous.

MARCIA (Latin) "warlike"; a feminine form of Mark (see also Marsha)

Image: Marcia is a fifties name that brings to mind a pretty, blonde, slim, old-fashioned girl who is quiet, serious, and studious.

Famous Marcias: TV's Marcia ("The Brady Bunch") Brady; actress Marcia ("The Bob Newhart Show") Wallace

MARCIE a short form of Marcella, Marcia

Image: Marcie is pictured as a cute, middle-class girl who is smart, caring, talkative, and friendly.

Famous Marcie: Marcie in "Peanuts" comics

MARGARET (Greek) "pearl"

Image: Despite all of the queens with this name, Margaret does not have a royal image. Rather, Margaret is seen as a solid, matronly woman who is smart, hard-working, quiet, and strong willed.

Famous Margarets: many Queen Margarets; novelist Margaret (*Gone with the Wind*) Mitchell; Senator Margaret Chase Smith; Britain's Prime Minister Margaret Thatcher; Britain's Princess Margaret; Margaret in "Dennis the Menace" comics; anthropologist Margaret Mead

MARGE a short form of Margery, Margaret

Image: The name Marge name has a homey flavor. People say Marge is a large, white-haired woman who is old-fashioned, down-to-earth, friendly, and happy.

Famous Marges: actress Marge Meadows; novelist Marge Piercy

MARGERY see Marjorie

MARGO, Margot (French) short forms of Margaret

Image: The name Margo calls to mind a dark, attractive woman who is strong willed and businesslike, yet kind.

Famous Margos: actresses Margaux (*Lipstick*) Hemingway, Margot (*Superman*) Kidder; dancer Dame Margot Fonteyn; producer/director Margo Jones; Margo (*All About Eve*) Channing

MARIA a form of Mary

Image: People say Maria is a petite, pretty, dark-haired Hispanic woman who is quiet, gentle, and sweet.

Famous Marias: singer Maria Callas; Maria (*The Sound of Music*) von Trapp; dancer Maria Tallchief; Maria in the musical *West Side Story*; TV newscaster Maria Shriver

MARIAN, Marion combinations of Mary and Ann

Image: The name Marian reminds people of an older woman who is smart, old-fashioned, competent, helpful, kind, and bookish. Marian is considered a perfect name for a librarian.

Famous Marians: Marian the librarian in the musical *The Music Man*; singer Marian Anderson; TV's Marian ("Happy Days") Cunningham; Robin

Hood's Maid Marian; Marion Davies, mistress of W. R. Hearst; novelist Marion Zimmer (*The Mists of Avalon*) Bradley

MARIE a French form of Mary

Image: Most people think of Marie as a pretty, fun-loving woman who is artistic, friendly, and sweet. Some, though, think of Marie as hardworking, dependable, and boring.

Famous Maries: singer Marie Osmond; France's Queen Marie Antoinette; scientist Marie Curie; poet Marie de France

MARILYN a form of Mary

Image: Marilyn Monroe is the dominant image for this name. People describe Marilyn as a beautiful blonde who is soft-spoken and very sexy.

Famous Marilyns: actresses Marilyn (*Gentlemen Prefer Blondes*) Monroe, Marilyn Miller; porn star Marilyn Chambers; Marilyn Quayle, wife of Vice President Dan Quayle

MARINA (Latin) "from the sea"

Image: Marina is pictured as an exotic, well-traveled woman who is sporty and athletic, yet feminine.

Famous Marinas: the song "Marina Del Ray"; Marina Oswald, Lee Harvey Oswald's widow

MARISA (Latin) "of the sea"; forms of Maris

Image: Marisa is pictured as a pretty Hispanic woman with dark hair and dark eyes who is charming and smart.

Famous Marisa: actress Marisa (*Barry Lyndon*) Berenson

MARJORIE, Margery familiar forms of Margaret

Image: Marjorie is usually thought to be a large, strong woman who is hardworking, sweet, and homey, like Ma Kettle. Some, though, think the name has a classy ring to it.

Famous Marjories: actresses Marjorie ("Make Room for Daddy") Lord, Marjorie ("Ma Kettle") Main; Herman Wouk's novel *Marjorie Morningstar;* children's story writer Marjorie Rawlings; the nursery rhyme "See-Saw, Margery Daw"

MARLENA, Marlene forms of Madeline

Image: Thanks to Marlene Dietrich, people describe Marlena as a sexy, sultry, sophisticated woman with a husky voice.

Famous Marlenes: actress Marlene (*The Blue Angel*) Dietrich

MARLO a form of Mary

Image: The name Marlo calls to mind a cute sexy blonde who is classy and strong willed.

Famous Marlo: actress Marlo ("That Girl") Thomas

MARNIE a short form of Marina

Image: The name Marnie has two different images: a glamorous, fun-loving blonde or a plain, bespectacled intellectual who is old-fashioned, quiet, and polite.

Famous Marnies: singer Marni Nixon; the movie *Marnie*

MARSHA a form of Marcia (see also Marcia)

Image: Marsha is described as a short, heavy blonde who is bubbly, fun loving, and loud. The name conveys the impression of a typical or average girl.

Famous Marsha: actress Marsha (*The Goodbye Girl*) Mason

MARTHA (Aramaic) "lady"

Image: Martha is described as an overweight, old-fashioned blonde who is strong, solid, likable, and loud.

Famous Marthas: the biblical Martha, Mary's sister; the Watergate era's Martha Mitchell; entertainer Martha Raye; entertaining expert Martha Stewart; First Lady Martha Washington; choreographer Martha Graham

MARTINA a form of Martha; a feminine form of Martin

Image: The name Martina has a Spanish or Eastern European flavor. Martina is pictured either as small and delicate, like a flamenco dancer, or as muscular, athletic, and somewhat masculine, like tennis player Martina Navratilova.

Famous Martinas: tennis's Martina Navratilova; dancer/ choreographer Martine Van Hamel

MARIBETH see Mary Beth

MARY (Hebrew) "bitter"

Image: Mary is thought of as a plain, ordinary girl who is dependable, quiet, and a bit dull.

Famous Marys: the biblical Mary, mother of Jesus; the biblical prostitute Mary Magdalene; actresses Mary Tyler Moore, Mary (*The Maltese Falcon*) Astor; Mary Queen of Scots; TV's "Mary Hartman, Mary Hartman"; the nursery rhymes "Mary, Mary, Quite Contrary," "Mary Had a Little Lamb"

MARY BETH, Marybeth, Maribeth combinations of Mary and Beth

Image: Most people think of Mary Beth as a small, pretty blonde. Some say Mary Beth is kind and likable; others see her as vain, snobby, and loud.

Famous Mary Beths: surrogate mother Marybeth Whitehead; actress Mary Beth (*The World According to Garp*) Hurt; TV's Mary Beth ("Cagney and Lacey") Lacey

MARY ELLEN, Maryellen combinations of Mary and Ellen

Image: Mary Ellen is described as a tall, plain, old-fashioned girl who is either folksy and good-natured or bossy and self-righteous.

Famous Mary Ellens: novelist Mary Ellen Chase; TV's Mary Ellen ("The Waltons") Walton

MARY LOU, Marylou combinations of Mary and Louise

Image: Most people picture Mary Lou as a short, cute,

athletic country girl who is helpful, smart, and nice. Some, though, picture Mary Lou as perky and bubbly; or quiet and shy.

Famous Mary Lous: gymnast Mary Lou Retton; Ricky Nelson's song "Hello, Mary Lou"; actress Marilu ("Taxi") Henner; jazz pianist Mary Lou Williams

MATILDA (Old German) "powerful in battle"

Image: Powerful in battle, indeed! Matilda is thought to be a big, heavy, old spinster who is old-fashioned and bossy. Some people also think Matilda is a great name for a witch.

Famous Matildas: Banjo Patterson's song "Waltzing Matilda"; Matilda Cuomo, politician Mario Cuomo's wife; Matilda, queen of William the Conqueror

MAUD, Maude short forms of Madeline, Matilda

Image: People say Maud is a large older woman who is loudmouthed and opinionated but nice.

Famous Mauds: actress Maud (*Man with the Golden Gun*) Adams; TV's "Maude"; Alfred, Lord Tennyson's poem *Maud*; the movie *Harold and Maude*

MAUREEN (Old French) "dark-skinned"; an Irish form of Mary; a feminine form of Maurice

Image: Most people picture Maureen as a beautiful, lusty redhead — a spunky woman with a fiery temper. Some, though, picture Maureen as quiet, sweet, and old.

Famous Maureens: Maureen, President Reagan's daughter; actresses Maureen (*Anna Karenina*) O'Sullivan, Maureen (*Rio Grande*) O'Hara, Maureen (*Cocoon*) Stapleton; tennis's Maureen (Little Mo) Connelly

MAVIS (French) "thrush"; a form of Damara

Image: Most people describe Mavis as a tall, heavyset, middle-aged black woman who is nice but boring. Some, though, say Mavis is a wealthy, bossy old maid.

Famous Mavis: novelist Mavis Gallant

MAXINE, Maxene (Latin) "greatest"; feminine forms of Max

Image: There are three different images of Maxine: a prim and proper, bespectacled schoolteacher; a popular, sweet, blonde homecoming queen; or a scrappy tomboy.

Famous Maxines: singer Maxene Andrews; actress Maxine Elliott; novelist Maxine Hong Kingston

MAY, Mae (Latin) "great"

Image: May calls two images to mind: a buxom, blonde tramp who is likable and funny, like Mae West, or a plain and boring old maid.

Famous Mays: Maia, Roman goddess of springtime; actress Mae West; poet May Sarton; short-story writer May Sinclair

MEG a short form of Margaret, Megan

> **Image:** Most people picture Meg as the female counterpart of Huck Finn — a redheaded, freckle-faced, pigtailed tomboy who is adventurous, creative, friendly, and funny. Some, though, see Meg as a quiet, shy, conservative homebody.

> **Famous Megs:** Meg (*Little Women*) March; actresses Meg (*When Harry Met Sally*) Ryan, Meg (*Agnes of God*) Tilly; columnist Meg Greenfield

MEGAN, Meghan (Greek) "great"; Irish forms of Margaret

> **Image:** The name Megan calls to mind a cute, young, red-headed pixie who is fun loving and headstrong.

> **Famous Megan:** actress Megan ("China Beach") Gallagher

MELANIE (Greek) "dark-clothed"

> **Image:** Most people think of Melanie as smart, sweet, shy, and quiet. Some, though, think Melanie is a wild, sexy flirt.

> **Famous Melanies:** Melanie (*Gone with the Wind*) Wilkes; actress Melanie (*Working Girl*) Griffith

MELINDA (Greek) "dark, gentle"

> **Image:** People have three different impressions of Melinda: a perky, open, fun girl; a sweet, shy dreamer; or a spoiled, self-centered brat.

MELISSA (Greek) "honey bee"

> **Image:** Melissa is described as a petite, pretty young girl who is sweet but spoiled.

> **Famous Melissas:** actresses Melissa ("Little House on the Prairie") Gilbert, Melissa Sue ("Little House on the Prairie") Anderson; singer Melissa ("Midnight Blue") Manchester; Melissa in the medieval epic *Orlando Furioso*

MERCEDES (Spanish) "mercies"

> **Image:** Mercedes is considered a good name for a socialite — a sleek, worldly sophisticate who is outgoing and lighthearted.

> **Famous Mercedes:** Santa Maria de Mercedes (Mary of Mercies); actress Mercedes (*All the King's Men*) McCambridge; Mercedes-Benz automobiles; Mercedes on TV's "Kukla, Fran, and Ollie"

MEREDITH (Welsh) "guardian from the sea"

> **Image:** Meredith is described as a pretty, classy woman who is smart, independent, and rich.

> **Famous Merediths:** actresses Meredith ("Family Ties") Baxter-Birney, Meredith ("Petticoat Junction") MacRea; playwright Meredith (*The Music Man*) Willson; TV reporter Meredith ("60 Minutes") Vieira

MERRY (Middle English) "merry"; a short form of Meredith

> **Image:** As you might expect, people think of Merry as cute, jolly, cheerful, and funny. People also think Merry is a shallow, self-centered show-off.

MIA (Italian) "mine, my"; a form of Michelle

> **Image:** Mia is pictured as a small, dark, pretty woman of foreign origin who is a quiet nonconformist with considerable depth.
>
> **Famous Mia:** actress Mia (*Hannah and Her Sisters*) Farrow

MICHELLE (Hebrew) "who is like the Lord"; a feminine form of Michael

> **Image:** Most people think of Michelle as a pretty, tall, snobby young upstart.
>
> **Famous Michelles:** actresses Michelle (*Dillinger*) Phillips, Michelle (*Dangerous Liaisons*) Pfeiffer, Michele ("Knots Landing") Lee; the Beatles' song "Michelle"

MICKIE, Mickey forms of Michelle

> **Image:** A girl named Mickie is described as a tomboy or boyish girl who is fun, friendly, funny, and full of energy.
>
> **Famous Mickeys:** Walt Disney's Mickey Mouse; baseball's Mickey Mantle; Mickey Vernon

MILDRED (Old English) "gentle counselor"

> **Image:** Mildred is reputed to be an old-fashioned shrew — a large older woman who is prim and stern.
>
> **Famous Mildreds:** TV's Mildred ("M*A*S*H") Potter; the movie *Mildred Pierce*; actress Mildred Dunnock; blues singer Mildred Bailey

MILLICENT (Old German) "industrious"; a form of Melissa

> **Image:** Millicent is an old-fashioned name that brings to mind a stereotypical librarian — a plain, prudish, old, bespectacled woman who is quiet, proper, and stuffy.
>
> **Famous Millicent:** congresswoman Millicent Fenwick

MILLIE, Milly short forms of Camille, Emily, Melissa, Mildred, Millicent

> **Image:** Millie strikes people as a good name for a big older woman who is talkative, friendly, lovable, and homey — a farmer, perhaps.
>
> **Famous Millies:** actress Millie (*The Diary of Anne Frank*) Perkins; the movie *Thoroughly Modern Millie*; TV's Millie ("The Dick Van Dyke Show") Helper

MIMI a French form of Miriam

> **Image:** People say Mimi is a stylish Frenchwoman who is rich, pampered, stuck-up, and prone to tantrums.
>
> **Famous Mimis:** Mimi in Puccini's opera *La Bohème*; Maurice Chevalier's song "Mimi"; actress Mimi (*Someone to Watch Over Me*) Rogers; opera singer Mimi Benzell

MINDY a short form of Melinda

> **Image:** To most people Mindy is a cute, dainty, perky child. To some, though, Mindy is a rich, spoiled snob.

Famous Mindys: actress Mindy ("Facts of Life") Cohn; TV's "Mork and Mindy"

MINERVA (Greek) "wisdom"

Image: The name Minerva is associated with wisdom and mythology. Minerva is described as an exotic, unconventional woman who is artistic, magical, or perhaps witchy.

Famous Minerva: the mythological Minerva, Roman goddess of wisdom

MINNIE a short form of Minerva, Minna, Wilhelmina

Image: The name Minnie brings to mind Minnie Mouse and Minnie Pearl. People expect a woman named Minnie to be either short and mousy or very old and grandmotherly.

Famous Minnies: Walt Disney's Minnie Mouse; country entertainer Minnie ("Hee Haw") Pearl; Cab Calloway's song "Minnie, the Moocher"; politician Minnie Fisher Cunningham

MIRA see Myra

MIRABEL (Latin) "of extraordinary beauty"

Image: When people think of Mirabel, they picture a chubby, older southern woman who is old-fashioned, proper, and quiet.

Famous Mirabels: author Marabel (*Total Woman*) Morgan; Mirabell in William Congreve's play *The Way of the World*

MIRANDA (Latin) "admirable"

Image: Most people describe Miranda as a tall, pretty, dark Hispanic woman who is exotic, mysterious, silent, and possibly stuck-up. Some, though, are reminded of the fruit-covered dancer Carmen Miranda.

Famous Mirandas: entertainer Carmen Miranda; *The U.S. vs. Miranda* Supreme Court decision; Miranda in Shakespeare's play *The Tempest*

MIRIAM (Hebrew) "bitter"

Image: Miriam is thought to be a plump, pretty, older woman who is motherly, soft-spoken, and refined.

Famous Miriams: the biblical Miriam, Moses' sister; actress Miriam Hopkins; Miriam in D. H. Lawrence's novel *Sons and Lovers*

MISSY a short form of Melissa, Millicent

Image: People say Missy is a spoiled brat who is mischievous, sassy, and annoying.

Famous Missy: actress Missy ("Benson") Gold

MITZI a form of Miriam

Image: People describe Mitzi as a petite blonde dancer who is cheerful, playful, and bubbly. Some think Mitzi is stuck-up.

Famous Mitzis: performer Mitzi (*South Pacific*) Gaynor; Mitzi, Mighty Mouse's girlfriend

MOIRA (Irish Gaelic) "great"; an Irish form of Mary

Image: The name Moira evokes an image of a plain woman with thick glasses who is highly religious, quiet, and reserved.

Famous Moiras: actress Moira (*The Red Shoes*) Shearer; Moira in Margaret Atwood's novel *The Handmaid's Tale*

MOLLY an Irish form of Mary

Image: People describe Molly as a pretty, plump, dark-haired girl who is perky, down-to-earth, and very likable.

Famous Mollys: the movie *The Unsinkable Molly Brown*; TV's "The Days and Nights of Molly Dodd"; the song "Sweet Molly Malone"; actress Molly (*Sixteen Candles*) Ringwald; Molly (*Ulysses*) Bloom; radio's "Fibber McGee and Molly"; feminist Molly Yard

MONA (Greek) "solitary"; (Irish Gaelic) "noble"; a short form of Monica

Image: Most people think of Mona as an old spinster who is plain, quiet, lackluster, and secretive. Some, though, see Mona as sophisticated and sexy.

Famous Monas: Leonardo da Vinci's painting Mona Lisa; actress Mona Barrie; TV's Mona ("Who's the Boss?") Robinson

MONICA (Latin) "advisor"

Image: Most people describe Monica as a beautiful blonde woman who is educated, fun loving, and friendly. Some, though, think of Monica as spoiled and snobby.

Famous Monicas: TV's Monica ("General Hospital") Quartermaine; Saint Monica, mother of Saint Augustine

MORGAN (Scottish Gaelic) "from the edge of the sea"

Image: This unisex name calls to mind a beautiful blonde who is witty, sophisticated, and successful, like Morgan Fairchild.

Famous Morgans: actresses Morgan ("Flamingo Road") Fairchild, Morgan ("Glitter") Brittany; Morgan horses; Wall Street tycoon J. P. Morgan

MORGANA (Welsh) "edge of the sea"; a feminine form of Morgan

Image: The name Morgana has two very different images: a flirtatious, buxom prostitute or porno star or a smart woman who is shy and well spoken.

Famous Morganas: Morgana Le Fay, King Arthur's evil sister; Morgana, baseball's "kissing bandit"; Morgana in the medieval epic *Orlando Furioso*; Ali Baba's slave Morgiana

MURIEL (Arabic) "myrrh"; (Irish Gaelic) "sea-bright"; a form of Mary

Image: Most people say Muriel is a plain-looking, older woman who is dignified and demure, but some say Muriel is an energetic, talkative, young playgirl.

Famous Muriels: Muriel Humphrey Brown, former vice president Hubert Humphrey's widow; novelist Muriel Spark; poet/activist Muriel Rukeyser; Muriel cigars

MYRA, Mira (Old French) "quiet song"; forms of Miranda

Image: Myra is regarded as a plain old maid, perhaps Jewish, who is either a bossy, snobby aristocrat or a sweet, silly scatterbrain.

Famous Myras: Gore Vidal's novel *Myra Breckinridge*; pianist Dame Myra Hess

MYRNA (Irish Gaelic) "polite, gentle"

Image: People picture Myrna as a frumpy, bespectacled old woman who is either bossy and domineering, silly and flaky, or nervous and withdrawn.

Famous Myrna: actress Myrna (*The Thin Man*) Loy

NADIA a Slavic form of Nadine

Image: Thanks to Nadia Comaneci, Americans picture Nadia as a small, cute, Eastern European athlete who is an enthusiastic, determined achiever.

Famous Nadias: gymnast Nadia Comaneci; conductor/composer Nadia Boulanger

NADINE (French Slavic) "hope"; a feminine form of Nathan

Image: Nadine is pictured as a thin, bespectacled, studious woman who is quiet, stodgy, and perhaps a bit stuck-up.

Famous Nadines: novelist Nadine Gordimer; opera singer Nadine Conner

NANCY a form of Nan

Image: Nancy is pictured as a pretty, dark-haired girl-next-door — a quiet, pleasant girl who is friendly and sweet.

Famous Nancys: Nancy in Charles Dickens's novel *Oliver Twist*; fictional detective Nancy Drew; First Lady Nancy Reagan; singer Nancy Sinatra; "Nancy" comics; actress Nancy ("The Beverly Hillbillies") Kulp

NANETTE a form of Nan

Image: Nanette is described as cute, funny, saucy, sexy, and talkative. Some people, though, think Nanette is quiet and mousy.

Famous Nanettes: actress Nanette Fabray; the musical *No, No, Nanette*

NAOMI (Hebrew) "pleasant"

Image: Naomi is pictured as a pretty woman dedicated to a noble or spiritual mission.

Famous Naomis: the biblical Naomi, Ruth's mother-in-law; country singer Naomi Judd; author Lady Naomi Mitchison

NATALIE (Latin) "Christmas, born on Christmas Day"

Image: When people think of Natalie, they imagine a dark, pretty woman who is fun and easy to get along with, like Natalie Wood.

Famous Natalies: actress Natalie (*Rebel Without a Cause*) Wood; singer Natalie

Cole; TV's Natalie ("Facts of Life") Green

NATASHA a Russian form of Natalie

Image: Natasha is described as a dark, beautiful, exotic, mysterious Russian with a queen-size ego.

Famous Natashas: TV's Natasha ("The Bullwinkle Show") Fatale; Natasha in Leo Tolstoy's novel *War and Peace*; Natassya in Fydor Dostoyevsky's *The Idiot*; actress Nastassja (*Tess*) Kinski

NELLIE, Nelly forms of Nell

Image: People think of Nellie as either jolly, good humored, and playful or rude, spoiled, and bratty. The name has an old-fashioned ring that makes it seem appropriate for an old lady.

Famous Nellies: TV's Nellie ("Little House on the Prairie") Oleson, Nell ("The Bullwinkle Show") Fenwick; the song "Wait Till the Sun Shines, Nellie"; opera singer Nellie Melba; Pat Brady's jeep, Nellybelle on TV's "Roy Rogers"

NETTIE a short form of Nan, Natalie, names ending with "nette"

Image: To most people Nettie is an old-fashioned, short, heavyset grandma who is bubbly, friendly, and sweet.

Famous Nettie: biologist Nettie Stevens

NICOLE (Greek) "victory of the people"; a feminine form of Nicholas

Image: Nicole is described as a china doll — a petite, pretty young girl who is sweet and romantic, but fragile.

Famous Nicoles: actress Nicola (*Anna Karenina*) Pagett; cartoonist Nicole ("Sylvia") Hollander

NIKKI, Nicky short forms of Nicole

Image: Nikki is pictured as a petite woman with lots of energy. People say Nikki is an athletic, outdoorsy woman who may be friendly and fun; or selfish and spoiled.

Famous Nikkis: Nikki (*Who's That Girl?*) Fenn; poet Nikki Giovanni; Nikki Porter, Ellery Queen's secretary; Nicky Smith, Vicky Buchanan's alter ego on TV's "One Life to Live"

NINA (Spanish) "girl"

Image: Most people picture Nina as a small, pretty blonde — an elegant, exotic woman who is quiet, aloof, and independent. Some see Nina as charming and easygoing.

Famous Ninas: Nina ("All My Children") Cortlandt; Nina Ricci perfume; blues singer Nina Simone; actress Nina Mae (*Sanders of the River*) McKinney

NOEL (Latin-French) "Christmas, born on Christmas day"

Image: Noel is increasingly viewed as a unisex name. A girl named Noel is pictured as cheerful, bookish, and sophisticated.

NORA a short form of Eleanor, Honora, Leonora

Image: Nora is considered an old-fashioned name suitable for an older farmer who is hard-working and serious.

Famous Noras: Nora (*The Thin Man*) Charles; novelist Nora (*Heartburn*) Ephron; Nora (*A Doll House*) Helmer; Nora Joyce, James Joyce's wife; comedienne Nora Dunn; TV's Nora ("The Carol Burnett Show") Desmond

NOREEN an Irish form of Norma

Image: The name Noreen has two very different images: an unattractive, stodgy goody-two-shoes or a pretty, vivacious woman who is smart and assertive.

NORMA (Latin) "rule, pattern"

Image: Norma is described as a plain, simple, homey, old-fashioned woman who is hardworking and nice (which explains why Norma Jean Baker's name was changed by the movie moguls to Marilyn Monroe).

Famous Normas: Norma Jean (Marilyn Monroe) Baker; singer Norma Zimmer; the movie *Norma Rae*; actress Norma (*The Women*) Shearer; designer Norma Kamali

NYSSA (Greek) "beginning"; (Scandinavian) "friendly elf or brownie"

Image: People say Nyssa sounds like a foreign name or a made-up Hollywood name (which it is). Nyssa is described as either an exotic, different, or perhaps wierd woman or an obnoxious, spoiled brat.

Famous Nyssa: Nyssa on TV's "Doctor Who"

OLGA (Scandinavian) "holy"

Image: Olga strikes people as a suitable name for a fat, older German blonde who is strict, cold, and nasty.

Famous Olga: gymnast Olga Korbut

OLIVIA (Latin) "olive tree"; an English form of Olga

Image: Some people say Olivia is a sexy blonde who is stuck-up and accustomed to getting her way. Others say Olivia is old-fashioned, motherly, and sweet.

Famous Olivias: actress Olivia (*Gone with the Wind*) de Havilland; singer Olivia ("Let's Get Physical") Newton-John; Olivia in Shakespeare's play *Twelfth Night*

OPAL (Hindu) "precious stone"

Image: Opal is pictured as an older black woman who is talkative, friendly, and a bit weird.

Famous Opals: Opal automobiles; TV's Opal ("All My Children") Gardner; opal, the precious stone

OPRAH (American) a form of Opera, Opie

> **Image:** This name is identified almost exclusively with TV entertainer Oprah Winfrey. The dominant impression of Oprah is that she is black, beautiful, aggressive, opinionated, flamboyant, bright, and sensitive.
>
> **Famous Oprah:** TV host Oprah Winfrey

PAIGE, Page (Old English) "child, young"; (French) "useful assistant"

> **Image:** People describe Paige as a sophisticated, upper-class woman who is independent, intelligent, and fun loving.
>
> **Famous Paiges:** actress Geraldine (*The Trip to Bountiful*) Page; singer Patti ("Tennessee Waltz") Page

PAM a short form of Pamela

> **Image:** Pam is pictured as a very sweet, cute, outgoing woman who is well mannered and kind.
>
> **Famous Pams:** actress Pam ("Mork and Mindy") Dawber; the Beatles' song "Polythene Pam"

PAMELA (Greek) "all-honey"

> **Image:** People describe Pamela as either an obnoxious, stuck-up princess or a lower-class, single pregnant woman.
>
> **Famous Pamelas:** the song "Pamela Brown"; TV's Pamela ("Dallas") Ewing; actress Pamela Sue ("Dynasty") Martin; Samuel Richardson's novel *Pamela*

PANDORA (Greek) "all-gifted"

> **Image:** Pandora is pictured as a blonde troublemaker whose curiosity is out of control.
>
> **Famous Pandora:** the mythological Pandora who opened a box full of trouble

PAT a short form of Patricia

> **Image:** Pat is described as a warm, independent tomboy with a good head on her shoulders.
>
> **Famous Pats:** First Lady Pat Nixon; rock singer Pat ("Hit Me with Your Best Shot") Benatar; politician Pat Schroeder; the movie *Pat and Mike*

PATRICIA (Latin) "of the nobility"; a feminine form of Patrick

> **Image:** People say Patricia is a pretty, petite, freckle-faced woman who is nice, friendly, popular, and smart.
>
> **Famous Patricias:** actress Patricia (*Hud*) Neal; heiress Patricia Hearst; former cabinet minister Patricia Roberts Harris

PATSY a short form of Patricia

> **Image:** People usually picture Patsy as a cute, spirited girl who is popular, self-confident, and down-to-earth — a cheerleader, perhaps.

Famous Patsy: country singer Patsy Cline

PATTI, Patty short forms of Patricia

Image: People think of Patti as either a chunky, likable, conventional woman or a pretty, vivacious, fun-loving girl.

Famous Pattis: singers Patti Smith, Patti ("On My Own") LaBelle, Patti ("Tennessee Waltz") Page; actress Patty Duke Astin; heiress Patti Hearst; Peppermint Patty in "Peanuts" comics

PAULA (Latin) "small"; a feminine form of Paul

Image: Paula is described as a strong-willed, authoritative woman who complains when she does not get what she wants.

Famous Paulas: actress Paula (*What's New, Pussycat?*) Prentiss; the song "Hey, Hey, Paula"; pop singer Paula ("Forever Your Girl") Abdul; TV host Paula ("CBS This Morning") Zahn

PAULINE a form of Paula

Image: Pauline is described as a smart, level-headed and mature woman who is straitlaced and proper.

Famous Paulines: film critic Pauline Kael; the movie *The Perils of Pauline*; Czech model/actress Paulina (*Her Alibi*) Porizkova; news analyst Pauline Frederick; Pauline Friedman (Dear Abby) Lederer Phillips

PEARL (Latin) "pearl"

Image: Pearl is pictured as a pretty, heavyset older woman who is outspoken and fun.

Famous Pearls: blues singer Pearl Bailey; country entertainer Minnie ("Hee Haw") Pearl; novelist Pearl S. (*The Good Earth*) Buck; Pearl in Nathaniel Hawthorne's novel *The Scarlet Letter*

PEGGY a short form of Margaret

Image: People think of Peggy as the girl-next-door — cute, pleasant, friendly, and average.

Famous Peggys: Buddy Holly's song "Peggy Sue"; singer Peggy ("Is That All There Is?") Lee; skater Peggy Fleming; actresses Dame Peggy (*The Jewel in the Crown*) Ashcroft, Peggy ("Women in Prison") Cass, Peggy ("The Mod Squad") Lipton; the movie *Peggy Sue Got Married*

PENELOPE (Greek) "weaver"

Image: People say the name Penelope evokes three different images: a strict school-teacher; a studious nerd; or a friendly, dim-witted bimbo.

Famous Penelopes: the mythological Penelope, wife of Ulysses; "Penelope Pitstop" cartoons; British actress Penelope Keith

PENNY a short form of Penelope

Image: Penny is pictured as an outgoing scatterbrain who loves to have a good time.

Famous Pennys: director/actress Penny ("Laverne and Shirley") Marshall; actress Penny Singleton, the voice of Jane Jetson on TV's "The Jetsons"; Penny on TV's "Sky King"

PHOEBE (Greek) "shining"

Image: Phoebe is pictured as an attractive but old-fashioned woman who is conservative, dowdy, prudish, and tight-fisted.

Famous Phoebes: actress/model Phoebe (*Lace*) Cates; gymnast Phoebe Mills; TV's Phoebe ("All My Children") Wallingford; singer Phoebe Snow

PHYLICIA see Felicia

PHYLLIS (Greek) "green bough"

Image: Most people picture Phyllis as a sickly older woman who is strict and fussy. Some, though, see Phyllis as a gaudy, outrageous divorcée.

Famous Phyllises: comedienne Phyllis Diller; sportscaster Phyllis George; TV's Phyllis ("The Mary Tyler Moore Show") Lindstrom; eighteenth-century poet Phillis Wheatley; right-to-life advocate Phyllis Schlafly

POLLY a form of Molly, Paula

Image: Polly is pictured as a real sweetheart — a cute, energetic woman with a cheerful and friendly manner.

Famous Pollys: Tom Sawyer's Aunt Polly; actress Polly (*War and Remembrance*) Bergen; H.G. Wells's *The History of Mr. Polly*; Polly, Jack Benny's parrot; nursery rhyme "Little Polly Flinders"; Sweet Polly Purebread, Underdog's girlfriend

PRISCILLA (Latin) "from ancient times"

Image: Most people picture Priscilla as a prude who is pretty, feminine, and uptight, but not above flirting.

Famous Priscillas: actresses Priscilla ("Dallas") Presley, Priscilla ("Three's Company") Barnes, Priscilla (*The Roaring Twenties*) Lane

PRUDENCE (Latin) "foresight, intelligence"

Image: People think of Prudence as very old-fashioned — a homely, stuffy, straitlaced, prudish introvert.

Famous Prudence: the Beatles' song "Dear Prudence"

QUEENIE (Old English) "queen"

Image: People think of Queenie as a heavy, tough, streetwise woman. Some also think Queenie is a great name for a dog.

Famous Queenies: Michael Korda's novel *Queenie*; actress Merle (*Queenie*) Oberon

RACHEL (Hebrew) "ewe"

Image: Rachel is pictured as a beautiful, small, dark-haired woman with quiet, intelligent strength.

Famous Rachels: the biblical Rachel, Joseph's mother; writer/environmentalist Rachel (*The Silent Spring*) Carson; the art world's Rachel Mellon, Paul's wife; actress Rachel (*Against All Odds*) Ward; children's story writer Rachel Field

RAE (Old English) "doe"; a short form of Rachel

Image: People think the unusual name Rae is suitable for an intelligent young girl with a sunny disposition.

Famous Raes: actress Rae Dawn (*The Color Purple*) . Chong; Elizabeth Ray, Wilber Mills's close friend; entertainer Martha Raye; the movie *Norma Rae*

RANDI, Randy feminine forms of Randall, Randolph

Image: Randi, a name increasingly used for girls, calls to mind a cute, young blonde who is lively and dependable — a hairdresser or waitress, perhaps.

Famous Randis: actress Randi ("CHIPS") Oakes; illusionist the Amazing Randi

RAQUEL a Spanish form of Rachel

Image: Raquel Welch is the dominant image for this name. People say Raquel is a beautiful, buxom woman who is lots of fun.

Famous Raquel: actress Raquel Welch

REBA a short form of Rebecca

Image: Reba strikes people as a good name for a smart, successful businesswoman or singer who is generous and nice.

Famous Reba: country singer Reba McIntyre

REBECCA, Rebekah (Hebrew) "bound"

Image: People think of Rebecca as a pretty, unpretentious young woman who is smart, well read, and either outspoken and strong willed or soft and sweet.

Famous Rebeccas: the biblical Rebekah, Isaac's wife; Kate D. Wiggin's novel *Rebecca of Sunnybrook Farm*; Daphne du Maurier's novel *Rebecca*; actress Rebecca (*Risky Business*) De Mornay; author Rebecca West

REGINA (Latin) "queen"

Image: People say Regina is an older, red- or auburn-haired woman who is classy, pompous, and very proper.

Famous Reginas: Latin designation used for England's queens, e.g., Elizabeth Regina; Regina (*The Little Foxes*) Giddens; the city of Regina, Saskatchewan

RENEE (Latin) "reborn"; a French form of Renata

> **Image:** Renee is described as a smart, trendy sophisticate who is ambitious, independent, and strong.

> **Famous Renees:** tennis's Renee Richards; comedienne Renee Taylor

RHEA (Greek) "earth, that which flows from the earth, as rivers"

> **Image:** The name Rhea calls to mind a short woman who is a real survivor — spunky, opinionated, and tough.

> **Famous Rheas:** the mythological Rhea Silvia, mother of Romulus and Remus; actress Rhea ("Cheers") Perlman; Rhea, Saturn's moon

RHODA (Greek) "roses, from Rhodes"; a form of Rose

> **Image:** When people hear the name Rhoda, they think of a Jewish woman who is strong, funny, and friendly, like Mary Tyler Moore's friend Rhoda.

> **Famous Rhodas:** TV's Rhoda ("The Mary Tyler Moore Show") Morgenstern; George Meredith's novel *Rhoda Fleming*

RHONDA a geographical name of southern Wales, possibly meaning "grand"

> **Image:** People say the name Rhonda reminds them of a round, beautiful, popular blonde with a sunny disposition.

> **Famous Rhondas:** the Beach Boys' song "Help Me, Rhonda"; actress Rhonda (*Pony Express*) Fleming

RITA a short form of Margaret

> **Image:** Most people think of Rita as a gorgeous, talented woman who is funny and outgoing but somewhat phony. Some, though, think Rita is quiet and saintly.

> **Famous Ritas:** Saint Rita, known for her austerity; singer Rita Coolidge; actress Rita (*Salome*) Hayworth; actress/dancer Rita (*West Side Story*) Moreno; the Beatles' song "Lovely Rita Meter Maid"; the movie *Educating Rita*

ROBERTA (Old English) "shining with fame"; a feminine form of Robert

> **Image:** People think of Roberta as an overweight, family-oriented woman who is strong willed yet supportive and sweet.

> **Famous Robertas:** pop singer Roberta ("Where Is the Love?") Flack; opera singer Roberta Peters

ROBIN, Robyn (Old English) "robin"; forms of Roberta

> **Image:** Though the name is often used for boys, a girl named Robin is described as petite, pretty, talented, interesting, and snobby.

> **Famous Robins:** comic actor Robin Williams; legendary hero Robin Hood; robin redbreast, the bird; actresses Robyn ("Houston Knights") Douglass; Robin ("Head of the Class") Givens

ROCHELLE (French) "from the little rock"; a form of Rachel

Image: The name Rochelle reminds many people of a pretty black woman who is quiet, kind, and motherly.

Famous Rochelle: the city of New Rochelle, New York

RONA (Old Norse) "mighty power"; a feminine form of Ronald

Image: Rona Barrett is the dominant image for this name. People say Rona is an inquisitive, hard-edged, abrasive gossip.

Famous Ronas: columnist Rona Barrett; author Rona Jaffe

RONNI, Ronnie forms of Roanna, Rowena, Veronica

Image: The name Ronni is considered appropriate for girls and boys. A girl named Ronni is pictured as a fun-loving, friendly, tomboy with a ponytail.

Famous Ronnie: singer Ronnie Spector of the Ronettes

ROSALIE an Irish form of Rose

Image: There are two different images of Rosalie: a confident go-getter who fights for what she wants or a heavy, old-fashioned homebody.

Famous Rosalies: nonsexist language expert Rosalie Maggio; Nelson Eddy's song "Rosalie"

ROSALIND, Rosalyn (Spanish) "beautiful rose"

Image: When people hear this name, they think of Rosalind Russell — happy, energetic,

and classy. They also think of Rosalynn Carter — southern, quiet, businesslike, and strong willed.

Famous Rosalinds: actresses Rosalind (*Auntie Mame*) Russell, Rosalind (*The Omega Man*) Cash; First Lady Rosalynn Carter; Rosalind in Shakespeare's play *As You Like It*; figure skater Rosalynn Sumners; physicist Rosalyn Yalow

ROSE (Greek) "rose"

Image: Rose is described as a real sweetie — a gentle, motherly woman who is warmhearted and kind.

Famous Roses: matriarch Rose Kennedy; author Dame Rose Macaulay; stripper Gypsy Rose Lee; World War II's Tokyo Rose

ROSEANNE a combination of Rose and Ann

Image: The name Roseanne has two different images: a pretty, feminine woman who is sweet and caring or a boisterous, loud comic, like Roseanne Barr.

Famous Roseannes: actresses Roseanne ("Roseanne") Barr, Rosanna (*Desperately Seeking Susan*) Arquette; country singer Roseanne Cash; TV's Roseanne ("Saturday Night Live") Roseannadanna

ROSE MARIE, Rosemary (Latin) "rosemary"

Image: Most people describe Rose Marie as a pretty, old-fashioned woman who is wholesome, quiet, loyal, and sweet. Some, though, say Rose Marie is a pushy know-it-all.

Famous Rose Maries: comic actresses Rose ("The Dick Van Dyke Show") Marie, Rosemary ("That Girl") De Camp; singer Rosemary Clooney; the movie *Rosemary's Baby*; tennis's Rosemary Casals; the light opera *Rose Marie*

ROSIE, Rosey forms of Rose

Image: Rosie is pictured as a cheerleader — an energetic girl who is bouncy, bubbly, and very happy.

Famous Rosies: skier Rosi Mittermaier; Rosie the robot on TV's "The Jetsons"; World War II's Rosie the Riveter; tennis's Rosie Casals; football's Rosey Grier

ROXANNE (Persian) "dawn"

Image: People think of Roxanne as a pretty, feminine blonde who is energetic and enthusiastic, though not too bright.

Famous Roxannes: Roxane in Edmond Rostand's play *Cyrano de Bergerac*; Sting's song "Roxanne"; TV's Roxanne ("L.A. Law") Melman

ROZ a short form of Rosalind

Image: Roz has a reputation as a real tough cookie — a big, strong, sexy woman who is outspoken, aggressive, and funny.

Famous Rozes: comic actress Roz ("Amen") Ryan; Roz on TV's "Night Court"

RUBY (Old French) "ruby"

Image: Ruby is pictured as a pretty, older black woman who is friendly, vivacious, and resilient.

Famous Rubys: entertainer Ruby Keeler; actress Ruby (*A Raisin in the Sun*) Dee; Ruby ("Amos 'n' Andy") Jones

RUTH (Hebrew) "friend of beauty"

Image: People say Ruth is a big, sturdy, average woman who is strong, dedicated, and well respected — a teacher or leader, perhaps.

Famous Ruths: the biblical Ruth, Naomi's daughter-in-law; comic actress Ruth ("Laugh-In") Buzzi; sex therapist Dr. Ruth Westheimer; baseball's Babe Ruth; actress Ruth (*Harold and Maude*) Gordon

SABRA (Hebrew) "thorny cactus, to rest"

Image: Most people picture Sabra as a dark, exotic Israeli beauty who is wild, sexy, and passionate.

Famous Sabra: Sabra, the term for a native-born Israeli girl

SABRINA (Latin) "from the boundary line"

Image: People say Sabrina is a pretty, sexy woman who is exotic, mischievous, and a bit of a tease.

Famous Sabrinas: the movie *Sabrina*; TV's Sabrina ("Charlie's Angels") Duncan; Sabrina, the cartoon witch on TV's "The Archies"

SADIE a form of Sarah

Image: Sadie is pictured as a big, plain, down-home, barefoot country girl who is vivacious and loud.

Famous Sadies: Sadie ("Li'l Abner") Hawkins; Sadie (*Rain*) Thompson; the Beatles' song "Sexy Sadie"; Sadie, Sad Sack's girlfriend

SALLY a form of Sarah

Image: The name Sally reminds people of the girl-next-door — a plain, blonde, old-fashioned girl who is lighthearted and fun.

Famous Sallys: actresses Sally (*Norma Rae*) Field, Sally ("All in the Family") Struthers, Sally (*M*A*S*H*) Kellerman; fan dancer Sally Rand; astronaut Sally Ride; TV host Sally Jessy Raphael; Sally Brown in "Peanuts" comics

SAMANTHA (Aramaic) "listener"

Image: The name Samantha has two different images: a bright, pretty, magical woman or a nondescript, middle-aged mom.

Famous Samanthas: TV's Samantha ("Bewitched") Stephens; actress Samantha (*Doctor Doolittle*) Eggar; 12-year-old goodwill ambassador Samantha Smith

SANDRA a short form of Alexandra

Image: Two different impressions of the name Sandra come to mind: an intelligent blonde who is determined and controlling or a plump woman who is soft-spoken and easygoing.

Famous Sandras: actress Sandra (*Gidget*) Dee; Supreme Court Justice Sandra Day O'Connor; electrical engineer Sandra Hawley

SANDY a short form of Sandra

Image: Sandy is described as a young blonde who is smart, playful, fun loving, friendly, and nice.

Famous Sandys: actresses Sandy (*Up the Down Staircase*) Dennis, Sandy ("The Hogan Family") Duncan; Sandy, Little Orphan Annie's dog

SARAH, Sara (Hebrew) "princess"

Image: The name Sarah calls to mind a short, pretty, curly-haired girl who is old-fashioned and nice.

Famous Sarahs: the biblical Sarah, Abraham's wife; Britain's Duchess Sarah, of York; actress Sarah (*Ryan's Daughter*) Miles; the movie *Two Mules for Sister Sarah*; TV host Sarah ("Real People") Purcell; Fleetwood Mac's song "Sara"

SASHA a Russian short form of Alexandra

   Image: People say Sasha is an exotic foreigner who is intriguing, yet cold and aloof.

   Famous Sashas: Sasha, Sylvester Stallone's ex-wife; Sasha the bird in *Peter and the Wolf*

SCARLETT (Middle English) "scarlet"

   Image: Scarlett's image comes straight from the movies. Scarlett is described as a very pretty, vivacious woman who is temperamental and conniving.

   Famous Scarlett: Scarlett (*Gone with the Wind*) O'Hara

SELMA (Scandinavian) "divinely protected"; a feminine form of Anselm

   Image: People say Selma is an old-fashioned name befitting an older, low-class southern woman who is a brassy know-it-all.

   Famous Selmas: actress Selma ("Night Court") Diamond; Swedish novelist Selma Lagerlof; the city of Selma, Alabama

SERENA (Latin) "calm, serene"

   Image: Serena has two different images: cute, lively, and full of surprises or quiet, timid, and religious.

   Famous Serena: Serena, Samantha's conniving cousin on TV's "Bewitched"

SHANNON (Irish Gaelic) "small, wise"

   Image: People picture Shannon as a cute, young, curly-haired, western blonde who is smart and serious and loves horses.

   Famous Shannons: actress Shannon (*Hot Dog*) Tweed; the Shannon River in Ireland

SHARI a Hungarian form of Sarah

   Image: People picture Shari as cute, blonde, fun loving, witty, and smart, like Shari Lewis.

   Famous Sharis: entertainer Shari Lewis; actress Shari ("Hotel") Belafonte-Harper

SHARLENE see also Charlene

SHARON (Hebrew) "a plain"; a form of Sarah

   Image: Most people expect Sharon to be a small, cute, middle-class brunette who is friendly, sweet, and bright. Some, though, think Sharon is shy and dull.

   Famous Sharons: actress Sharon ("Cagney and Lacey") Gless; actress Sharon Tate, murdered by Charles Manson

SHAUNA, Shawna feminine forms of John (through Sean)

   Image: The name Shauna reminds most people of a beautiful woman who is soft-spoken, sweet, and quiet. Some people, though, see Shauna as vibrant and exciting.

SHEENA an Irish form of Jane

   Image: Thanks to Sheena Easton, people picture Sheena as a singer who is sexy, stylish, and slender.

Famous Sheenas: singer Sheena ("For Your Eyes Only") Easton; the movie *Sheena, Queen of the Jungle*

SHEILA an Irish form of Cecilia

Image: People say Sheila is an overweight blonde who is spunky, boisterous, and wild.

Famous Sheilas: gossip columnist Sheila Graham; writer Sheila Kaye-Smith; rock musician Sheila ("Glamorous Life") E.; playwright Shelagh Delaney

SHELLEY (Old English) "from the meadow on the ledge"; a form of Rachel, Sheila, Shelby, Shirley

Image: Shelley is described in two different ways: a cute, blonde, witty, stuck-up preppy or a silly, pudgy, talkative blonde.

Famous Shelleys: actresses Shelley (*The Diary of Anne Frank*) Winters, Shelley ("Cheers") Long, Shelley (*Popeye*) Duvall, Shelley ("Coach") Fabares

SHERRY, Cherie forms of Charlotte, Cher, Sarah, Shirley

Image: People picture Sherry as a cute, short, plump blonde who is nice, flirtatious, and somewhat scatterbrained.

Famous Sherrys: actress Sheree ("Big Eddie") North; Stevie Wonder's song "Ma Cherie Amour"; the Four Seasons' song "Sherry"

SHERYL a form of Shirley (see also Cheryl)

Image: Sheryl is pictured as a fat, homely, bespectacled girl-next-door who is quiet and intelligent.

SHIRLEY (Old English) "from the bright meadow"

Image: People picture Shirley as a gray-haired version of Shirley Temple — cute, sweet, curly-haired, baby-faced, and overweight.

Famous Shirleys: entertainer/ diplomat Shirley Temple Black; actresses Shirley ("Hazel") Booth, Shirley (*The Music Man*) Jones, Shirley (*Steel Magnolias*) MacLaine; congresswoman Shirley Chisholm

SIMONE (Hebrew) "one who hears"; a feminine form of Simon

Image: People say Simone is a French or black woman who is a pretty, elegant, and sexy coquette.

Famous Simones: writers Simone (*The Second Sex*) de Beauvoir, Simone Weil; actress Simone (*Room at the Top*) Signoret; singer Nina Simone; TV's Simone ("Head of the Class") Foster

SISSY (American) a short form of Cecilia, Cecily

Image: People picture Sissy as a youthful, down-home, freckled country girl who is funny, bouncy, and childlike.

Famous Sissys: actress Sissy (*Coal Miner's Daughter*) Spacek; TV's Cissy ("Family Affair") Davis

SONIA, Sonya Slavic and Scandinavian forms of Sophie

Image: Sonia is described as an active, outdoorsy foreign woman who is gentle and sweet.

Famous Sonias: actress Sonia (*The Milagro Beanfield War*) Braga; skater Sonja Henie; Sonya in Fyodor Dostoyevsky's novel *Crime and Punishment*; Sonia the duck in *Peter and the Wolf*

SOPHIE, Sophia (Greek) "wisdom"

Image: Sophie strikes people as a good name for a big old-fashioned, black woman who is extremely talkative.

Famous Sophies: singer Sophie Tucker; Sophie, Archduke Franz Ferdinand's wife; actress Sophia (*Two Women*) Loren; Sophia Smith, founder of Smith College

STACY a short form of Anastasia

Image: Stacy is described as a short, cute, young redhead who is active, outgoing, and flirtatious.

Famous Stacys: actor Stacy ("Mike Hammer") Keach; singer Stacey Q

STEFFI a short form of Stephanie

Image: Most people think of Steffi as a cute, athletic girl who is a bubbly, popular free spirit. Some say Steffi is also stuck-up.

Famous Steffi: tennis's Steffi Graf

STELLA (Latin) "star"; a short form of Estelle

Image: Most people regard Stella as a dowdy, old-fashioned, and hardworking but slow-witted old crab. Some, though, think Stella is pretty, seductive, and worldly.

Famous Stellas: actress Stella (*Girls! Girls! Girls!*) Stevens; Stella (*A Streetcar Named Desire*) Kowalski; Jonathan Swift's novel *Journal to Stella*

STEPHANIE (Greek) "crowned"; a feminine form of Stephen

Image: Most people think Stephanie is a thin, pretty, feminine woman who is sophisticated and self-centered — a model, perhaps. Some think Stephanie is very kind.

Famous Stephanies: actresses Stephanie ("Hart to Hart") Powers, Stephanie ("Remington Steele") Zimbalist; Princess Stephanie of Monaco; TV's Stephanie ("Newhart") Vanderkellen Harris

SUE a short form of Susan

Image: The name Sue has two different images: a homely, all-American girl who is sweet and considerate or a gorgeous, seductive woman who wants it all.

Famous Sues: actresses Sue (*Lolita*) Lyon, Melissa Sue ("Little House on the Prairie") Anderson

SUNNY (English) "bright, cheerful"; a short form of Sonia

Image: As the name suggests, Sunny is regarded as bright and happy — an outgoing, pleasant, sexy, and somewhat airheaded party girl.

Famous Sunnys: the song "Sunny"; heiress Sunny von Bulow

SUSAN (Hebrew) "lily"

Image: Susan is described as an average woman who is wholesome, pleasant, and down-to-earth. Some people, though, think Susan is whiny and fussy.

Famous Susans: actresses Susan ("Kate and Allie") Saint James, Susan (*Bull Durham*) Sarandon, Susan (*Straw Dogs*) George, Susan (*Goldengirl*) Anton, Susan (*I'll Cry Tomorrow*) Hayward; suffragist Susan B. Anthony; director Susan (*Desperately Seeking Susan*) Seidelman

SUZANNE, Susannah forms of Susan

Image: Many people picture Suzanne as a cute, sassy woman who is fun loving and mischievous — a French maid, perhaps. Some think Suzanne is a hardworking bore.

Famous Suzannes: the biblical Susannah, falsely accused of adultery; actresses Suzanne ("The Bob Newhart Show") Pleshette, Suzanne ("Three's Company") Somers; philosopher Susanne Knauth Langer; the song "Oh, Susannah"

SUZIE, Susie short forms of Susan

Image: Suzie is described as a cute, bouncy girl who is a popular, fun-loving, cheerleader type.

Famous Suzies: the songs "If You Knew Suzie," "Wake Up Little Susie"; generic Suzie Q; skier Suzy Chaffee

SYBIL, Cybil (Greek) "prophetess"; forms of Sibyl

Image: The name Sybil has three different images: a beautiful, cool jet-setter; a prim, prudish spinster; or a strange and scary woman of mystery.

Famous Sybils: the book and movie *Sybil*; Sybil, Richard Burton's first wife; actresses Cybill ("Moonlighting") Shepherd, Dame Sybil (*Major Barbara*) Thorndike; TV's Sybil ("Fawlty Towers") Fawlty

SYLVIA (Latin) "from the forest"

Image: People see Sylvia as a beautiful, wealthy woman who is poised, proper, shrewd, and businesslike.

Famous Sylvias: Silvia in Shakespeare's play *Two Gentlemen of Verona*; newscaster Sylvia Chase; columnist Sylvia Porter; actress Sylvia (*An Early Frost*) Sidney; poet Sylvia Plath

TABITHA (Aramaic) "gazelle"

Image: Thanks to TV's "Bewitched," Tabitha is perceived as a childlike, silly airhead with an air of mystery. Tabitha is also considered a great name for a cat.

Famous Tabithas: TV's Tabitha ("Bewitched") Stephens; Tabitha (*Humphrey Clinker*) Bramble; the biblical Tabitha, raised from the dead

TALIA (Greek) "blooming"

Image: Talia Shire is the dominant image for this name. People describe Talia as a skinny, cute, dark-skinned Italian who is somewhat offbeat.

Famous Talias: the mythological Thalia, Greek muse of comedy; actress Talia (*Rocky*) Shire

TALLULAH (North American Indian) "leaping water"

Image: Tallulah is an oldfashioned name that calls to mind a strange-looking older woman who is serious, superstitious, and weird or a sexy black woman who is giddy and playful.

Famous Tallulah: actress Tallulah Bankhead

TAMARA (Hebrew) "palm tree"

Image: Most people picture Tamara as a dark, pretty, athletic woman who is sexy, caring, and fun. Tamara may be a business-minded achiever or a bit of an airhead.

Famous Tamaras: skier Tamara McKinney; Russian ballerina Tamara Karsavina

TAMMY a short form of Tamara

Image: People think of Tammy as a cute young blonde who is sweet, playful, and extravagant.

Famous Tammys: TV evangelist Tammy Faye Bakker; actress Tammy Grimes; country singer Tammy ("Stand By Your Man") Wynette; the movie *Tammy and the Bachelor*

TANYA, Tonya (Slavic) meaning unknown

Image: People say Tanya is a fitting name for a big, pretty, blonde country girl who is sexy, boisterous, wild, and not too bright.

Famous Tanyas: actresses Tonya Crowe, Tanya ("Charlie's Angels") Roberts; country singer Tanya Tucker; Tonia, Doctor Zhivago's wife

TARA (Irish Gaelic) "rocky pinnacle"

Image: Tara is described a petite, beautiful brunette southern belle who is quiet, elegant, and earthy.

Famous Taras: Tara, the O'Hara plantation in *Gone with the Wind*; the mythological Tara, home of ancient Irish kings

TERESA, Theresa (Greek)
"reaper"

Image: Teresa is pictured as a pretty, dark-haired woman who is quiet, straitlaced, and highly religious.

Famous Teresas: singer Teresa Brewer; Nobel Prize recipient Mother Teresa; Saint Theresa of Spain; actress Theresa (*Blind Ambition*) Russell

TERI, Terry short forms of Theresa; feminine forms of Terence

Image: People say Teri is an attractive, outdoorsy tomboy who is capable, average, and nice.

Famous Teris: actresses Teri (*Tootsie*) Garr, Terry (*Two of a Kind*) Moore; actor Terry (*It's a Mad Mad Mad Mad World*) Thomas; "Terry and the Pirates" comics

TESS a short form of Tessa, Teresa

Image: There are two different images of the name Tess: a fat, homey, country grandma or a small, shy, pretty, long-haired girl.

Famous Tesses: Thomas Hardy's novel *Tess of the D'Urbervilles*; actress Tess (*Tender Mercies*) Harper; Tess Trueheart, Dick Tracy's girlfriend; poet Tess Gallagher

TESSA (Greek) "fourth child"; a short form of Teresa

Image: Tessa is pictured as a pretty, dainty woman who is quiet and well read.

THELMA, Telma (Greek)
"nursling"

Image: When people think of Thelma, they imagine an unattractive older woman who is quite old-fashioned.

Famous Thelmas: actress Thelma (*Rear Window*) Ritter; singer/actress Telma ("Bosom Buddies") Hopkins

THEODORA (Greek) "gift of God"; a feminine form of Theodore

Image: Theodora is described as a tall, slender, awkward older woman who is formal, quiet, and boring.

Famous Theodora: Byzantine Empress Theodora

THERESA see Teresa

TIFFANY (Greek) "appearance of God"

Image: Tiffany strikes people as a good name for a petite, pretty woman who is rich, sophisticated, frivolous, and snotty.

Famous Tiffanys: the movie *Breakfast at Tiffany's*; skater Tiffany Chin; singer Tiffany Darwich; TV's Tiffany ("Charlie's Angels") Wells; artist Louis Comfort Tiffany; the Tiffany & Co. jewelry stores

TINA a short form of names ending in "tina" or "tine"

Image: Most people describe Tina as a little bundle of energy who is talented and fun. Some, though, picture Tina as spoiled and shy.

Famous Tinas: singer Tina ("Proud Mary") Turner; actresses Tina ("Gilligan's Island") Louise, Tina ("Family Ties") Yothers

TONI a short form of Antoinette

Image: A girl named Toni is pictured as tall, dark, and boyish — an athletic rich kid who is sneaky and troublesome.

Famous Tonis: singers Toni ("Love Will Keep Us Together") Tennille, Toni Childs; novelist Toni (*Beloved*) Morrison

TONYA see Tanya

TRACY, Tracey (Irish Gaelic) "battler"; (Latin) "courageous"; short forms of Teresa

Image: Tracy is described as a cute, blonde, athletic preppy with curly hair, who may be confident and in charge; giggly and fun loving; or well mannered and mild.

Famous Tracys: singer Tracy Chapman; tennis's Tracy Austin; comic actress Tracey Ullman; actresses Tracey ("Growing Pains") Gold, Tracy ("Mr. Belvedere") Wells, Tracy ("Father Dowling Mysteries") Nelson

TRICIA a short form of Patricia

Image: People say Tricia is a thin blonde who is rich, well mannered, and sweet — maybe too sweet.

Famous Tricia: Tricia Nixon Cox, President Nixon's daughter

TRIXIE a short form of Beatrice

Image: Trixie is described as a blonde airhead who is funny, sexy, and flirty — a stand-up comic, perhaps.

Famous Trixies: TV's Trixie ("The Honeymooners") Norton; fictional detective Trixie Belden; Trixie in "Hi and Lois" comics

TRUDY (Old German) "beloved"; a short form of Gertrude

Image: Trudy strikes people as a good name for a cute woman who is a serious, loyal teacher.

TUESDAY (Old English) "Tuesday"

Image: Tuesday is pictured as cute, blonde, sexy, flighty, quirky, and self-conscious, like actress Tuesday Weld.

Famous Tuesdays: actress Tuesday Weld; rock band 'Til Tuesday

TWYLA (Middle English) "woven of double thread"

Image: People consider Twyla a good name for a flighty, insecure, shy girl who is either rebellious or dopey.

Famous Twyla: choreographer Twyla Tharp

TYNE (Old English) "river"

Image: Thanks to Tyne Daly's TV roles, Tyne is pictured as a sturdy woman who is intelligent, interesting, and strong.

Famous Tyne: actress Tyne ("Cagney and Lacey") Daly

URSULA (Latin) "little bear"

Image: Because Ursula Andress quickly comes to mind, people picture Ursula as a sexy, shapely, German or Scandinavian beauty who is graceful, quiet, and self-assured.

Famous Ursulas: Saint Ursula, legendary Cornish princess; actress Ursula (*Dr. No*) Andress; science fiction novelist Ursula K. LeGuin; Ursula (*Women in Love*) Brangwen

VAL a short form of Valerie

Image: Val is described as a sensible, caring woman who is loud but nice and who has her priorities in order.

Famous Vals: TV's Val ("Knots Landing") Ewing; actor Val Kilmer

VALERIE (Latin) "strong"

Image: The name Valerie has two different images: an elite, high-society woman who is studious and soft-spoken or a happy, funny, middle-class career woman.

Famous Valeries: actresses Valerie ("One Day at a Time") Bertinelli, Valerie ("Rhoda") Harper; runner Valerie Briscoe-Hooks

VANESSA invented by Jonathan Swift for Esther Vanhomrigh ("van" plus "essa")

Image: Most people think of Vanessa as a slim, attractive woman who is intelligent, wealthy, stately, and snobby. Some also think of Vanessa as seductive.

Famous Vanessas: actress Vanessa (*Playing for Time*) Redgrave; model Vanessa Williams; TV's Vanessa ("The Cosby Show") Huxtable

VANNA a short form of Vanessa

Image: Thanks to TV's Vanna White, the name Vanna has a "dumb blonde" image. Vanna is pictured as pretty, blonde, sexy, shapely, likable, and empty-headed.

Famous Vanna: TV host Vanna ("Wheel of Fortune") White

VELMA (Old German) "determined guardian"; a short form of Wilhelmina; a feminine form of William

Image: The old-fashioned name Velma is considered suitable for a plump, frumpy old woman who is mean and controlling.

VERA (Latin) "true"; (Slavic) "faith"; a short form of Veronica

Image: People describe Vera as an old-fashioned worrywart who is two-faced, bitter, and sharp-tongued.

Famous Veras: TV's Vera ("Alice") Gorman; actress Vera Miles; Vera, Norm Peterson's wife on TV's "Cheers"

VERNA, Virna (Latin) "springlike"

Image: Most people picture Verna as a big, strong older woman who is old-fashioned, loud, and self-assured. Some, though, see Verna as a soft-spoken loner.

Famous Virna: actress Virna (*Night Flight from Moscow*) Lisi

VERONICA (Latin-Greek) "true image"; a form of Bernice

Image: Veronica is described as a tall, pretty, long-haired blonde who is a flighty, self-absorbed, sexy cheerleader.

Famous Veronicas: Saint Veronica; actresses Veronica (*I Married a Witch*) Lake, Veronica ("Hill Street Blues") Hamel; Veronica in "Archie" comics

VICKI a short form of Victoria

Image: People picture Vicki as a small, plain tomboy who is caring and who smokes heavily.

Famous Vickis: singer Vicki Carr; comic actress Vicki ("The Carol Burnett Show") Lawrence; Austrian novelist Vicki (*Grand Hotel*) Baum; Miss Vicki, Tiny Tim's wife

VICTORIA (Latin) "victory"; a feminine form of Victor

Image: Victoria is pictured as a stately, sophisticated brunette who is rich, conservative, ambitious, elegant, and aloof.

Famous Victorias: Britain's Queen Victoria; actress Victoria ("Dallas") Principal; novelists Victoria Holt, Victoria (*Vita*) Sackville-West; the movie *Victor/Victoria*

VIOLET (Latin) "violet flower"

Image: Violet is pictured as a delicate older woman who is old-fashioned, quiet, and not too bright, like a "shrinking violet."

Famous Violets: English writer Violet Hunt; English actress Violet ("Coronation Street") Carson; Violet in "Peanuts" comics; Violet (*It's a Wonderful Life*) Bick

VIRGINIA (Latin) "virginal, maidenly"

Image: Virginia is described as a heavy, old-fashioned woman who is prim, proper, prudish, and polite. To some, though, Virginia is a moody prima donna who is overpowering and explosive.

Famous Virginias: early settler Virginia Dare; actresses Virginia (*Slam Dance*) Madsen, Virginia (*The Best Years of Our Lives*) Mayo; novelist Virginia (*To the Lighthouse*) Woolf; tennis's Virginia Wade; the state of Virginia

VIRNA see Verna

VIVIAN, Vivien (Latin) "full of life"

Image: Full of life? You bet! People say Vivian is vivacious, cultured, funny, friendly, and active.

Famous Vivians: actresses Vivien (*Gone with the Wind*) Leigh, Vivian ("I Love Lucy") Vance

WANDA (Old German) "wanderer"

> **Image:** Wanda is described as a hefty, frumpy woman who is terribly sweet and well liked, though perhaps not too bright.
>
> **Famous Wandas:** the movie *A Fish Called Wanda*; Polish film director Wanda Jakubowska; children's story writer Wanda (*Millions of Cats*) Gag

WENDY a short form of Gwendolyn, Wanda

> **Image:** Most people see Wendy as a short, cute, cuddly woman who is friendly and sweet. Some, though, see Wendy as ambitious, rude, or arrogant.
>
> **Famous Wendys:** Wendy (*Peter Pan*) Darling; actress Dame Wendy (*A Man for All Seasons*) Hiller; "Wendy, the Good Little Witch" comics; Wendy's hamburgers; singers Wendy O. Williams, Wendy Wall

WHITNEY (Old English) "from the white island, from fair water"

> **Image:** People picture Whitney as a tall, thin, pretty, young black woman who is talented, chic, rich, outgoing, and successful, like Whitney Houston.
>
> **Famous Whitneys:** singer Whitney ("Saving All My Love For You") Houston; inventor Eli Whitney; civil rights leader Whitney Young

WILLA (Old German) "determined guardian"; a short form of Wilhelmina; a feminine form of William

> **Image:** Willa is pictured as a plain, thin black woman — a down-home country girl who is practical and boring.
>
> **Famous Willa:** novelist Willa (*My Ántonia*) Cather

WILMA a short form of Wilhelmina; a feminine form of William

> **Image:** People describe Wilma as a stocky old lady who is old-fashioned, quiet, and nervous.
>
> **Famous Wilmas:** Wilma, Fred Flintstone's wife; runner Wilma Rudolph; TV's Wilma ("Buck Rogers") Deering

WINONA (Sioux Indian) "first-born daughter"

> **Image:** People think of Winona as an old-fashioned name that suits a southern black farm girl who is friendly and soft-spoken.
>
> **Famous Winonas:** country singer Wynona Judd; actress Winona (*Beetlejuice*) Ryder

WYNNE (Welsh) "fair"; a short form of Gwendolyn

Image: People say Wynne is an overweight, older woman — a simple homebody who is silly and whiny.

Famous Wynnes: actor Keenan (*Dr. Strangelove*) Wynn; comic actor Ed (*Mary Poppins*) Wynn

XAVIERA (Arabic) "brilliant"; (Spanish Basque) "owner of the new house"; a feminine form of Xavier

Image: When people hear the name Xaviera, they imagine an exotic Latin American woman who is rich, sexy, and extravagant.

Famous Xaviera: writer/prostitute Xaviera (*The Happy Hooker*) Hollander

XENIA (Greek) "hospitable"

Image: Xenia is regarded as a trendy, even futuristic name, suitable for an artistic person who is flamboyant and outrageous.

Famous Xenia: the city of Xenia, Ohio

YETTA (Old English) "to give, giver"; a short form of Henrietta

Image: The name Yetta calls to mind an old-fashioned Jewish grandmother who is caring, kind, and warm.

YOKO (Japanese) "the positive (female)"

Image: Yoko's image comes straight from Yoko Ono. People say Yoko is a dark-haired Asian woman who is strong willed, strange, and quiet.

Famous Yoko: Yoko Ono, John Lennon's widow

YVETTE, Ivette forms of Yvonne

Image: People describe Yvette as a petite French brunette — a high-society sophisticate who is smart and friendly, though a bit snobby.

Famous Yvette: actress Yvette (*Where the Boys Are*) Mimieux

YVONNE, Evonne (Old French) "archer"; feminine forms of Ivar, Ives

Image: People imagine Yvonne as a fair-skinned woman with long black hair who is easygoing, likeable, and smart.

Famous Yvonnes: actress Yvonne ("The Munsters") De Carlo; tennis's Evonne Goolagong; Miss Yvonne on TV's "Pee Wee's Playhouse"

ZELDA (Old German) "gray woman warrior"; a short form of Griselda

Image: Two images of the name Zelda come to mind: a large, loud, and frumpy old woman or a flamboyant and untrustworthy eccentric.

Famous Zelda: Zelda, F. Scott Fitzgerald's wife

ZENA, Zina forms of Xenia

Image: The name Zena has two different images: a sultry, foreign gypsy or fortune-teller; or a short, heavy, enthusiastic, well-organized woman who likes to cook.

Famous Zenas: tennis's Zina Garrison; Zena jeans

ZOË (Greek) "life"

Image: To most people Zoë is a pretty, artistic flower child who is fun and somewhat weird. To some, though, Zoë is careful, reliable, and boring.

Famous Zoës: actress Zoë Caldwell; playwright Zoë Akins; J. D. Salinger's novella *Frannie and Zooey*

ZOLA (Italian) "ball of earth"

Image: Zola is pictured as an exotic, foreign woman with dark hair, a slender, athletic body, and wild clothes. Zola is thought to be a forceful, goal-oriented individual.

Famous Zolas: runner Zola Budd; French novelist Émile Zola

ZSA ZSA a Hungarian form of Susan

Image: Zsa Zsa's image comes straight from Zsa Zsa Gabor. A girl with this name is described as pretty, wealthy, spacey, sexy, extravagant, and spoiled.

Famous Zsa Zsa: celebrity Zsa Zsa Gabor

PERSONALITY PROFILES
OF BOYS' NAMES

AARON (Hebrew) "enlightened"

Image: Aaron is described as a small and nice-looking man who is honest, hardworking, and responsible — an effective leader with a quiet manner.

Famous Aarons: the biblical priest Aaron, brother of Moses; former vice president Aaron Burr; TV producer Aaron Spelling; composer Aaron (*Appalachian Spring*) Copland; tennis's Aaron Krickstein

ABBOTT (Hebrew) "father, abbot"

Image: Thanks to comedian Bud Abbott, most people describe Abbott as a fast-talking funny man who is tall and slender. Some, though, believe Abbott is fat and dumb, possibly confusing Bud Abbott with his longtime sidekick, Lou Costello.

Famous Abbotts: comic actor Bud Abbott; educator Abbott Kaplan

ABE a short form of Abel, Abelard, Abraham, Abram

Image: "Honest Abe" Lincoln is the dominant image for this old-fashioned name — a strong, lanky outdoorsman who is honest, hardworking, and kind.

Famous Abes: President Abe Lincoln; actor Abe ("Barney Miller") Vigoda; former

Supreme Court justice Abe Fortas

ABEL (Hebrew) "breath"; a short form of Abelard

Image: Most people think Abel is a tall, strong athlete who is capable, dependable, and extremely smart. Some, though, think Abel is skinny and meek.

Famous Abels: the biblical Abel, Cain's brother; explorer Abel Tasman; Soviet spy Colonel Rudolf Abel

ABNER (Hebrew) "father of light"

Image: The name Abner calls to mind the strong, backward, and very dense hillbilly hero of "Li'l Abner" comics.

Famous Abners: Al Capp's "Li'l Abner"; baseball's Abner Doubleday; TV's Abner ("Bewitched") Kravitz; the biblical Abner, who commanded King Saul's army

ABRAHAM (Hebrew) "father of the multitude"

Image: Most people describe Abraham as a tall, strong, bearded leader who is honest, solemn, and wise, like President Abraham Lincoln.

Famous Abrahams: the biblical Abraham, first Hebrew patriarch; President Abraham Lincoln

ACE (Latin) "unity"

Image: Most people see Ace as a hotshot jock you find at the card table or on the playing field. Some people also say Ace is stupid and kind of a jerk.

Famous Aces: rock musician Ace Frehley of Kiss; soccer's Ace Ntsoelengoe

ADAM (Hebrew) "man of the red earth"

Image: Adam is described as a tall, dark, handsome, and masculine man who is quiet and smart.

Famous Adams: the biblical Adam, first man; actors Adam ("Batman") West, Adam (*My Bodyguard*) Baldwin; TV's Adam ("Dynasty") Carrington, Adam ("Bonanza") Cartwright, "Adam-12"; rock singer Adam Ant

ADDISON (Old English) "son of Adam"

Image: Addison is described as a handsome, professional, politically conservative yuppie who reads a lot of books.

Famous Addisons: TV's David ("Moonlighting") Addison; the cities of Addison, Texas, and Addison, Illinois; publisher Addison-Wesley; essayist/poet Joseph Addison

ADLAI (Hebrew) "my witness"

Image: The name Adlai evokes an image of a highly intelligent, politically minded man who might be stuffy or pompous, like the famous "egghead" who lost the presidential election to Eisenhower in 1956.

Famous Adlais: Senators Adlai Stevenson, Sr. and Jr.

ADOLPH (Old German) "noble wolf, noble hero"

Image: Noble? Not to most people! World War II gave the name Adolph a very bad name. People describe Adolph as evil incarnate — a maniacal, egotistical, murdering tyrant.

Famous Adolphs: Nazi leaders Adolph Hitler, Adolph Eichmann; brewer Adolph Coors; actor Adolphe (*The Front Page*) Menjou

ADRIAN (Latin) "dark"

Image: People picture Adrian as an attractive, perhaps effeminate, man who is sensitive, loving, thoughtful, and rich.

Famous Adrians: Popes Adrian I-VI; actor Adrian ("T.J. Hooker") Zmed; the movie *The List of Adrian Messenger*; Adrian (*Good Morning, Vietnam*) Cronauer; designer Adrien Arpel; basketball's Adrian Dantley

AL a short form of names beginning with "Al"

Image: Al is described as a chunky older guy who is happy, talkative, and tough — a balding short-order cook, perhaps, with tattoos and a beer belly.

Famous Als: gangster Al Capone; trumpeter Al Hirt; singers Al Jolson, "Weird Al" Yankovic; actor Al (*Dog Day Afternoon*) Pacino; auto racer Al Unser; former senator Al Smith

ALAN see Allen

ALASTAIR a Scottish form of Alexander

Image: Thanks to Alistair Cooke, most people think

of Alastair as a classic British aristocrat who is elegant, proper, and cerebral.

Famous Alastairs: TV host Alistair ("Masterpiece Theatre") Cooke; British actor Alastair (*A Christmas Carol*) Sim; occult writer Aleister Crowley

ALBERT (Old English) "noble and bright"

Image: The name Albert calls to mind three different images: fat, clumsy, and slow, like Fat Albert; brainy and nerdy, like Albert Einstein; or formal and dignified, like Prince Albert.

Famous Alberts: physicist Albert Einstein; physician Albert Schweitzer; Bill Cosby's cartoon character, "Fat Albert"; actors Albert (*Tom Jones*) Finney, Eddie ("Green Acres") Albert; Britain's Prince Albert; Prince Albert pipe tobacco; tennis's Alberto Mancini

ALEC a short form of Alexander

Image: Alec strikes people as a good name for a wealthy intellectual who is a bit of a rogue.

Famous Alecs: actors Alec (*The Bridge on the River Kwai*) Guinness, Alec (*The Hunt for Red October*) Baldwin; Alec in *St. Elmo's Fire*; the city of Aleck Island, Georgia; the proverbial smart aleck

ALEX a short form of Alexander

Image: People say Alex is a strong, athletic man of Greek descent who is smart, nice, and happy.

Famous Alexs: football's Alex Karras; TV's Alex ("Family Ties") Keaton; novelist Alex (*Roots*) Haley; game show host Alex Trebek; Alex the "Stroh's Beer" dog; Alex in the movie *The Black Stallion*

ALEXANDER (Greek) "helper of mankind"

Image: Alexander is pictured as an influential leader — a tall, thin, highly intelligent man with a majestic or military bearing.

Famous Alexanders: King Alexander the Great of Macedonia; statesman Alexander Hamilton; telephone inventor Alexander Graham Bell; former secretary of state Alexander Haig; French novelist Alexandre (*The Three Musketeers*) Dumas; Alexander Bumstead of "Blondie" comics

ALFRED (Old English) "elf counselor, wise counselor"

Image: The name Alfred has two very different images: an overweight older man who is stuffy and secretive, like Alfred Hitchcock, or a weak, wimpy, and brainy nerd.

Famous Alfreds: director Alfred (*Psycho*) Hitchcock; Alfred E. (*MAD Magazine*) Neuman; Alfred, Batman's butler; psychiatrist Alfred Adler; poet Alfred ("The Charge of the Light Brigade") Lord Tennyson; King Alfred the Great of Wessex; auto executive Alfred P. Sloan

ALLEN, Allan, Alan (Irish Gaelic) "handsome, cheerful"

Image: Most people describe Allen as extremely smart, funny, and friendly. Some, though, think of Allen as effeminate, gentle, and dull.

Famous Allens: actors Alan ("M*A*S*H") Alda, Alan (*Shane*) Ladd, Alan (*Catch-22*) Arkin, Alan (*Memories of Me*) King, Alan (*An Unmarried Woman*) Bates, Alan ("Growing Pains") Thicke; TV hosts Allen ("Candid Camera") Funt, Allen ("Password") Ludden; poet/writer Edgar Allan ("The Raven") Poe; football's Alan Page; Wall Street's Allen & Co.; revolutionary soldier Ethan Allen; actor/director Woody Allen; humorist Steve Allen

ALONZO a form of Alphonse

Image: Alonzo is pictured as a dark, handsome, spirited, and loving young man of Hispanic descent.

Famous Alonzo: football's Amos Alonzo Stagg

ALPHONSE, Alfonso (Old German) "noble and eager"

Image: Most people see Alphonse as a strong, handsome black man who is hardworking but not very bright. Some, though, see Alphonse as a skinny, smart nerd who might be homosexual.

Famous Alphonses: gangster Alphonse Capone; Senator Alfonse D'Amato; King Alfonso of Spain; French comedians Alphonse and Gaston; French author Alphonse Dandet

ALVIN (Old German) "beloved by all"

Image: Alvin's image comes straight from David Seville's singing chipmunks. People describe Alvin as a cute, mischievous comic with a very squeaky voice.

Famous Alvins: Alvin and the Chipmunks; writer Alvin (*Future Shock*) Toffler; choreographer Alvin Ailey; rock musician Alvin Lee; World War I hero Sergeant Alvin York

AMOS (Hebrew) "burden"

Image: People say Amos is an older black man who might not be sophisticated but is strong and hardworking.

Famous Amoses: the biblical prophet Amos; Amos ("Amos 'n' Andy") Jones; football's Amos Alonzo Stagg; actor John ("Good Times") Amos; cookie mogul Willie (Famous Amos) Amos; Jerry Reed's song "Amos Moses"

ANDRÉ a French form of Andrew

Image: People describe André as the strong, silent type — a rich, sophisticated, talented, and romantic French playboy.

Famous Andrés: pianist André Previn; André champagne; wrestler André the Giant; French author André Gide; tennis's André Agassi; the movie *My Dinner with André*

ANDREW (Greek) "strong, manly"

Image: The name Andrew has two different images: a big, strong, jolly guy you can count on when the chips are down or a smart but wimpy preppy.

Famous Andrews: the biblical disciple Andrew; Presidents Andrew Jackson, Andrew Johnson; Britain's Prince Andrew; industrialist Andrew Carnegie; actor Andrew (*St. Elmo's Fire*) McCarthy; composer Andrew (*Cats*) Lloyd Webber

ANDY a short form of Andrew

Image: Andy is pictured as a tall, blond, boyish, and ordinary man who is happy, easygoing, and dense.

Famous Andys: actor Andy ("Matlock") Griffith; TV pundit Andy Rooney; singers Andy Williams, Andy Gibb; pop artist Andy ("Campbell's Soup Cans") Warhol; TV and radio's Andy ("Amos 'n' Andy") Brown; Raggedy Ann's friend Andy

ANGELO (Greek) "angel"

Image: The name Angelo calls to mind a thin, tough, lower-class Italian who is a smooth-talking ladies' man.

Famous Angelos: Angelo in Shakespeare's play *Measure for Measure*; Angelo (Charles Atlas) Siciliano; boxing's Angelo Dundee; Pope John XXIII, Angelo Roncalli

ANGUS (Scottish Gaelic) "unique choice, one strength"

Image: Angus is pictured as an awkward, troublemaking jerk. Despite the name's Scottish origin, some people think Angus is Italian.

Famous Anguses: Celtic god Angus Og, spirit of laughter, love, and wisdom; author Sir Angus Wilson; Black Angus cattle

ANTHONY (Latin) "priceless"

Image: People imagine Anthony as a tall, dark Italian man who is smart, strong, and tough.

Famous Anthonys: actors Anthony (*Zorba the Greek*) Quinn, Anthony (*Psycho*) Perkins, Anthony (*Doctor Doolittle*) Newley, Anthony (*International Velvet*) Hopkins, Anthony (*Top Gun*) Edwards; British statesman Anthony Eden; Marc Antony, lover of Cleopatra; playwright Anton (*Uncle Vanya*) Chekhov

ARCHIBALD (Old German) "genuinely bold"

Image: Archibald is considered a good name for a fat, balding scholar who is snooty and terribly stuffy.

Famous Archibalds: Solicitor General Archibald Cox; author Archibald (*J.B.*) MacLeish; Archibald (Cary Grant) Leach

ARCHIE a short form of Archer, Archibald

Image: The name Archie has two different images: a goofy, all-American, redheaded teenager, like Archie in "Archie" comics, or a lazy, bullheaded bigot, like TV's Archie Bunker.

Famous Archies: TV's Archie ("All in the Family") Bunker; Archie Andrews of "Archie" comics; Don Marquis's poetry book *Archy and Mehitabel*; boxer Archie Moore; football's Archie Griffin

ARLEN (Irish Gaelic) "pledge"

Image: The name Arlen calls to mind a strong, distinguished, and articulate aristocrat.

Famous Arlens: Senator Arlen Specter; English author Michael Arlen; actor Richard Arlen

ARLO (Spanish) "the barberry"

Image: Thanks to folk singer Arlo Guthrie, people picture Arlo as a pot-smoking, musical hippie.

Famous Arlo: folk singer Arlo ("Alice's Restaurant") Guthrie

ARMAND (Old German) "army man"; a French form of Herman

Image: People describe Armand as a tall, skinny black or foreign man who is an aristocrat or a diplomat.

Famous Armands: business tycoon Armand Hammer; actor Armand (*Napoleon and Josephine: A Love Story*) Assante; Armand (*Camille*) Duval

ARNE (Old German) "eagle"

Image: The name Arne has two very different images: a nerdy intellectual or a beer-bellied couch potato with an abrasive personality.

Famous Arnes: Norwegian writer Arne Garbourg; Swedish biochemist Arne Tiselius

ARNIE a short form of Arne, Arnold

Image: Most people say Arnie is a friendly, outgoing, working-class guy — a pizza maker perhaps. Some, though, think of Arnie as the class nerd.

Famous Arnie: TV's Arnie ("L.A. Law") Becker

ARNOLD (Old German) "strong as an eagle, eagle-ruler"

Image: People picture Arnold as a strong, working-class black man who is short, fat, and jolly.

Famous Arnolds: actor Arnold (*The Terminator*) Schwarzenegger; TV's Arnold ("Diff'rent Strokes") Jackson; Arnold the pig of TV's "Green Acres"; traitor Benedict Arnold; golfer Arnold Palmer

ART a short form of Artemus, Arthur

Image: The name Art has two different images: an old, funny man who is full of stories and always wants to be the center of attention or a quiet, distinguished, wise man who keeps to himself.

Famous Arts: humorist Art Buchwald; actor Art ("The Honeymooners") Carney; singer Art Garfunkel; radio/TV host Art Linkletter

ARTHUR (Celtic) "noble"; (Welsh) "bear-hero"

Image: Most people say Arthur is a bespectacled old bookworm who is serious, dull, and proper. Some, though, say Arthur is a comic or a rat.

Famous Arthurs: England's legendary King Arthur; economist Arthur Burns; actor Arthur Kennedy; tennis's Arthur Ashe; *Sherlock Holmes's* creator Sir Arthur Conan Doyle; playwright Arthur (*Death of a Salesman*) Miller; President Chester A. Arthur; the movie *Arthur*

ARTIE a short form of Artemus, Arthur

Image: People picture Artie as the average guy-next-door — unpretentious, casual, good-natured, and funny.

Famous Arties: comedian Arte ("Laugh-In") Johnson; bandleader Artie Shaw

AUSTIN a form of August, Augustine

Image: Austin is described as intelligent, straightforward, polite, and snobby — a wealthy oil baron, perhaps.

Famous Austins: Austin-Healy automobiles; the city of Austin, Texas; TV's Colonel Steve ("The Six Million Dollar Man") Austin; diplomat Sir Austen Layard; patriot Stephen F. Austin

AVERILL (Middle English) "born in April"

Image: Averill is pictured as a reserved, highly distinguished intellectual.

Famous Averill: diplomat William Averell Harriman

AVERY an English form of Alfred, Aubrey

Image: Most people describe Avery as a sociable, happy-go-lucky comedian. Some, though, say Avery is an uptight nerd.

Famous Averys: actor Avery ("A Man Called Hawk") Brooks; comic actor Avery ("My Mother, the Car") Shreiber; Avery Brundage, longtime coordinator of the Olympic Games

BARNABAS (Greek) "son of prophecy"

Image: People have two different images of Barnabas: a grandfatherly man who is kind, honest, and highly religious or a man like the "Dark Shadows" TV character who is sinister, scary, and very mysterious.

Famous Barnabases: the biblical Barnabas, Paul's associate; TV's Barnabas ("Dark Shadows") Collins; attorney Barnabas Sears

BARNABY an English form of Barnabas

Image: Barnaby's image comes straight from the character "Barnaby Jones." People describe Barnaby as a lanky country boy with an old-fashioned style and a razor-sharp wit.

Famous Barnabys: TV's "Barnaby Jones"; Charles Dickens's novel *Barnaby Rudge*; Barnaby in the musical *Hello Dolly!*

BARNEY a short form of Barnabas, Barnett, Bernard

Image: Thanks to TV portrayals of men with the name Barney, people imagine a comic character who is fat, nervous, silly, and not too bright.

Famous Barneys: TV's Barney ("The Flintstones") Rubble, Barney ("The Andy Griffith Show") Fife, "Barney Miller"

BARRY (Irish Gaelic) "spearlike, pointed"; (Welsh) "son of Harry"

> **Image:** People describe Barry as a cute, working-class guy who is either soft-spoken and nice or demanding and rude.

> **Famous Barrys:** Senator Barry Goldwater; singers Barry ("Mandy") Manilow, Barry White, Barry Gibb of the Bee Gees; actors Barry (*The Rocky Horror Picture Show*) Bostwick, Barry (*The Bad and the Beautiful*) Sullivan; humorist Dave Barry; William Thackeray's novel *Barry Lyndon*; children's story writer James M. (*Peter Pan*) Barrie; Motown record producer Berry Gordy, Jr.

BART a short form of Bartholomew, Barton, Bertram

> **Image:** Bart is described as a tall, dark, and handsome athlete who is either shy and polite or bold and assertive.

> **Famous Barts:** football's Bart Starr; gymnast Bart Connor; TV cowboy Bart Maverick; TV's Bart ("The Simpsons") Simpson

BARTHOLOMEW (Hebrew) "son of a farmer"

> **Image:** People think of Bartholomew as a grandfatherly gentleman who is religious, old-fashioned, stuffy, and very rich.

> **Famous Bartholomews:** the biblical disciple Bartholomew; Dr. Seuss's character Bartholomew Cubbins; explorer Bartholomew Dias

BARTON (Old English) "from the barley farm"

> **Image:** Most people picture Barton as a highly intelligent aristocrat who is formal to the point of stuffiness. Some, though, see Barton as a tough cowboy.

> **Famous Bartons:** actor Barton ("The Outlaws") MacLane; Red Cross founder Clara Barton

BASIL (Latin) "magnificent, kingly"

> **Image:** The name Basil usually calls to mind a British blue blood or butler who is bookish, snooty, and dull. Some, though, think Basil is strange and wild, like Basil Fawlty.

> **Famous Basils:** actor Basil (*The Adventures of Sherlock Holmes*) Rathbone; TV's Basil ("Fawlty Towers") Fawlty; Saint Basil of Caesarea; the spice basil

BEAU (Old French) "handsome"; a short form of Beauregard

> **Image:** Handsome? You bet! People think Beau is a pretty boy — a good-looking sissy who is either gentle and charming or cold and vain.

> **Famous Beaus:** actor Beau (*The Fabulous Baker Boys*) Bridges; TV cowboy Beau Maverick; English dandy Beau Brummel; P.C. Wren's novel *Beau Geste*

BEN (Hebrew) "son"; a short form of names beginning with "Ben"

Image: Ben is described as a big, strong, dark-haired bear of a man who is quiet, lovable, and easygoing, like Gentle Ben.

Famous Bens: American revolutionary/diplomat Ben Franklin; TV's "Gentle Ben"; the movies *Ben*, *Ben and Me*, *Ben-Hur*; TV's Ben ("Bonanza") Cartwright; actor Ben (*Gandhi*) Kingsley; golfers Ben Crenshaw, Ben Hogan; Scottish mountain peak Ben Nevis; London's Big Ben clocktower

BENEDICT (Latin) "blessed"

Image: Even memories of an infamous traitor have not destroyed people's image of Benedict. They say Benedict is quiet, refined, and serious.

Famous Benedicts: traitor Benedict Arnold; fifteen popes named Benedict; Saint Benedict, founder of the Benedictine Order; Eggs Benedict

BENJAMIN (Hebrew) "son of the right hand"

Image: People think of Benjamin as a smart and inventive man who is tall, strong, and cute.

Famous Benjamins: the biblical Benjamin, Joseph's younger brother; American revolutionary/diplomat Benjamin Franklin; President Benjamin Harrison; the movie *Private Benjamin*; baby expert/author Dr. Benjamin

(*Baby and Child Care*) Spock; actor Richard (*Goodbye, Columbus*) Benjamin; bandleader Benny Goodman

BENSON (Hebrew-English) "son of Benjamin"

Image: Thanks to TV's Benson Dubois, Benson is described as a witty black butler who is intelligent, caring, and funny.

Famous Bensons: TV's Benson ("Benson") Dubois; Benson and Hedges cigarettes

BERNARD (Old German) "brave bear"

Image: Most people say Bernard is a big, happy, outdoorsy, and easygoing guy with the loyalty of a Saint Bernard dog. Some, though, think he is distinguished and stuffy, like an aristocrat or butler.

Famous Bernards: Saint Bernard of Clairvaux; Saint Bernard dogs; novelist Bernard (*The Natural*) Malamud; playwright George Bernard (*Man and Superman*) Shaw; basketball's Bernard King; presidential advisor Bernard Baruch; subway vigilante Bernard Goetz

BERT (Old English) "bright"; a short form of names containing "bert" (see also Burt)

Image: Bert is pictured as a dumpy guy who is a sincere, hardworking nerd.

Famous Berts: TV host Bert ("Miss America") Parks; comic actors Bert (*The Wizard of Oz*) Lahr, Bert ("The Snoop Sisters") Convy; muppet Bert on TV's "Sesame Street"

BERTRAND (Old English)
"glorious raven"

Image: The name Bertrand calls to mind an old intellectual who is analytical and boring — a mathematician or teacher, perhaps.

Famous Bertrand: philosopher Bertrand Russell

BILL a short form of William

Image: Bill is described as an average working guy who is likable, intelligent, and handsome.

Famous Bills: actor Bill ("The Incredible Hulk") Bixby; comic actors Bill ("The Cosby Show") Cosby, Bill ("Saturday Night Live") Murray; the Wild West's Buffalo Bill Cody, Wild Bill Hickok; Senator Bill Bradley; Bill the Cat in "Bloom County" comics; cartoonist Bill Mauldin

BILLY a short form of William

Image: The name Billy has two very different images: a shy kid who is gentle and sweet or a mischievous kid who is a troublemaker.

Famous Billys: outlaw Billy the Kid; Billy Carter, President Carter's brother; the Reverend Billy Graham; singer Billy ("Piano Man") Joel; comic actor Billy (*When Harry Met Sally*) Crystal; baseball's Billy Martin; Herman Melville's novella *Billy Budd*

BING (Old German) "kettle-shaped hollow"

Image: People say Bing is an easygoing older man who is friendly and lots of fun, like Bing Crosby.

Famous Bings: singer/actor Bing ("White Christmas") Crosby; Bing cherries

BIRCH (Old English) "birch tree"

Image: Birch is an old-fashioned name that calls to mind a lanky, down-home outdoorsman or a strong-willed, rabble-rousing fascist.

Famous Birches: right-winger John Birch; Senator Birch Bayh

BJORN (Old German) "bear"; a Scandinavian form of Bern

Image: People picture Bjorn as a strong, manly athlete with blond hair and Scandinavian features.

Famous Bjorn: tennis's Bjorn Borg

BLAKE (Old English) "fair-haired and fair-complexioned"

Image: People describe Blake as tall, handsome, manly, and rich. Some, though, see Blake as proud and domineering, like TV's Blake Carrington.

Famous Blakes: TV's Blake ("Dynasty") Carrington; poet William ("The Tyger") Blake; director Blake (*10*) Edwards; actress Amanda ("Gunsmoke") Blake; actor Robert ("Baretta") Blake

BOB a short form of Robert

Image: Most people consider Bob an all-American good guy — tall, easygoing, friendly, confident, and successful. To some, though, Bob is studious, quiet, and boring. Others describe him as lazy, selfish, and whiny.

Famous Bobs: comic actors Bob Hope, Bob ("Newhart") Newhart, Bob ("The Bob Cummings Show") Cummings; TV host Bob ("The Price Is Right") Barker; baseball's Bob Uecker; Senator Bob Dole; columnist Bob Greene; magazine publisher Bob (*Penthouse*) Guccione

BOBBY a short form of Robert

Image: Most people picture Bobby as a boyish version of all-American Bob: a good-looking, freckle-faced kid who is friendly, playful, mischievous, and energetic. Some, though, think Bobby is a fat, stuffy nerd.

Famous Bobbys: Senator Bobby Kennedy; auto racer Bobby Unser; basketball coach Bobby Knight; tennis's Bobby Riggs; singer Bobby ("Don't Worry, Be Happy") McFerrin; hockey's Bobby Hull, Bobby Orr; golfer Bobby Jones; TV's Bobby ("Dallas") Ewing; bobbies, London's policemen; Janis Joplin's song "Me and Bobby McGee"

BOONE (Old French) "good"

Image: Thanks to Daniel Boone, people describe Boone as a tall, good-looking, out-doorsy man who is rugged and aggressive.

Famous Boones: pioneer Daniel Boone; singers Pat Boone, Debby ("You Light Up My Life") Boone; actor Richard ("Have Gun Will Travel") Boone; computer raider T. Boone Pickens

BORIS (Slavic) "battler, warrior"

Image: Horror movies and KGB agents have shaped the image of the name Boris. Boris is pictured as a big, heavy Russian or German man who is scary and sinister.

Famous Borises: actor Boris (*Frankenstein*) Karloff; Russian Czar Boris Godunov; TV's Boris ("The Bullwinkle Show") Badunov; Russian novelist Boris (*Doctor Zhivago*) Pasternak; tennis's Boris Becker

BOYD (Irish Gaelic) "yellow-haired"; an Irish form of Bowie

Image: People think of Boyd as a tall, awkward, and well-educated snob — a college professor, perhaps.

Famous Boyds: actors William ("Hopalong Cassidy") Boyd, Stephen (*The Fall of the Roman Empire*) Boyd; jazz bandleader Boyd Raeburn; TV's Woody ("Cheers") Boyd

BRAD (Old English) "broad"; a short form of names beginning with "Brad"

Image: Brad is pictured as a muscular, good-looking guy who is either hardworking and good natured or a conceited playboy.

Famous Brads: football's Brad Budde; actor Brad (*Midnight Express*) Davis; tennis's Brad Gilbert

BRADFORD (Old English) "from the broad river crossing"

Image: Most people think of Bradford as an upper-class

snob who is intelligent, proper, and boring — an Ivy League educated lawyer, perhaps.

Famous Bradfords: actor Bradford (*The Way We Were*) Dillman; Massachusetts colony Governor William Bradford; TV's Tom ("Eight Is Enough") Bradford

BRADLEY (Old English)
"from the broad meadow"

Image: Most people picture Bradley as a blond rich kid who is spoiled but sensitive. Some, though, see Bradley as an outgoing, fun-loving tease.

Famous Bradleys: General Omar Bradley; the Milton Bradley game company; Senator Bill Bradley

BRANDON (Old English)
"from the beacon hill"

Image: People think Brandon is tall, strong, good-looking, and masculine — an all-American boy who might be student-body president in college and a yuppie after graduation.

Famous Brandons: actor Brandon (*The Member of the Wedding*) de Wilde; NBC executive Brandon Tartikoff

BRENDAN (Irish Gaelic)
"little raven"

Image: Brendan is regarded as a well-to-do, scholarly preppy or young professional who is nice and rather dashing.

Famous Brendans: Saint Brendan of Ireland; author Brendan Gill; Irish playwright Brendan Behan

BRENT (Old English) "steep hill";
a short form of Brenton

Image: Most people say Brent is a tall, good-looking, preppy intellectual who is thoughtful and nice. To some, though, he is spoiled and effeminate.

Famous Brents: sportscaster Brent Musburger; Brent (*Gone with the Wind*) Tarleton; football's Brent Fullwood; Security Advisor Brent Scowcroft

BRETT, Bret (Celtic) "Briton"

Image: People describe Brett as a slender, blond athlete who is handsome, masculine, and strong. They imagine Brett as either a wild, uncontrollable brat or a smart, businesslike yuppie.

Famous Bretts: TV cowboy Bret Maverick; short story writer Bret Harte; novelist Bret (*Less Than Zero*) Easton Ellis; Lady Brett (*The Sun Also Rises*) Ashley; baseball's George Brett; hockey's Brett Hull

BRIAN, Bryan (Irish Gaelic)
"strength, virtue"

Image: Most people think of Brian as an Irish he-man who is smart, athletic, and sociable. Some, though, think Brian is a drab mama's boy.

Famous Brians: Irish King Brian Boru; actors Brian ("Family Affair") Keith, Brian (*Cocoon*) Dennehy; Monty Python's movie *The Life of Brian*; football's Brian Piccolo; the movie *Brian's Song*; director Brian (*The Untouchables*) De Palma; Canadian Prime Minister Brian Mulroney

BRICE, Bryce (Welsh) "son of the ardent one"; form of Price

Image: Brice is pictured as a spoiled rich kid who is good-looking in an effeminate way and icy in manner.

Famous Brices: comic actress Fanny (*The Ziegfeld Follies*) Brice; Bryce Canyon, Utah

BROCK (Old English) "badger"

Image: People think of Brock as a strong, good-looking man who is wealthy, intelligent, and tough.

Famous Brocks: actor Brock (*The Adventures of Huckleberry Finn*) Peters; Senator Brock Adams, baseball's Lou Brock

BRONSON (Old English) "son of the dark-skinned one"

Image: Thanks to TV and the movies, Bronson is pictured as a dark, strong, sexy he-man who is rich, tough, ruthless, and, like Charles Bronson, associated with crime and revenge.

Famous Bronsons: actors Charles (*Death Wish*) Bronson, Bronson ("Perfect Strangers") Pinchot; TV's "Then Came Bronson"

BRUCE (Old French) "from the brushwood thicket"

Image: Most people picture Bruce as a big, dark, good-looking hunk. Some people think Bruce is too good-looking — maybe gay. Bruce is considered an all-brawn, no-brains guy who is either funny and nice or tough and bullying.

Famous Bruces: actors Bruce ("Scarecrow and Mrs. King") Boxleitner, Bruce (*Enter the Dragon*) Lee, Bruce (*Coming Home*) Dern, Bruce ("Moon-lighting") Willis; decathlete Bruce Jenner; singer Bruce ("Born in the U.S.A.") Spring-steen; King Robert the Bruce of Scotland; Civil War expert Bruce Catton

BRUNO (Italian) "brown-haired"

Image: Bruno's image comes straight from old gangster movies — a big, dark, muscle-bound Italian who is rough, tough, mean, and stupid. Some people think Bruno is a great name for a dog.

Famous Brunos: kidnapper Bruno Hauptmann; Bruno in the movie *Fame*; nicknames of baseball's Tom Brunansky and actor Bruce Willis; conductor Bruno Walter

BRYAN see Brian

BRYCE see Brice

BUCK (Old English) "buck deer"

Image: Buck is pictured as a big, dark, outdoorsy tough guy who is athletic and lighthearted but not too bright.

Famous Bucks: TV's space hero Buck Rogers; TV writer Buck Henry; country singer Buck Owens; TV's Frank ("Bring 'Em Back Alive") Buck

BUD (Old English) "herald, messenger"

Image: Bud is described as a handsome young blond who is cheerful, not too serious, and not too smart.

Famous Buds: football coach Bud Grant; "Bud" beer; comedians Larry Bud ("Late Night with David Letterman") Melman, Bud ("Abbott and Costello") Abbott; TV's Bud ("Father Knows Best") Anderson

BURKE, Berke (Old French) "from the fortress"

Image: Burke is usually pictured as a wealthy, distinguished professional who is a bit of a snob. Some, though, view Burke as rough and tough — a lumberjack, perhaps.

Famous Burkes: TV's Amos ("Burke's Law") Burke; cartoonist Berke ("Bloom County") Breathed; former attorney general Burke Marshall

BURL (Old English) "cup-bearer"

Image: The name Burl calls to mind folk singer Burl Ives — a bearded older man who is big, heavy, strong, and nice.

Famous Burls: folk singer Burl Ives; comedian Milton Berle

BURT a short form of Burton (see also Bert)

Image: Burt is pictured as a very handsome, masculine guy who is easygoing, funny, and short.

Famous Burts: actors Burt (*The Longest Yard*) Reynolds, Burt (*Elmer Gantry*) Lancaster, Burt (*Rocky*) Young; songwriter Burt Bacharach

BURTON (Old English) "from the fortress"

Image: Thanks to Richard Burton, most people think of Burton as a wealthy British man who is a handsome, talented, well-educated ladies' man.

Famous Burtons: actors Richard (*The Spy Who Came in from the Cold*) Burton, LeVar (*Roots*) Burton; singer Burton Cummings of the Guess Who; composer Burton (*Finian's Rainbow*) Lane

BUTCH a form of Bert, Burt

Image: The name Butch calls to mind either a tough, mean bully or a chubby bully who tries to act tough.

Famous Butches: outlaw Butch Cassidy; jazz musician Butch Thompson; hockey's Butch Goring

BYRON (Old French) "from the cottage"

Image: The name Byron has several images: a wealthy, British, high-class snob; a romantic dreamer, like the poet Lord Byron; or a feisty hotshot, like golfer Byron Nelson.

Famous Byrons: poet George Gordon Byron (Lord Byron); golfer Byron Nelson; Supreme Court Justice Byron White; media host Byron Allen

CAESAR, Cesar (Latin)
"long-haired"

Image: Caesar is pictured as a tall, sexy European man who is a ruthless, rich, and powerful leader. Some also say Caeser is fun, like comedian Sid Caesar.

Famous Caesars: Roman leaders Julius Caesar, Augustus Caesar; farm labor leader Cesar Chavez; actor Cesar ("Batman") Romero; comedian Sid ("Your Show of Shows") Caesar; the movie *Little Caesar*; composer Cesar Franck

CAIN, Caine (Hebrew) "a spear"

Image: Some people picture Cain as dark, strong, good-looking, and mild mannered, like Caine of TV's "Kung Fu" series. Others picture Caine as a hateful, ruthless murderer, like Cain in the Bible.

Famous Cains: the biblical Cain, Abel's brother; Caine on TV's "Kung Fu"; actor Michael Caine

CAL a short form of names beginning with "Cal"

Image: Most people think of Cal as a big heavyset guy who is friendly, likable, and funny — a football coach, perhaps. There are three other images of Cal, however: a rough-and-ready outdoorsman; a cool, slick politician; or a distinguished doctor.

Famous Cals: Cal in John Steinbeck's novel *East of Eden*; President Calvin (Silent Cal) Coolidge

CALEB, Kaleb (Hebrew)
"bold one, dog"

Image: Caleb is pictured as a tall, religious, honest, and strict Quaker or Amish farmer.

Famous Calebs: the biblical Caleb, Hebrew leader; former senator J. Caleb Boggs

CALHOUN (Celtic) "warrior"

Image: Most people think of Calhoun as a strong but aging hick who is a drinker or a ne'er-do-well. Some, though, picture Calhoun as a stuffy, wealthy WASP.

Famous Calhouns: actor Rory (*How to Marry a Millionaire*) Calhoun; former vice president John C. Calhoun; Calhoun on TV's "Amos 'n' Andy"

CALVIN (Latin) "bald"

Image: There are several different views of Calvin: fat, slovenly, and mean, like baseball owner Calvin Griffith; cute, thin, and successful, like designer Calvin Klein; or deeply religious, like Protestant reformer John Calvin.

Famous Calvins: Protestant reformer John Calvin; President Calvin Coolidge; baseball's Calvin Griffith; "Calvin and Hobbes" comics; designer Calvin Klein; basketball's Calvin Murphy

CAMERON (Scottish Gaelic) "crooked nose"

Image: the name Cameron calls to mind a rich, sociable, and good-looking reporter. Some, though, view Cameron as short tempered and untrustworthy.

Famous Camerons: actors Cameron ("Swiss Family Robinson") Mitchell, Kirk ("Growing Pains") Cameron; TV announcer John Cameron Swayze; Cameron in the movie *Ferris Bueller's Day Off*

CARL, Karl (Old German) "farmer"; forms of Charles

Image: Most people picture Carl as a straight shooter — a thoughtful, caring, polite man who is intelligent, steady, and quiet. Some people, less impressed with Carl, view him as a bossy know-it-all with a bad temper.

Famous Carls: rock singer Carl ("Blue Suede Shoes") Perkins; director/comic actor Carl (*Oh, God!*) Reiner; actors Karl ("The Streets of San Francisco") Malden, Carl (*Rocky*) Weathers; astronomer Carl Sagan; baseball's Carl Yastrzemski; political philosopher Karl Marx; track and field's Carl Lewis; poet Carl Sandburg

CARLETON (Old English) "farmer's town"

Image: Most people view Carleton as a big, stuffy, upper-class intellectual. Some TV watchers, however, remember him as a nosy doorman who is not very bright.

Famous Carletons: baseball's Carlton Fisk, Steve Carlton; painter Carleton Wiggins; Carleton the doorman on TV's "Rhoda"

CARLOS a Spanish form of Charles

Image: Most people describe Carlos as a dark, good-looking Hispanic gentleman who is terribly rich.

Famous Carloses: Spanish King Juan Carlos; Spanish leader Don Carlos; rock singer Carlos ("Black Magic Woman") Santana; guitarist Carlos Montoya; author Carlos Castenada; Italian movie producer Carlo Ponti; Verdi's opera *Don Carlos*

CARMINE (Latin) "song"

Image: People think of Carmine as a dark Italian or Latin man who is either small, nice, and soft-spoken or heavyset, loud, and brassy.

Famous Carmines: TV's Carmine ("Laverne and Shirley") Ragusa; political boss Carmine DeSapio; bandleader Carmen Dragon

CARROLL (Irish Gaelic) "champion"; a form of Charles

Image: Two very different images of Carroll come to mind: a slim, polite, devout man or a strong, loud, and funny character, like the one Carroll O'Connor plays on TV's "All in the Family".

Famous Carrolls: actor Carroll ("All in the Family") O'Connor; Karol (Pope John Paul II) Wojtyla; children's story writer Lewis (*Alice's Adventures in*

Wonderland) Carroll; actresses Diahann ("Dynasty") Carroll, Carol (*The Four Seasons*) Burnett, Carol (*Hello Dolly!*) Channing

CARSON (Old English)
"son of the family on the marsh"

Image: Carson is pictured as a macho cowboy of the Old West, like Kit Carson. Carson is also viewed as rich, good-looking, and very funny, like Johnny Carson.

Famous Carsons: Johnny ("The Tonight Show") Carson; frontiersman Kit Carson; short story writer Carson McCullers; Carson Drew, father of fictional detective Nancy Drew; Carson City, Nevada

CARY, Carey (Welsh) "from near the castle" (see also Kerry)

Image: Cary is viewed as a good name for a movie star who is suave, friendly, care-free, and nice. Some people also think the name sounds feminine.

Famous Carys: actors Cary (*North by Northwest*) Grant, Cary (*The Princess Bride*) Elwes; golfer Cary Middlecoff; baseball announcer Harry Carey

CASEY (Irish Gaelic) "brave"

Image: Casey is pictured as a good-looking Irish athlete — a fiery competitor who is warm and friendly off the playing field.

Famous Caseys: baseball's Casey Stengel; engineer Casey Jones; the poem "Casey at the Bat"; radio's Casey ("American Top 40") Kasem; TV's "Ben Casey"

CASPER, Caspar (Persian) "treasurer"

Image: The name Casper has two different images: friendly, shy, and helpful, like Casper the Friendly Ghost, or old and religious, like the biblical Caspar.

Famous Caspers: Caspar, traditionally one of the biblical Three Wise Men; TV's Casper the Friendly Ghost; former secretary of defense Caspar Weinberger; comic strip character "Casper Milquetoast"

CASSIUS (Latin) "vain"

Image: Cassius reminds people of boxer Cassius Clay — a big, tough, mouthy fighter.

Famous Cassiuses: Roman General Cassius Longinus; boxer Cassius (Muhammad Ali) Clay; abolitionist Cassius Marcellus Clay

CECIL (Latin) "blind"

Image: Some view Cecil as an older, aristocratic, wimpy bookworm who is stern, self-centered, and whiny. Others see Cecil as an all-around good guy who is nice, well mannered, and steady.

Famous Cecils: director Cecil B. DeMille; Idaho Governor Cecil Andrus; author Cecil Day Lewis; Cecil the Seasick Sea Serpent on TV's "Beanie and Cecil"; photographer Cecil Beaton; Cecil in the movie *A Room with a View*

CEDRIC (Old English) "battle chieftain"

Image: Most people picture Cedric as a thin, stuffy Englishman who might be either a well-educated aristocrat or a snotty butler. Some, though, picture Cedric as witty and charming.

Famous Cedrics: actor Sir Cedric (*Nicholas Nickleby*) Hardwicke; basketball's Cedric Maxwell; Cedric in Sir Walter Scott's novel *Ivanhoe*

CHAD (Old English) "warlike"; a form of Charles

Image: Warlike? Hardly! People describe Chad as a young, handsome, muscular, outdoorsy blond who is happy, intelligent, helpful, and nice.

Famous Chads: actor Chad ("Medical Center") Everett; singers Chad and Jeremy; musical group The Chad Mitchell Trio; Chad, a country in Africa

CHARLES (Old German) "manly, strong"

Image: Charles is viewed as either a hardworking, loyal friend and leader or as a smart, pompous nitpicker.

Famous Charleses: Britain's Prince Charles; actors Charles (*Death Wish*) Bronson, Charles (*Midnight Run*) Grodin, Charles (*Mutiny on the Bounty*) Laughton; comedian Charles Nelson Reilly; novelist Charles (*A Tale of Two Cities*) Dickens; cartoonist Charles ("Peanuts") Schulz; TV's "Charles in Charge"; basketball's Charles Barkley, Charles Oakley; cartoonist Charles Addams; TV newscaster Charles Osgood

CHARLIE, Charley short forms of Charles

Image: Thanks to the advertising campaign for Charlie perfume, Charlie has become a unisex name. A boy named Charlie is pictured as active, outgoing, friendly, and footloose.

Famous Charlies: actors Charlie (The Little Tramp) Chaplin, Charlie (*Wall Street*) Sheen; country singer Charlie Pride; Charlie ("Peanuts") Brown; movie detective Charlie Chan; Charlie the "Star-Kist" Tuna; Charlie perfume

CHASE (Old French) "hunter"

Image: Most people say Chase is a strong, good-looking athlete who is successful, intelligent, and, like Chevy Chase, funny.

Famous Chases: comic actor Chevy (*National Lampoon's Vacation*) Chase; Chase Manhattan Bank; Chase ("The Young and the Restless") Benson; Chase ("Falcon Crest") Gioberti

CHAUNCEY (Middle English) "chancellor, church official"

Image: Chauncey is described as a rich, stuck-up British intellectual or chauffeur who is well dressed, proper, and quiet.

Famous Chaunceys: Chauncey (*Being There*) Gardner; lawyer Chauncey Depew

CHESTER (Old English) "from the fortified camp"; a short form of Rochester

Image: Thanks to Marshal Dillon's deputy, most people picture Chester as a gangly, limping cowboy who is backward and slow. Some, though, see Chester as a fat, learned old man.

Famous Chesters: President Chester A. Arthur; adman/diplomat Chester Bowles; Admiral Chester Nimitz; author Chester Himes; TV's Chester ("Gunsmoke") Goode

CHET (Old English) a short form of Chester

Image: People have two different images of Chet: a clean-cut, wealthy man or a loud, dark-haired, macho country boy.

Famous Chets: country singer Chet Atkins; newscaster Chet Huntley; baseball's Chet Lemon

CHICK a short form of Charles

Image: Chick is described as a cute, thin blond with loose morals — a slick mafioso or a trendy gigolo, perhaps.

Famous Chicks: jazz pianist Chick Corea; drummer Chick Webb

CHICO a Spanish form of Francis

Image: People think of Chico as a small, dark Hispanic man who is a shifty tough guy.

Famous Chicos: TV's "Chico and the Man"; Marx Brother Chico Marx; the city of Chico, California

CHIP a short form of names beginning with "Ch"

Image: Chip is pictured as a good-looking, fun-loving athlete who is popular though not too bright. Chip might be a sixties surfer or a preppy with a boyish face.

Famous Chips: Chip Carter, President Carter's son; TV's Chip ("My Three Sons") Douglas; Walt Disney's "Chip 'n' Dale" cartoons

CHRIS a short form of Christian, Christopher

Image: Chris is described as a clean-cut, average, all-American blond boy who is smart, likable, and lots of fun.

Famous Chrises: tennis's Chris Evert; actor Chris Lemmon, son of Jack Lemmon; basketball's Chris Mullin

CHRISTIAN (Greek) "follower of Christ"

Image: The name Christian calls to mind a small, highly religious man who is honest, kind, and well mannered — a minister, perhaps.

Famous Christians: designer Christian Dior; cardiologist Dr. Christian Barnard; children's story writer Hans Christian (*The Ugly Duckling*) Andersen; actor Christian ("High Mountain Rangers") Conrad; Christian in Edmond Rostand's play *Cyrano de Bergerac*

CHRISTOPHER (Greek) "Christ-bearer"

Image: People view Christopher as a strong, handsome man who is smart, determined, independent, and nice. Christopher is also a good name for an explorer or an inventor.

Famous Christophers: Saint Christopher, patron saint of travelers; explorer Christopher Columbus; actors Christopher (*The Sound of Music*) Plummer, Christopher (*Superman*) Reeve, Christopher (*Back to the Future*) Lloyd; Christopher (*Winnie the Pooh*) Robin

CHUCK a short form of Charles

Image: Most people picture Chuck as a tall, athletic, and muscular man who is either a party animal and all-around good guy or a beady-eyed bully.

Famous Chucks: singer Chuck Berry; trumpeter Chuck Mangione; actor Chuck (*Missing in Action*) Norris; TV host Chuck ("The Love Connection") Woolery; football's Chuck Foreman; basketball's Chuck Person

CLAIBORNE see Clayborne

CLARENCE (Latin) "bright, famous"

Image: Clarence is described as a big, stooped, bespectacled nerd who is a bright, quiet mama's boy.

Famous Clarences: rock musician Clarence Clemons of the E Street Band; lawyer Clarence (*Inherit the Wind*) Darrow; novelist Clarence (*Life with Father*) Day; the Duke of Clarence, later William IV; Clarence the cross-eyed lion on TV's "Daktari"; guardian angel Clarence (*It's a Wonderful Life*) Oddbody

CLARK (Old French) "scholar"

Image: The name Clark calls to mind Clark Kent: a tall man with a dual personality. Clark is said to be prissy, intelligent, and introverted one day and muscular and macho the next.

Famous Clarks: actor Clark (*Gone with the Wind*) Gable; Clark (*Superman*) Kent; former presidential advisor Clark Clifford; explorers Lewis and Clark; the Dave Clark Five band; TV host Dick ("American Bandstand") Clark; former U.S. attorney general Ramsey Clark

CLAUDE (Latin) "lame"

Image: Most people picture Claude as a real clod — a big, kindly dolt with two left feet. Some, though, picture Claude as a suave, dark-haired Frenchman.

Famous Claudes: actors Claude (*Rio Bravo*) Akins, Claude (*Casablanca*) Rains; composers Claude Bolling, Claude Debussy; painter Claude Monet; former senator Claude Pepper; skier Jean-Claude Killy

CLAY (Old English) "from the earth"; a short form of Clayborn, Clayton

Image: Clay is described as a down-to-earth, rugged, handsome, and easygoing guy who is both a hardworker and a devoted family man. To some, though, Clay is a wealthy, suave smooth-talker.

Famous Clays: boxer Cassius (Muhammad Ali) Clay; statesman Henry Clay; General Lucius Clay

CLAYBORNE, Claiborne (Old English) "born of the earth"

Image: The name Clayborne calls to mind someone who has had a wealthy, pampered, and spoiled upbringing. Some people picture Clayborne as a senator or a bird-watching yuppie.

Famous Claibornes: Senator Claiborne Pell; chef Craig Claiborne; fashion designer Liz Claiborne

CLAYTON (Old English) "from the farm built on clay"

Image: The name Clayton evokes several different images: a rich, conservative snob; a smart, egotistical know-it-all; a strong, temperate leader; or a shy, mild-mannered nerd.

Famous Claytons: actor Clayton ("The Lone Ranger") Moore; TV's Clayton ("Dallas") Farlow; politician Adam Clayton Powell

CLEM a short form of Clement, Clemont

Image: Remember Red Skelton's portrayal of the bumbling hayseed, Clem Kadiddle-hopper? The name Clem reminds people of this klutzy old hillbilly.

Famous Clems: Red Skelton's Clem Kadiddlehopper; basketball coach Clem Haskins

CLEMENT, Clemont (Latin) "merciful"

Image: Most people describe Clement as an affluent man who is highly inventive, ethical, and outspoken. Some people also picture Clement as black or as a southern hick.

Famous Clements: Saint Clement, patron saint of tanners; fourteen popes named Clement; theologian Clement of Alexandria; British statesman Clement Atlee; poet Clement ("The Night Before Christmas") Moore; tycoon W. Clement Stone

CLEON (Greek) "famous"

Image: The name Cleon has two different images: a soft-spoken, rural black man or a man from outer space in a sci-fi movie.

Famous Cleons: Cleon, Athenian politician; stage designer Cleon Throckmorton

CLETUS (Greek) "summoned"

Image: Cletus is pictured as a heavyset hillbilly who is friendly but not too bright.

Famous Cletus: baseball's Cletis Boyer; Deputy Cletus on TV's "The Dukes of Hazzard"

CLIFF (Old English) "steep rock, cliff"; a short form of Clifford

Image: Cliff is generally described as tall, dark, and handsome. People say Cliff may be a happy-go-lucky, sexy ego-tripper; a kind, ethical hardworker; or an older man with limited mental capacity.

Famous Cliffs: TV's Cliff ("The Cosby Show") Huxtable, Cliff ("Cheers") Claven; actors Cliff (*Charly*) Robertson, Cliff ("Charlie Weaver") Arquette

CLIFFORD (Old English) "from the cliff at the river crossing"

Image: People describe Clifford as either a highly intelligent, friendly, and popular guy or as a nerdy, pudgy bookworm.

Famous Cliffords: playwright Clifford Odets; jazz trumpeter Clifford Brown; Senator Clifford Case; author Clifford Irving

CLIFTON (Old English) "from the town near the cliffs"

Image: Clifton is pictured in several ways: a well-heeled, upper class, sophisticated snob; a popular, good-looking athlete; or a nerdy bookworm. People often identify Clifton as a Hollywood name.

Famous Cliftons: actors Clifton ("Amen") Davis, Clifton (*Laura*) Webb; TV quiz master Clifton Fadiman; musician Clifton Chenier; journalist Clifton Daniels

CLINT a short form of Clinton

Image: Thanks to Clint Eastwood, Clint is described as a strong but silent, tall, and ruggedly handsome outdoorsman who is mighty rough and tough.

Famous Clints: actors Clint (*Dirty Harry*) Eastwood, Clint ("Cheyenne") Walker, Clint ("Gentle Ben") Howard; TV's Clint ("One Life to Live") Buchanan

CLINTON (Old English) "from the headland farm"

Image: The name Clinton has two very different images:

a tall, rugged rodeo rider or a rich, quiet, boring, sensitive, and well-educated nerd.

Famous Clintons: statesman DeWitt Clinton; Clinton ("Judd, for the Defense") Judd; Clinton's Folly (the Erie Canal); physicist Clinton Davisson

CLIVE (Old English) "from the cliff"

Image: People think Clive is a good name for a British gentleman who is either a serious, mustachioed patron of the arts or a slow-witted twit.

Famous Clives: novelists Clive Cussler, Clive Barker; children's story writer Clive Staples (*The Lion, the Witch, and the Wardrobe*) Lewis; critic Clive Barnes; Robert Clive, British conqueror of India

CLYDE (Scottish Gaelic) "rocky eminence, heard from afar"; (Welsh) "warm"

Image: Most people say Clyde is a clumsy hillbilly or a manual laborer with a small brain. To some, though, he is a sneaky crook, like Clyde Barrow.

Famous Clydes: rock singer Clyde ("A Lover's Question") McPhatter; bank robber Clyde Barrow of Bonnie and Clyde; astronomer Clyde Tombaugh; Clyde, "Ahab the Arab's" camel; basketball's Clyde Drexler; animal trainer Clyde Beattie; Scotland's River Clyde

CODY (Old English) "a cushion"

Image: The name Cody has a real Western flavor. Most people think of Cody as a rugged, handsome cowboy who is independent, adventurous, and outgoing. Some, though, picture Cody as a sweet, shy mama's boy.

Famous Codys: Buffalo Bill Cody; the city of Cody, Wyoming

COLE a short form of Nicholas

Image: Some people think of Cole as a friendly, personable, dependable chap ("a merry old soul") while others picture a smart man who is calculating, shifty, and mysterious.

Famous Coles: songwriter Cole Porter; singers Nat King Cole, Natalie Cole; the nursery rhyme "Old King Cole"

COLEMAN (Old English) "adherent of Nicholas"

Image: The name Coleman calls to mind a dignified, cultured man — a banker, perhaps. Some, though, think of Coleman as a bouncy, energetic comic. Others are simply reminded of camping supplies.

Famous Colemans: Coleman camping equipment; jazz musician Coleman Hawkins; actors Gary ("Diff'rent Strokes") Coleman, Dabney (*Tootsie*) Coleman, Ronald (*Lost Horizon*) Colman

COLIN (Irish Gaelic) "child"; a form of Nicholas.

Image: People picture Colin as a rich, blond flirt who is a smart professional man by day and a charming playboy at night.

Famous Colins: English actor Colin (*Frankenstein*) Clive; authors Colin Dexter, Colin MacInnes, Colin Wilson; conductor Colin Davis; General Colin Powell

CONNOR (Irish Gaelic) "wise aid"

Image: Connor is described as a dashing, athletic, upper-class man who is either witty and fun or spoiled and bratty.

Famous Connors: U.N. Secretary General Conor Cruise O'Brien; tennis's Jimmy Conners; actors Chuck ("The Rifleman") Connors, Mike ("Mannix") Connors

CONRAD (Old German) "honest counselor"

Image: The name Conrad has several images: a short, macho tough guy with a crew-cut, like actor Robert Conrad; a rich, aristocratic snob; or an intelligent, naive, and boring scientist.

Famous Conrads: novelist Joseph (*Heart of Darkness*) Conrad; author Konrad Lorenz; actors Conrad ("Diff'rent Strokes") Bain, Robert ("The Wild, Wild West") Conrad, William ("Jake and the Fatman") Conrad; West German Chancellor Konrad Adenauer; poet Conrad Aiken; hotel magnate Conrad Hilton; Conrad in Judith Guest's novel *Ordinary People*; Conrad *Bye Bye Birdie*) Birdie

CONSTANTINE (Latin)
"firm, constant"

Image: The name Constantine calls to mind Old World wealth and royalty. Constantine is described as a Greek or Roman man who is a strong, arrogant leader.

Famous Constantines: Roman emperor Constantine; actor Michael ("Room 222") Constantine; Greece's prime minister Constantine Karamanlis

CONWAY (Irish Gaelic) "hound of the plain"

Image: People think of Conway as an entertainer — a country-western singer or comedian, perhaps.

Famous Conways: country singer Conway Twitty; comic actor Tim ("McHale's Navy") Conway

COOPER (Old English) "barrelmaker"

Image: The name Cooper has several images: a tall, quiet man, like Gary Cooper; a rich intelligent snob; a happy-go-lucky, clean-cut athlete; or a wild and restless tough guy.

Famous Coopers: actor Gary (*High Noon*) Cooper; novelist James Fenimore (*The Deerslayer*) Cooper; basketball's Michael Cooper; rock singer Alice Cooper

COREY (Irish Gaelic) "from the hollow"

Image: People picture Corey as a nice-looking girl-chaser — a sun-tanned beach bum, perhaps. Corey is also

described as a smart, well-read, and unusual person.

Famous Coreys: actors Corey (*Lucas*) Haim, Corey (*Stand By Me*) Feldman; comedian "Professor" Irwin Corey; Canadian singer Corey (*Never Surrender*) Hart

CORNELIUS (Latin) "horn-colored, having horn-colored hair"

Image: Cornelius is pictured as a man of refinement who is either an intellectual, philosopher, abstract poet, or pompous poseur.

Famous Corneliuses: Roman historian Cornelius Tacitus; shipping magnate Cornelius Vanderbilt; Cornelius in the movie *Planet of the Apes*; football's Cornelius Bennett; Yukon ("Rudolph, the Red-Nosed Reindeer") Cornelius; baseball's Cornelius (Connie Mack) McGillicuddy

CORNELL a French form of Cornelius

Image: The name Cornell calls to mind a preppy scholar from an upper-crust family.

Famous Cornells: Cornell University; actor Cornel (*The Greatest Show on Earth*) Wilde; opera singer Cornell MacNeil; actress Katherine Cornell; football's Cornell Green

CORT (Old German) "bold"; (Scandinavian) "short"

Image: Most people think of Cort as a rugged, independent, carefree kind of guy — a cowboy, perhaps. Some, though, think Cort is a name befitting a fancy-dressing Tinseltown executive.

Famous Cort: actor Bud (*Harold and Maude*) Cort

COSMO (Greek) "order, harmony, the universe"

Image: Cosmo is described as a weird, spacy (but happy) airhead. Cosmo is also imagined as a quiet, dark loner of Greek descent.

Famous Cosmos: the movie *Topper*'s hero Cosmo Topper; Cosmo Lang, Archbishop of Canterbury; Florentine politician Cosimo de Medici; Cosmo in the movie *Moonstruck*; a nickname for *Cosmopolitan* magazine; TV's Cosmo ("The Jetsons") Spacely

CRAIG (Irish Gaelic) "from near the crag"

Image: Most people say Craig is a tall, athletic, good-looking blond who is smart, quiet, nice, casual, and bighearted.

Famous Craigs: country singer Craig Statler of the Statler Brothers; baseball's Roger Craig; football's Roger Craig; actor Craig ("Peter Gunn") Stevens

CREIGHTON (Old English) "from the estate near the creek"

Image: Creighton is pictured as a short, nerdy southern intellectual with a tendency to tell tall tales.

Famous Creightons: Creighton University; General Creighton Abrams

CULLEN (Irish Gaelic) "handsome"

Image: The name Cullen calls to mind a curious collection of relatively unflattering adjectives: mysterious, sullen, forgetful, wimpy, myopic, bony, effeminate, interesting, and lost.

Famous Cullens: TV host Bill Cullen; football's Cullen Bryant; poet William Cullen Bryant

CURT a short form of Courtney, Curtis (see also Kurt)

Image: Curt is described as a dark-haired, athletic, exceedingly good-looking guy who is warm, loving, and considerate.

Famous Curts: business tycoon Curt Carlson; sportscaster Curt Gowdy

CURTIS (Old French) "courteous"

Image: People think of Curtis as a heavy, handsome, quiet man who is hardworking, dependable, and rich — a businessman or pilot, perhaps.

Famous Curtises: General Curtis LeMay; actor Tony (*Some Like It Hot*) Curtis; golfer Curtis Strange

CY a short form of Cyril, Cyrus

Image: Cy is pictured as a small older man who is quiet, helpful, and loves outdoor sports — especially baseball.

Famous Cys: baseball's Cy Young; composer Cy Coleman

CYRIL (Greek) "lordly"

Image: Cyril is pictured as a tall, stately aristocrat or upper-class professional who is stuffy and meek.

Famous Cyrils: Saint Cyril, Slavic apostle; singer Cyril Paul

CYRUS (Persian) "sun"

Image: Cyrus is described as a big, solid farmer who is an old-fashioned, quiet, and dependable homebody.

Famous Cyruses: Persian King Cyrus the Great; inventor Cyrus McCormick; diplomat Cyrus Vance; educator Cyrus Adler

DAG (Scandinavian) "day of brightness"

Image: Most people imagine Dag as a Swedish diplomat who is socially prominant, highly intellectual, and easy to get along with.

Famous Dag: former U. N. secretary general Dag Hammarskjold

DALE (Old English) "from the valley"

Image: Dale is pictured as a short, thin country boy who is quiet and nice but also nerdy and dumb.

Famous Dales: singer Dale Evans; actor Dale (*The Last Ride of the Dalton Gang*) Robertson; Chip 'n' Dale cartoons; baseball's Dale Murphy; motivator Dale (*How to Win Friends and Influence People*) Carnegie

DALLAS (Irish Gaelic) "wise"

Image: Most people see Dallas as a big, tall designer cowboy who is about as flashy as he is rough. Some, though, see Dallas as a quiet, likable, middle-class PTA president.

Famous Dallases: former vice president George M. Dallas; baseball's Dallas Green; the city of Dallas, Texas; TV's "Dallas"

DAMIEN a German form of Damon

Image: Most people describe Damien as a dark, handsome sophisticate who is gifted but also devilish — perhaps even evil. To some, though, Damien is a courageous, sympathetic priest.

Famous Damiens: Damien in the movie *The Omen*; Father Damien (*The Exorcist*) Karras; Father Damien of Molokai, missionary to lepers

DAMON (Greek) "constant, tamer"

Image: Most people associate the name Damon with the devil — dark, aloof, evil. Some people merely picture Damon as a sneaky brat.

Famous Damons: short story writer Damon Runyon; mythical Greek friends Damon and Pythias

DAN a short form of Daniel or Riordan

Image: People think of Dan as a big, strong athlete who is friendly, kind, intelligent, and fun.

Famous Dans: Vice President Dan Quayle; comic actors Dan ("Saturday Night Live") Aykroyd, Dan ("Laugh-In") Rowan; actor Dan ("Bonanza") Blocker; newscaster Dan Rather; the biblical tribe of Dan; football's Dan Fouts, Dan Pastorini; TV's Dan ("Roseanne") Connor

DANA (Scandinavian) "from Denmark"

Image: Dana has become a name for both girls and boys. A boy named Dana is pictured as tall, strong, athletic, and friendly.

DANE (Old English) "from Denmark"

Image: Dane is considered a good name for a tall, lanky, athletic Scandinavian who is a self-assured, rich snob.

Famous Danes: actor Dane ("Bold Venture") Clark; Great Dane dogs; pop singer Taylor Dayne; Dane (*The Thorn Birds*) O'Neill

DANIEL (Hebrew) "God is my judge"

Image: Daniel is pictured as a good-looking, strong all-American boy scout who is athletic, brave, kind, friendly, trustworthy, well-bred, intelligent, and easygoing.

Famous Daniels: the biblical Hebrew prophet Daniel; statesman Daniel Webster; Nicaragua's former president Daniel Ortega; frontiersman Daniel Boone; actors Daniel J. ("Hill Street Blues") Travanti, Daniel Day (*A Room with a View*) Lewis; novelist Daniel (*Robinson Crusoe*) Defoe

DANNY a short form of Daniel

Image: Danny is described as a small, cute, boyish redhead who is kind, friendly, carefree, and lots of fun.

Famous Dannys: comic actors Danny ("Taxi") DeVito, Danny ("Make Room for Daddy") Thomas, Danny (*Hans Christian Andersen*) Kaye; football's Danny White; the song "Danny Boy"

DANTE (Latin) "lasting"; an Italian form of Durant

Image: Most people say Dante is a wealthy European man who is strong, thoughtful, and charming.

Famous Dantes: epic writer Dante (*The Divine Comedy*) Alighieri; poet Dante Gabriel Rossetti; football's Dante Lavelli

DARBY (Irish Gaelic) "free man"; (Old Norse) "from the deer estate"

Image: The name Darby calls to mind the happy, hardworking "wee folk" of Ireland.

Famous Darbys: the movie *Darby O'Gill and the Little People*; actress Kim (*True Grit*) Darby

DARRELL, Daryl (French) "beloved"

Image: Darrell is pictured as a tall, thin, passive mama's boy who is either an intelligent computer whiz or a lazy dimwit.

Famous Daryls: the silent Darryl brothers on TV's "Newhart"; baseball's Darryl Strawberry; singers Daryl Hall

of Hall and Oates, Daryl
Dragon of Captain and Tenille;
actress Daryl (*Splash*) Hannah;
movie producer Darryl F.
Zanuck

DARREN, Darrin (Irish Gaelic)
"great"; forms of Dorian

Image: Most people think of
Darren as a slim, dark-haired,
young scholar who is shy,
gentle, and wimpy. Some,
though, see him as handsome,
strong willed, and adventurous.

Famous Darrens: actor Darren
("Kolchak: The Night Stalker")
McGavin; TV's Darrin
("Bewitched") Stephens;
football's Darrin Nelson;
singer Bobby ("Mack the
Knife") Darrin

DARYL see Darrell

DAVE a short form of David

Image: People say Dave is a
really fun guy — a tall, good-
looking, well-built man who is
easygoing, outgoing, and
popular.

Famous Daves: TV host Dave
("The Today Show") Garroway;
writer Dave (*Dave Barry Slept
Here*) Barry; baseball's Dave
Winfield; jazz pianist/composer
Dave Brubeck

DAVID (Hebrew) "beloved"

Image: David is described as
a strong, handsome, intelligent
man who is friendly, good
humored, and dependable.

Famous Davids: the biblical
David, king of Israel; TV hosts
David ("Good Morning
America") Hartman, David
("Late Night with David

Letterman") Letterman; actors
David ("Kung Fu") Carradine,
David Niven; philosopher
David Hume; Michelangelo's
statue "David"; singer David
Bowie; Israel's Premier David
Ben-Gurion; newscaster David
("NBC Nightly News") Brinkley

DAVIS (Old English)
"son of David"

Image: Most people think of
Davis as a quiet, formal, upper-
class bore. To some, though,
Davis is cocky, active, and
mischievous.

Famous Davises: Confederate
president Jefferson Davis;
activist Angela Davis; actress
Bette (*All About Eve*) Davis;
actor Clifton ("Amen") Davis;
entertainer Sammy Davis, Jr.

DEACON (Greek)
"servant, messenger"

Image: Deacon is pictured
as a tall older man who is
righteous, stern, and downright unlikable — a priest
or minister, perhaps.

Famous Deacons: football's
Deacon Jones; Steely Dan's
song "Deacon Blues"

DEAN (Old English)
"from the valley"

Image: People think of Dean
as a tall young man who might
be either wild, daring, and
independent; outgoing and
easy to get along with; or a
hardworker and perfectionist.

Famous Deans: actors Dean
(*The Love Bug*) Jones, James
(*Rebel without a Cause*) Dean,
Richard Dean ("MacGyver")
Anderson; singer/actor Dean

("That's Amore") Martin; singers Jan and Dean; Watergate's John Dean; baseball's Dizzy Dean and Daffy Dean; Jimmy Dean sausages

DEL a short form of names beginning with "Del"

Image: Del is pictured as a wimpy, country-style farm boy who is still hanging on to his mother's apron strings.

Famous Dels: singer Del Shannon; basketball's Dell Curry

DELBERT (Old English) "bright as day"

Image: Delbert is described as a strong sportsman and sincere friend.

Famous Delberts: singer Delbert McClinton; director Delbert (*Marty*) Mann

DENNIS (Greek) "of Dionysus"

Image: Most people describe Dennis as a mischievous little brat like Dennis the Menace. Some, though, see Dennis as a tall, tan blond who is outgoing and fun loving — a lifeguard, cardshark, or race car driver, perhaps.

Famous Dennises: comedian Dennis ("The Jack Benny Show") Day; actors Dennis ("McCloud") Weaver, Dennis (*Easy Rider*) Hopper; "Dennis the Menace" comics; basketball's Dennis Rodman, Dennis Hopson; actress Sandy (*Up the Down Staircase*) Dennis

DENNY a short form of names beginning with "Den"

Image: The name Denny calls to mind the class clown — a fun-loving, friendly young guy with a high-powered sense of humor and a low-powered brain.

Famous Dennys: baseball's Denny McLain; Denny's restaurants

DENVER (Old English) "green valley"

Image: Most people think of Denver as the sturdy, rugged, outdoorsy type who is either a nice, dependable, and loving man or an arrogant braggart.

Famous Denvers: actors Denver ("The Dukes of Hazzard") Pyle, Bob ("Gilligan's Island") Denver; singer John ("Rocky Mountain High") Denver; TV's Denver ("Dynasty") Carrington; the city of Denver, Colorado

DEREK, Derrick (Old German) "ruler of the people"; short forms of Theodoric

Image: Derek is described as a tall, good-looking, masculine, and athletic blond who is either tough or quiet and shy.

Famous Dereks: actor Derek (*Inside the Third Reich*) Jacobi; director John (*Bolero*) Derek; Eric Clapton's rock group Derek ("Layla") and the Dominoes

DESMOND (Irish Gaelic) "man from South Munster"

Image: There are two contrasting views of Desmond: a middle- or lower-class black man who is studious, upright, hardworking, and drab or a rich man who is moody, ostentatious, and effeminate.

Famous Desmonds: South African civil rights advocate Desmond Tutu; anthropologist Desmond Morris

DEVIN (Irish Gaelic) "poet"

Image: People picture Devin as a cute, tall, well-to-do Irishman who is either charming and sweet or spoiled, evil, and bratty.

DEWEY (Welsh) "prized"

Image: Most people imagine Dewey as cute, mischievous, and fun, like Donald Duck's nephew. Some, though, describe Dewey as a careful, intelligent sissy.

Famous Deweys: educator John Dewey; politician Thomas Dewey; Donald Duck's nephew Dewey; Admiral George Dewey

DeWITT, Dewitt (Flemish) "blond"

Image: Most people describe DeWitt as a high-society gentleman who is classy, intelligent, and successful. Some people also describe DeWitt as a flake.

Famous DeWitts: politician DeWitt Clinton; publisher DeWitt Wallace; actress Joyce ("Three's Company") DeWitt

DEXTER (Latin) "dexterous"

Image: Most people view Dexter as a skinny, bespectacled, redheaded nerd who is brainy, studious, and whiny. Some, though, view Dexter as strong and handsome.

Famous Dexters: jazz musician Dexter Gordon; football's Dexter Manley; Dexter in the movie *The Philadelphia Story*

DICK a short form of Richard

Image: People say Dick is a tall, handsome, ordinary guy who is either fun loving, friendly, and easygoing or vulgar, cocky, and opinionated.

Famous Dicks: "Dick Tracy" comics; TV hosts Dick ("American Bandstand") Clark, Dick Cavett; actor Dick (*Gold Diggers of 1933*) Powell; comic actor Dick Van Dyke; President Richard (Tricky Dick) Nixon

DILLON (Irish Gaelic) "faithful" (see also Dylan)

Image: The name Dillon is strongly identified with Dodge City's famous marshal — a rugged, handsome Westerner who is easygoing and very strong. Unlike the marshal, however, Dillon is also thought to be rich.

Famous Dillons: TV's Marshal Matt ("Gunsmoke") Dillon; former Secretary of the Treasury Douglas Dillon; actor Matt (*The Flamingo Kid*) Dillon

DIRK a short form of Derek, Theodoric

Image: People think of Dirk as a rough, rugged jock who is cool, tactless, and very much the playboy.

Famous Dirks: actors Dirk (*The Servant*) Bogarde, Dirk ("The A-Team") Benedict; Clive Cussler's character Dirk Pitt

DMITRI (Greek) "belonging to Demeter"; a Russian form of Demetrius

Image: People picture Dmitri as a Greek statue come to life — a dark, handsome, sexy Greek hunk who might be a powerful leader or a shipping magnate.

Famous Dmitris: composer Dmitry Shostakovich; Russian chemist Dmitry Mendeleyev; conductor Dimitri Mitropoulous

DOLPH a short form of Adolph

Image: Most people picture Dolph as a big German muscleman who is a rigid, rude executive. Some, though, say Dolph is a shy, overweight wimp.

Famous Dolphs: basketball's Dolph Schayes; football's Dolph Briscoe; actor Dolph (*Rocky IV*) Lundgren; journalist Dolph Honicker

DOMINIC (Latin) "belonging to the Lord"

Image: People think of Dominic as a short Italian or Hispanic man who is either rich, powerful, and unemotional or quiet, simple, and highly religious.

Famous Dominics: Saint Dominic, founder of the Dominican order; TV's Dominic ("Airwolf") Santini; baseball's Dominic DiMaggio, Joe's brother; composer Domenico Scarlatti; the movie *Dominick and Eugene*

DON a short form of names beginning with "Don"

Image: The name Don evokes two very different images:

a spindly, unattractive geek, like Don Knotts, or a tall, handsome, sexy show-off, like Don Johnson.

Famous Dons: actors Don (*Cocoon*) Ameche, Don ("Miami Vice") Johnson; comic actors Don ("The Andy Griffith Show") Knotts, Don ("Get Smart") Adams; comedian Don Rickles; legendary ladies' man Don Juan; baseball's Don Drysdale; TV announcer Don Pardo; Don Diego de Vega (*Zorro*); poet Don (*Archy and Mehitabel*) Marquis

DONALD (Irish Gaelic) "world ruler"

Image: Take your pick! People have three different images of Donald: a goofy, dumb comic, like Donald Duck; a quiet, intelligent, bland middle-class family man; or a tall, strong, hotheaded troublemaker.

Famous Donalds: actor/dancer Donald (*Francis, the Talking Mule*) O'Connor; actor Donald (*Klute*) Sutherland; Walt Disney's Donald Duck; real estate tycoon Donald Trump

DONNY a short form of Donald

Image: Donny is imagined as a cute, baby-faced boy-next-door who is either friendly and popular, like Donny Osmond, or shy and wimpy.

Famous Donny: singer Donny Osmond

DORIAN (Greek) "from the sea"

Image: Dorian strikes people as an old-fashioned name befitting a curly-haired, elegant man who is vain but has great strength of character. Some people also think the name might suit a strong, vain woman.

Famous Dorians: the Dorian invaders of Greece; Oscar Wilde's novel *The Picture of Dorian Gray*; TV's Dorian ("One Life to Live") Lord

DOUG a short form of Douglas

Image: The name Doug calls to mind a masculine, athletic, average all-American guy or a middle-class businessman.

Famous Dougs: actor Doug ("The Virginian") McClure; football's Doug Flutie

DOUGLAS (Scotch Gaelic) "from the dark water"

Image: People say Douglas is a strong and handsome man who is either is a smart, sensitive, and quiet type or a bold, extroverted guy who gets into more than his fair share of trouble.

Famous Douglases: General Douglas MacArthur; actors Douglas (*The Mark of Zorro*) Fairbanks, Sr., Douglas (*The Corsican Brothers*) Fairbanks, Jr., Kirk (*Gunfight at the O.K. Corral*) Douglas, Michael (*Romancing the Stone*) Douglas; TV newsman Douglas Edwards; politician Stephen A. Douglas

DOYLE (Irish Gaelic) "dark stranger"

Image: Many people describe Doyle as a fat, balding, bespectacled scientist or accountant who is meticulous

and boring. Others describe Doyle as an off-beat, restless guy looking for trouble — a detective, perhaps.

Famous Doyles: baseball's Doyle Alexander; writer Sir Arthur (*The Adventures of Sherlock Holmes*) Conan Doyle; actor Brian Doyle-Murray; Doyle (*The Sting*) Lonnigan

DRAKE (Middle English) "owner of the 'Sign of the Dragon' inn"

Image: Drake is pictured as a tall, dark, handsome, and rich man who is either friendly, capable business executive or an elegant, snobby socialite.

Famous Drakes: TV's Paul ("Perry Mason") Drake, Evan ("Cheers") Drake; explorer Sir Francis Drake; Chicago's Drake Hotel

DREW (Old French) "sturdy"; (Old Welsh) "wise"; a short form of Andrew

Image: Drew is viewed as a dark, trim, attractive man who is nice, but highly independent — a wealthy lawyer, perhaps.

Famous Drews: actress Drew (*E.T. — The Extra-Terrestrial*) Barrymore; newscaster Drew Pearson; fictional detective Nancy Drew

DUANE (Irish Gaelic) "little and dark" (see also Dwayne)

Image: People think of Duane as a lanky man who is either an easygoing, helpful neighbor or a quiet, moody social dud.

Famous Duanes: musician Duane Allman; football's Duane Bickett, Duane Thomas

DUDLEY (Old English) "from the people's meadow"

Image: The name Dudley calls to mind a short, talented, and terribly funny man, like Dudley Moore.

Famous Dudleys: actor Dudley (*Arthur*) Moore; "Dudley Do-Right" cartoons; Dudley Nightshade, Crusader Rabbitt's foe

DUKE (Old French) "leader, duke"

Image: A leader? You bet! Duke is considered the perfect name for a big, strong, dominant he-man, like John (Duke) Wayne.

Famous Dukes: the Duke, John (*True Grit*) Wayne; the song "Duke of Earl"; musician Duke ("Satin Doll") Ellington; TV's "The Dukes of Hazzard"; Duke in "Doonesbury" comics; baseball's Duke Snider; Hawaiian swimmer Duke Kahanamoku; Massachusetts governor Michael ("Duke") Dukakis; Duke ("General Hospital") Lavery

DUNCAN (Scottish Gaelic) "dark-skinned warrior"

Image: Duncan is pictured as a Scottish or Irish man who is either a rich, spoiled ladies' man or an indecisive, mild-mannered nerd.

Famous Duncans: Duncan in Shakespeare's play *Macbeth*; Duncan Hines cake mixes; furniture maker Duncan Phyfe; actor Duncan ("The Cisco Kid") Renaldo; Duncan in John Irving's novel *The World According to Garp*

DUSTIN (Old German) "valiant fighter"

Image: Dustin is described as cute, short, intelligent, funny, quiet, and affected, like Dustin Hoffman.

Famous Dustin: actor Dustin (*The Graduate*) Hoffman

DUSTY a short form of Dustin

Image: Dusty strikes people as a good name for a modern cowboy who is outgoing, carefree, contemporary, and very sexy.

Famous Dustys: singer Dusty Springfield; TV's Dusty ("Dallas") Farlow; baseball's Dusty Baker

DWAYNE a form of Duane (see also Duane)

Image: People picture Dwayne as a slow-witted cowboy with curly blond hair who is either shy and vulnerable or friendly and outgoing.

Famous Dwaynes: football's Dwayne Woodruff; actor Dwayne ("Dobie Gillis") Hickman; TV's Dwayne ("A Different World") Wayne

DWIGHT a form of DeWitt

Image: Dwight is pictured as a strong, wise leader who is a soft-spoken yet powerful man, like President Dwight Eisenhower.

Famous Dwights: President Dwight Eisenhower; football's Dwight Clark; baseball's Dwight Gooden; columnist Dwight Chapin; high jumper Dwight Stones

145

DYLAN (Old Welsh) "from the sea" (see also Dillon)

Image: Most people see Dylan as a long-haired sixties rebel who is a serious, sensitive, and talented artist, like Bob Dylan.

Famous Dylans: poet Dylan ("A Child's Christmas in Wales") Thomas; singer Bob ("Blowin' in the Wind") Dylan

EARL (Old English) "nobleman"

Image: The name Earl calls to mind two different images: a tall, elderly, British nobleman who is rich, intelligent, dignified, and rather stuffy or a big, friendly, honest, hardworking guy who is ordinary in every way.

Famous Earls: country singer Earl Scruggs; actors Earl ("Police Woman") Holliman, James Earl (*The Great White Hope*) Jones; the song "Duke of Earl"; former chief justice Earl Warren; football's Earl Morrall; writer Erle (Perry Mason's creator) Stanley Gardner

EBENEZER (Hebrew) "stone of help"

Image: Charles Dickens's Scrooge is the prototypical Ebenezer — a skinny old geezer who is crotchety, cranky, mean, rich, and miserly.

Famous Ebenezer: Ebenezer (*A Christmas Carol*) Scrooge

ED a short form of names beginning with "Ed"

Image: Ed is pictured as a tall, heavy, balding older man who is an honest, friendly, kind hardworker and devoted father.

Famous Eds: actors Ed ("Lou Grant") Asner, Ed (*The Accidental Tourist*) Begley, Jr.; comic actor Ed (*The Absent-Minded Professor*) Wynn; TV's Ed ("The Honeymooners") Norton; Mr. Ed, TV's talking horse; TV hosts Ed Sullivan, Ed ("Star Search") McMahon

EDGAR (Old English) "successful spearman"

Image: Edgar is an old-fashioned name that calls to mind three different images: a grandfatherly, balding ventriloquist, like Edgar Bergan; a dark, frightening poet, like Edgar Allan Poe; or an insecure tyrant, like J. Edgar Hoover.

Famous Edgars: poet/writer Edgar Allan ("The Raven") Poe; ventriloquist Edgar Bergen; the FBI's J. Edgar Hoover; painter/sculptor Edgar Degas; poet Edgar Guest

EDMUND (Old English) "prosperous protector"

Image: Edmund is described as a large, distinguished man who is intelligent and charming — a political leader, like Senator Edmund Muskie, or a daring explorer, like Sir Edmund Hillary, perhaps.

Famous Edmunds: the ship-wrecked *Edmund Fitzgerald*; Mount Everest climber Sir Edmund Hillary; former senator Edmund Muskie; playwright Edmond (*Cyrano de Bergerac*) Rostand; English poet Edmund (*The Faerie Queene*) Spenser

EDSEL (Old English) "from the rich man's house"

Image: Edsel is pictured as a rich tycoon who, like the car that flopped soon after it was introduced, is a loser.

Famous Edsels: automaker Edsel Ford; the car Edsel

EDWARD (Old English) "happy protector"

Image: People say Edward is a good name for an intelligent, straitlaced, bespectacled bookworm who dresses well — a writer or businessman, perhaps.

Famous Edwards: Senator Edward Kennedy; actors Edward ("The Equalizer") Woodward, Edward G. (*Little Caesar*) Robinson; newscaster Edward R. Murrow; painter Edward Hopper; limerick writer Edward Lear

EDWIN (Old English) "rich friend"

Image: People picture Edwin as an older man who is stuffy and exceedingly brainy. To some, though, Edwin has a spooky or evil side.

Famous Edwins: former Attorney General Edwin Meese; TV pundit/writer Edwin Newman; hurdler Edwin

Moses; astronaut Edwin (Buzz) Aldrin; poet Edwin Arlington Robinson

EFREM see Ephraim

EGBERT (Old English) "bright as a sword"

Image: Egbert is considered a good name for a nerdy, homely, wimpy egghead with glasses and a bow tie.

Famous Egbert: Egbert, first English king

ELI (Hebrew) "height"; a short form of Eleazer, Elijah, Elisha

Image: Eli is described as an old-fashioned name appropriate for a strong, stout, independent thinker — a farmer or inventor, perhaps. Some, though, think of Eli as a cunning devil.

Famous Elis: the biblical priest Eli; cotton gin inventor Eli Whitney; actor Eli (*The Magnificent Seven*) Wallach; the Three Dog Night's song "Eli's Coming"

ELIAS a Greek form of Elijah

Image: Most people picture Elias as an old, wise, and deeply religious man.

Famous Eliases: inventor Elias Howe; Austrian writer Elias Canetti; Elias in the movie *Platoon*

ELIJAH (Hebrew) "Jehovah is God"

Image: The name Elijah calls to mind the biblical prophet Elijah — a humble man with strong faith who would not win a popularity contest.

Famous Elijahs: the biblical Hebrew prophet Elijah; Elijah Blue Allman, Gregg Allman and Cher's son; black nationalist leader Elijah Muhammad

ELLERY (Old English) "from the elder tree island"

Image: People describe Ellery as a tall, handsome man who is smart and mysterious, like Ellery Queen.

Famous Ellery: detective Ellery Queen

ELLIOTT a modern English form of Elijah

Image: The name Elliott has two different images: an attractive, dignified professional who is smart, personable, and witty or a myopic, brainy recluse who is stuffy and precise, like T. S. Eliot.

Famous Elliotts: actors Elliott (*M*A*S*H*) Gould, Denholm (*A Room with a View*) Elliott; Elliott in the movie *E.T. — 52The Extra-Terrestrial*; TV's Elliott ("thirty-something") Weston; Eliot (*The Untouchables*) Ness; poet T. S. (*The Waste Land*) Eliot; novelist George (*Silas Marner*) Eliot

ELMER (Old English) "noble, famous"

Image: Elmer is pictured as a dumb, goofy farmer who is laughed at, not with.

Famous Elmers: cartoon character Elmer Fudd; Sinclair Lewis's novel *Elmer Gantry*; football's Elmer Layden; dramatist Elmer (*The Adding Machine*) Rice; gyroscope inventor Elmer Sperry; the song "Elmer's Tune"; Elmer's glue

ELMO (Italian) "helmet, protector"; a form of Anselm

Image: The name Elmo evokes two images: a chubby awkward guy who is funny, chatty, and dumb or a nice, well-educated man that you could trust enough to buy a used car from him.

Famous Elmos: pollster Elmo Roper; actor Elmo (*Tarzan of the Apes*) Lincoln; Elmo in "Blondie" comics; the movie *St. Elmo's Fire*; Admiral Elmo Zumwald

ELROY a form of Leroy

Image: People think of Elroy as an uneducated country boy who is not very bright. Elroy is also described as an easy-going farmer or a loud-mouthed con man.

Famous Elroys: cartoon spaceboy Elroy Jetson; football's Elroy (Crazy Legs) Hirsch

ELSTON (Old English) "nobleman's town"

Image: Elston is pictured as either a bright nerd who wears taped glasses and plaid shirts or as a sophisticated, proper Englishman.

Famous Elstons: author Elston (*The Man Who Ruined Football*) Brooks; baseball's Elston Howard

ELTON (Old English) "from the old town"

Image: People describe Elton as a creative musical showman who is unusual and brash, like Elton John.

Famous Elton: rock singer Elton ("Crocodile Rock") John

ELVIS (Old Norse) "all-wise"; a form of Elwin

    Image: Elvis Presley is the dominant image for this name. Elvis is pictured as a handsome, generous southern rock star who sings the blues.

    Famous Elvises: singers Elvis ("Love Me Tender") Presley, Elvis Costello

ELWOOD (Old English) "from the old wood"

    Image: Elwood is an old-fashioned name that calls to mind a freckled, helpful, and slow-witted wimp.

    Famous Elwoods: Elwood P. (*Harvey*) Dowd; inventor Elwood Haynes; Elwood of the Blues Brothers

EMERSON (Old German-English) "son of the industrious ruler"

    Image: Emerson is described as a tall British Secret Service agent who has plenty of savoir faire or as a quiet, intelligent writer.

    Famous Emersons: poet/essayist Ralph Waldo Emerson; keyboardist Keith Emerson of Emerson, Lake and Palmer; auto racer Emerson Fittipaldi; preacher Harry Emerson Fosdick; Emerson College

EMERY (Old German) "industrious ruler"

    Image: Emery is viewed as a gentle, well-educated black man who might be a bookish writer, a dorky computer nerd, or an attentive salesman.

    Famous Emory: Emory University

EMIL, Emile (Latin) "flattering, winning"

    Image: Emil is pictured as a tall, strong, square-jawed man of German or Scandinavian descent who is friendly and dependable, though perhaps a bit boring.

    Famous Emils: French writer Émile (*Germinal*) Zola; sociologist Emile Durkheim; actor Emil (*The Blue Angel*) Jannings

EMMANUEL (Hebrew) "God is with us"

    Image: Emmanuel is described as a dark, good-looking, intelligent man who is righteous and highly religious.

    Famous Emmanuels: actor Emmanuel ("Webster") Lewis; pianist Emmanuel Ax; composer Emmanuel Chabrier; philosopher Immanuel Kant; Italy's Kings Victor Emanuel I, II, III

EMMETT a name that honors Irish patriot Robert Emmett

    Image: Emmett is imagined as a goofy-looking farmer or hillybilly who is nervous, short tempered, and of average or lower intelligence.

    Famous Emmetts: clown Emmett Kelly; Irish patriot Robert Emmett

ENGELBERT (Old German) "bright as an angel"

> **Image:** There are two distinct impressions of Engelbert: a handsome, romantic singer with lots of personality or a foolish, funny-looking egghead.

> **Famous Engelberts:** singer Engelbert Humperdinck; composer Engelbert (*Hansel and Gretel*) Humperdinck

ENOS (Hebrew) "man"

> **Image:** People picture Enos as a skinny southern athlete who is fast around the bases but slow on the uptake.

> **Famous Enoses:** the biblical Enos, Seth's son; baseball's Enos Cabell, Enos Slaughter; TV's Deputy Enos ("Dukes of Hazzard") Slate

EPHRAIM, Efrem (Hebrew) "very fruitful"

> **Image:** People identify Ephraim with the sophisticated, intelligent, middle-aged detective played by Efrem Zimbalist, Jr. on TV.

> **Famous Ephraims:** the biblical Ephraim, Joseph's son; actor Efrem ("The F.B.I.") Zimbalist, Jr.; violinist Efrem Zimbalist

ERASMUS (Greek) "lovable"

> **Image:** People think of Erasmus as a wise, honest, and loyal, old black man.

> **Famous Erasmuses:** Renaissance humanist Desiderius Erasmus; Brooklyn's Erasmus High School; physiologist/poet Erasmus Darwin

ERIC, Erik, Erich (Old Norse) "ever-ruler, ever-powerful"; short forms of Frederick

> **Image:** Eric is pictured as an extremely popular Scandinavian blond who is confident, intelligent, and nice.

> **Famous Erics:** actor Erik ("CHIPS") Estrada; skater Eric Heiden; newscaster Eric Sevareid; Norwegian explorer Eric the Red; composer Erik Satie; football's Eric Dickerson; novelists Erich (*Love Story*) Segal, Erich Maria (*All Quiet on the Western Front*) Remarque; singer Eric Clapton

ERNEST (Old English) "earnest"

> **Image:** People say Ernest is a big, plain, tubby guy who is even tempered, smart, and dependable.

> **Famous Ernests:** actor Ernest (*Marty*) Borgnine; novelist Ernest (*The Sun Also Rises*) Hemingway; TV host Ernie Kovacks; Oscar Wilde's play *The Importance of Being Earnest*

ERROL a German form of Earl

> **Image:** Errol is described as handsome, dashing, flamboyant, debonair, shallow, and vain, like swashbuckler Errol Flynn.

> **Famous Errols:** actor Errol (*The Adventures of Robin Hood*) Flynn; jazz pianist Errol Garner; football's Errol Mann

ERSKINE (Scottish Gaelic) "from the height of the cliff"

> **Image:** People picture Erskine as a smart, old-fashioned, lanky outdoorsman.

Famous Erskines: novelist Erskine (*Tobacco Road*) Caldwell; political pamphleteer Erskine Childers; educator John Erskine

ERWIN see Irwin

ETHAN (Hebrew) "firm"

Image: The name Ethan has two different images: a small, smart, upper-class straight-shooter or a big, tubby clown.

Famous Ethans: Revolutionary soldier Ethan Allen; Edith Wharton's novel *Ethan Frome*; Ethan Allen furniture

EUGENE (Greek) "well-born"

Image: Eugene is described as an introverted intellectual with inherited money. People say Eugene is either an old-fashioned, formal older man or a nerdy young man who is teased in gym class.

Famous Eugenes: playwrights Eugene (*Desire Under the Elms*) O'Neill, Eugene (*The Rhinoceros*) Ionesco; politician Eugene McCarthy; actor Eugene ("SCTV Network") Levy; painter Eugene Delacroix; poet Eugene (*Wynken, Blynken, and Nod*) Field; football's Eugene (Spider) Lockhart; the city of Eugene, Oregon

EVAN (Welsh) "young warrior"; a Welsh form of John

Image: People describe Evan as a well-dressed young man with boyish good looks who is intelligent enough to finish medical school and

imaginative enough to write books.

Famous Evans: Evan-Picone clothes; baseball's Dwight Evans

EVERETT (Old English) "strong as a boar"

Image: Everett is pictured as a smart, discerning, reliable small-town businessman or politician with square-jawed good looks.

Famous Everetts: former Senator Everett Dirksen; actors Chad ("Medical Center") Everett, Everett (*Citizen Kane*) Sloane; narrator Edward Everett ("Fractured Fairy Tales") Horton

EZEKIEL (Hebrew) "strength of God"

Image: For many people the name Ezekiel has strong biblical associations. Ezekiel is described as a deeply religious old man.

Famous Ezekiels: the biblical Hebrew prophet Ezekiel; football's Ezekiel (Zeke) Moore, Jr.

EZRA (Hebrew) "helper"

Image: Most people say Ezra is a strange old individualist — a poet or farmer, perhaps.

Famous Ezras: the biblical Israelite leader Ezra; former secretary of agriculture Ezra Taft Benson; poet Ezra Pound; college founder Ezra Cornell; children's story writer Ezra Jack (*The Snowy Day*) Keats; Robert Browning's poem "Rabbi Ben Ezra"

FABIAN (Latin) "bean grower"

Image: The name Fabian calls to mind a good-looking, vain young man with a slick dark pompadour and a comb in his back pocket.

Famous Fabians: rock singer Fabian Forte; Roman General Fabius; the Fabian Society of socialists

FAIRFAX (Old English) "fair-haired"

Image: People think Fairfax is a perfect name for a snobby British aristocrat or prep-school boy who practically lives at the country club when he is not playing polo.

Famous Fairfaxes: English General Baron Fairfax; adman Fairfax Cone; Edward Fairfax (*Jane Eyre*) Rochester

FARLEY (Old English) "from the bull or sheep meadow"

Image: Farley is pictured as a dark man who might be a rugged rancher, a handsome country gentleman, or an aging soap opera star.

Famous Farleys: actor Farley (*Strangers on a Train*) Granger; novelist Farley (*Never Cry Wolf*) Mowat; Farley, the dog in "For Better or For Worse" comics

FELIX (Latin) "fortunate"

Image: Felix's image comes right from "The Odd Couple" —

a thin, intelligent man who is a fussy, meticulous busybody.

Famous Felixes: TV's Felix ("The Odd Couple") Unger; "Felix the Cat" comics; Felix Leiter, James Bond's CIA contact; composer Felix Mendelssohn

FERDINAND (Old German) "world-daring, life-adventuring"

Image: Most people describe Ferdinand as a strong, dark man with an air of royalty and a selfish, overbearing nature, like dictator Ferdinand Marcos. To some, though, he is sensitive and withdrawn, like Ferdinand the bull.

Famous Ferdinands: Spain's King Ferdinand; the Philippines' dictator Ferdinand Marcos; Austria's Archduke Franz Ferdinand; explorer Ferdinand Magellan; Munro Leaf's children's story *Ferdinand the Bull*

FERRIS (Irish Gaelic) "Peter, the Rock"

Image: Ferris is pictured as a strong, brawny, happy-go-lucky cowboy; a lying, cheating rat; an absent-minded bookworm; or a pretentious, wealthy eccentric.

Famous Ferrises: the movie *Ferris Bueller's Day Off*; the ferris wheel

FIDEL (Latin) "faithful"

Image: The name Fidel calls to mind a rugged, bearded dictator who is powerful, ruthless, and smokes lots of cigars, like Fidel Castro.

Famous Fidel: Cuba's Premier Fidel Castro

FILBERT (Old English) "brilliant"

Image: Filbert is pictured as an introverted, weak, effeminate, and nutty man who wears his hair parted down the middle.

Famous Filbert: filbert nuts

FLETCHER (Middle English) "arrow-featherer, fletcher"

Image: People have four different images of Fletcher: a tough, funny detective, like Fletch; a heroic, seagoing adventurer, like Fletcher Christian; a rich and pompous author or journalist; or a friendly, earthy farmer.

Famous Fletchers: Fletcher (*Mutiny on the Bounty*) Christian; actress Louise (*One Flew over the Cuckoo's Nest*) Fletcher; TV's Fletcher ("Kukla, Fran, and Ollie") Rabbit, Fletcher ("Hill Street Blues") Daniels; the movie *Fletch*

FLINT (Old English) "stream"

Image: People picture Flint as a handsome, rugged adventurer who would make a great cowboy or secret agent.

Famous Flints: Derek (*Our Man Flint*) Flint; Captain Flint in Robert Louis Stevenson's novel *Treasure Island*; TV's Flint ("Wagon Train") McCullough; the city of Flint, Michigan

FLOYD an English form of Lloyd

Image: Floyd is described as either a tough, sneaky gangster or a rich, whiny, over-weight sissy.

Famous Floyds: gangster "Pretty Boy" Floyd; pianist

Floyd Kramer; boxer Floyd Patterson; football's Floyd Little; Floyd the barber on TV's "The Andy Griffith Show"; rock band Pink Floyd

FORREST (Old French) "forest, woodsman"

Image: The name Forrest calls to mind two different images: a big, strong outdoorsman who is quiet and happy or a wealthy, distinguished professional who is a capable winner — a Beverly Hills doctor, perhaps.

Famous Forrests: actor Forest (*The Adventures of Huckleberry Finn*) Tucker; newscaster Forrest Sawyer; football's Forrest Gregg; Confederate general Nathan Forrest; author Forrest Wilson

FOSTER (Latin) "keeper of the woods"; a form of Forrest

Image: People think Foster is either an older, gray-haired bank president who is well educated and socially adept or a sentimental, old boozer who is often obnoxious, like Foster Brooks.

Famous Fosters: comedian Foster Brooks; Foster Grant sunglasses; actress Jodie (*The Accused*) Foster; composer Stephen ("Old Folks at Home") Foster

FRANCIS (Latin) "Frenchman"

Image: The name Francis evokes an image of a quiet scholar or deeply religious man who lacks self-confidence.

Famous Francises: Saint Francis of Assisi; director

Francis Ford (*The Godfather*) Coppola; navigator Sir Francis Drake; composer Francis Scott ("The Star-Spangled Banner") Key; Francis the Talking Mule movies; football's Francis (Fran) Tarkenton; English essayist Francis Bacon

FRANK a short form of Francis, Franklin

Image: The name Frank calls to mind two different images: a hardworking older man who is dependable, kind, and gentle or a tall, strong, blue-collar guy who is lazy, unpopular, and careless.

Famous Franks: singer/actor Frank Sinatra; baseball's Frank Viola; architect Frank Lloyd Wright; TV's Frank ("M*A*S*H") Burns, Frank ("Hill Street Blues") Furillo; sportscaster Frank ("Monday Night Football") Gifford

FRANKLIN "free landowner"

Image: Franklin is viewed in two ways: a large, powerful, well-bred achiever or a dull, quiet, intelligent scientist.

Famous Franklins: Presidents Franklin D. Roosevelt, Franklin Pierce; founding father Benjamin Franklin; journalist Franklin Pierce (*The Conning Tower*) Adams

FRED a short form of names containing "Fred"

Image: Fred is described as friendly and funny. People picture Fred as either a short, fat, and clumsy type, like Fred Flinstone, or a graceful dancer, like Fred Astaire.

Famous Freds: cartoon caveman Fred Flintstone; entertainer Fred Astaire; actors Fred ("My Three Sons") MacMurray, Fred ("Hunter") Dryer; bandleader Fred Waring; Fred ("Mister Rogers' Neighborhood") Rogers; TV's Fred ("I Love Lucy") Mertz

FREDERICK (Old German) "ruler in peace"

Image: Frederick is viewed as a good name for a handsome, older, wealthy socialite or distinguished professional. Some people, though, picture Frederick as an obnoxious, insecure ladies' man or a stuffy snob.

Famous Fredericks: abolitionist Frederick Douglass; actor Frederic (*Inherit the Wind*) March; painter/sculptor Frederic Remington; Frederick's of Hollywood lingerie; Prussia's King Frederick the Great

FREEMAN (Old English) "free man"

Image: People picture Freeman as a handsome, neat, well-dressed, proud, and wealthy black man.

Famous Freemans: actors Freeman ("Amos 'n' Andy") Gosden, Morgan (*Driving Miss Daisy*) Freeman; football's Freeman McNeil

FRITZ a German short form of Frederick

Image: Fritz is described as a quiet man who is a brave leader or politician, like former vice president Walter Mondale.

Fritz is also a good name for a dog.

Famous Fritzes: former vice president Walter (Fritz) Mondale; "Fritz the Cat" cartoons; violinist Fritz Kreisler; director Fritz (*The Big Heat*) Lang

GABRIEL (Hebrew) "devoted to God"

Image: Gabriel is pictured as a small, delicate man with an angelic face who is kind, quiet, courageous, and one heck of a trumpet player.

Famous Gabriels: the biblical archangel Gabriel; radio personality Gabriel Heatter; football's Roman Gabriel; South American novelist Gabriel Garcia (*One Hundred Years of Solitude*) Marquez; physicist Gabriel Fahrenheit

GALE (Old English) "gay, lively"; (Irish Gaelic) "stranger"; a short form of Galen

Image: The name Gale reminds some people of a friendly, quick-moving, slow-thinking football player. Others associate the name with windy, stormy weather.

Famous Gales: comic actor Gale ("Our Miss Brooks") Gordon; football's Gale Sayers; basketball's Gale Goodrich; actress Gale Storm

GARDNER (Middle English) "gardener"

Image: Gardner is described as an older, balding British man who is a wealthy, distinguished, and straitlaced professional.

Famous Gardners: writer Erle Stanley (Perry Mason's creator) Gardner; actor Gardner ("Adventures in Paradise") McKay; actress Ava (*The Barefoot Contessa*) Gardner

GARETH (Welsh) "gentle"

Image: Most people say Gareth is an old-fashioned name that reminds them of a wealthy dud — a small, plain man who is reliable but dull. Some, though, see Gareth as a strong, wild, and rough fantasy character.

Famous Gareth: King Arthur's knight Sir Gareth

GARFIELD (Old English) "battlefield"

Image: Many people picture Garfield like the cartoon cat — a fat, fun-loving goof. Others think Garfield is good presidential material — smart, sophisticated, and boring.

Famous Garfields: cartoon cat Garfield; President James A. Garfield

GARRETT (Old English) "with a mighty spear"

Image: Garrett is described as a wild, tall man with a rakish mustache who is smart, interesting, and nice.

Famous Garretts: comic actor Garrett ("Saturday Night Live") Morris; pop singer Leif Garrett

GARRICK (Old English) "oak spear"

Image: Garrick is pictured as tall, rugged, handsome, and suave, like a tough-guy hero from a romance novel.

Famous Garrick: newscaster Garrick Utley

GARTH (Scandinavian) "grounds keeper"

Image: The name Garth calls to mind a noble and romantic hero. To some people, though, Garth is a different kind of fantasy character — a dwarf or deranged monster.

Famous Garths: Lord Garth on TV's "Star Trek"; Mary (*Middlemarch*) Garth; children's book illustrator Garth Williams

GARY, Garry (Old English) "spear-carrier"; short forms of Gerald

Image: People think of Gary as a tall, strong, regular guy who is friendly, nice, and funny.

Famous Garys: TV hosts Garry Moore, Gary Collins; actor Gary (*High Noon*) Cooper; former senator Gary Hart; cartoonist Garry ("Doonesbury") Trudeau; TV's Gary ("Knots Landing") Ewing

GAVIN (Welsh) "white hawk"

Image: Gavin is pictured as an older, balding, sexy sophisticate who is sporty, well spoken, and sometimes phony, like the Captain on TV's "The Love Boat" played by Gavin MacLeod.

Famous Gavins: actor Gavin ("The Love Boat") MacLeod; actor/ambassador John Gavin; Gavin (*The Little Minister*) Dishart

GAYLORD (Old French) "gay lord, jailer (gaoler)"

Image: People say Gaylord is a good name for a stuffy, old-fashioned, aristocratic bookworm in a silk smoking jacket.

Famous Gaylords: pitcher Gaylord Perry; former senator Gaylord Nelson; Gaylord (*Show Boat*) Ravenal

GENE a short form of Eugene

Image: Gene is pictured as a middle-aged, plain, balding, overweight man who is either funny and outgoing or boring and bookish.

Famous Genes: singer/actor Gene (*Singing in the Rain*) Kelly; singing cowboy Gene Autry; TV host Gene Rayburn; TV critic Gene ("The Today Show") Shalit; former senator Gene McCarthy; TV producer Gene ("Star Trek") Roddenberry; actors Gene (*The French Connection*) Hackman, Gene (*Young Frankenstein*) Wilder; boxer Gene Tunney

GEOFFREY an English form of Godfrey, Jeffrey (see also Jeffrey)

Image: Geoffrey strikes people as a classy name suitable for a rich, snooty English aristocrat or his chauffeur.

Famous Geoffreys: designer Geoffrey Beene; medieval English poet Geoffrey (*The Canterbury Tales*) Chaucer

GEORGE (Greek) "farmer"

Image: Most people think of George as an ordinary guy — a short, heavy, plain older man who is quiet, kind, friendly, reliable, and slow.

Famous Georges: Presidents George Washington, George Bush; comic actor George (*Oh, God!*) Burns; actors George C. (*Patton*) Scott, George ("The A-Team") Peppard, George (*Love at First Bite*) Hamilton, George (*Cool Hand Luke*) Kennedy; singer Boy George; former Beatle George Harrison; Generals George S. Patton, George A. Custer; basketball's George (Iceman) Gervin

GERALD (Old German) "spear-ruler"

Image: The name Gerald calls to mind a tall man who is strong but clumsy; and quiet but short tempered.

Famous Geralds: President Gerald Ford; actor Gerald ("Simon & Simon") McRaney; Canadian financier Gerald W. Schwartz

GERALDO a variant of Gerald

Image: People picture Geraldo as a muscular Hispanic man who is cocky, conceited, sly, and tough, like Geraldo Rivera, the mustachioed TV muckraker.

Famous Geraldo: TV host Geraldo Rivera

GERARD (Old English) "spear-hard"

Image: Gerard is pictured as a tall, strong, rich kid who is either funny, good-looking, and superficial or quiet, stuffy, hardworking, and nerdy.

Famous Gerards: actor Gil ("Buck Rogers in the 25th Century") Gerard; poet Gerard Manley ("God's Grandeur") Hopkins

GERRY see Jerry

GIDEON (Hebrew) "feller of trees, destroyer"

Image: A destroyer? Hardly! People think of Gideon as a tall, quiet do-gooder who is a peaceful, religious philanthropist.

Famous Gideons: the biblical Gideon, Hebrew liberator; the Society of Gideons; the movie *Gideon's Trumpet*

GIL a short form of Gilbert

Image: The name Gil calls to mind two different images: a tall, ruggedly handsome, soft-spoken outdoorsman or cowboy, like Gil Favor on TV's "Rawhide," or a fun-loving older guy whose sole aim in life is to have a good time.

Famous Gils: actor Gil ("Buck Rogers in the 25th Century") Gerard; TV's Gil ("Rawhide") Favor; jazz pianist Gil Evans

GILBERT (Old English) "trusted"

Image: Gilbert is described as a plain, bespectacled older man who is a real Victorian — distinguished, stuffy, introverted, and old-fashioned.

Famous Gilberts: singer Gilbert O'Sullivan; actor Gilbert

(*Captain Kidd*) Roland; lyricist Sir William Gilbert of Gilbert and Sullivan; geographer Gilbert Grosvenor; architect Cass Gilbert; mystery writer Gilbert K. Chesterton

GILES (Greek) "shield-bearer"

Image: Most people say Giles is a stuffy, stately, soft-spoken Englishman — a butler or polo player, perhaps. To some, though, Giles is a loud, beer-drinking cowboy.

Famous Giles: Saint Giles, patron saint of cripples; poet Giles Fletcher; John Barth's novel *Giles Goat Boy*

GINO, Jeno short forms of Ambrogino, Luigino

Image: People describe Gino as a short, dark, muscular Italian man who is friendly, energetic, and fun loving.

Famous Ginos: pizza king Jeno Paulucci; musician Gino Vanelli; football's Gino Marchetti

GLEN, Glenn (Irish Gaelic) "valley"; short forms of Glendon

Image: Glen is described as either a friendly, simple, down-to-earth, middle-class guy or a bold, innovative, wealthy intellectual.

Famous Glens: singers Glen ("Rhinestone Cowboy") Campbell, Glenn Frey of the Eagles; bandleader Glenn Miller; physicist Glen Seaborg; basketball's Glen Rice; actor Glenn (*Superman*) Ford

GODFREY a German form of Jeffrey

Image: Godfrey is pictured as an older British man who is quiet and formal — a wealthy businessman or his butler, perhaps.

Famous Godfreys: radio/TV host Arthur Godfrey; actor Godfrey (*The President's Analyst*) Cambridge; seventeenth-century English painter Sir Godfrey Kneller; W. C. Fields's exclamation "Godfrey Daniels!"

GORDON (Old English) "hill of the plains"

Image: Most people view Gordon as a strong, athletic, clean-cut boy-next-door — an outgoing, warm, down-to-earth guy who makes friends easily. Some, though, view Gordon as a short, tubby, quiet, older rocket scientist.

Famous Gordons: Watergate's G. Gordon Liddy; singers Gordon ("Lonesome Highway") Lightfoot, Gordon (Sting) Sumner; actor Gordon (*Oklahoma!*) MacRae; spaceman Flash Gordon

GORDY, Gordie short forms of Gordon

Image: Most people describe Gordy as a fun-loving practical joker who might strike some shady deals on the used-car lot. Some, though, say Gordy is an intelligent, rugged outdoorsman.

Famous Gordys: hockey's Gordie Howe; Motown's Berry Gordy

GRADY (Irish Gaelic) "noble, illustrious"

Image: People see Grady as a handsome, funny Irishman who is poor but has many friends.

Famous Grady: TV's Grady ("Sanford and Son") Wilson

GRAHAM (Old English) "the gray home"

Image: Graham is imagined as either a handsome, distinguished, intellectual British aristocrat or a skinny, average bloke who fades into the scenery.

Famous Grahams: singer Graham Nash of Crosby, Stills, Nash, and Young; comic actor Graham ("Monty Python's Flying Circus") Chapman; Graham (Galloping Gourmet) Kerr; inventor Alexander Graham Bell; novelist Graham (*The Quiet American*) Greene; graham crackers

GRANT (French) "great"; a short form of Grantland

Image: People describe Grant as a tall, handsome, sophisticated professional who is well dressed, well liked, witty, and sexy.

Famous Grants: TV producer Grant Tinker; President Ulysses S. Grant; painter Grant (*American Gothic*) Wood; actors Cary (*To Catch a Thief*) Grant, Grant ("Eight Is Enough") Goodeve

GREG a short form of Gregory

Image: Greg is pictured as a tall, blond, athletic boy-next-door — a wholesome, plain,

honest kid who takes directions well. Some also see him as a funny, cute, conceited pest.

Famous Gregs: diver Greg Louganis; TV's Greg ("The Brady Bunch") Brady; rock singer Gregg Allman of the Allman Brothers; actor Greg ("My Two Dads") Evigan

GREGORY (Latin) "watchman, watchful"

Image: People describe Gregory as a rich, sophisticated businessman — a tall, strong, attractive man who is smart and successful in business as well as a suave man about town. Gregory is also described as spoiled and short tempered.

Famous Gregorys: dancer/actor Gregory (*White Knights*) Hines; actors Gregory (*Moby Dick*) Peck, Gregory ("Trapper John, M.D.") Harrison; sixteen popes named Gregory

GROVER (Old English) "from the grove"

Image: Most people describe Grover as a big, heavy, older black man who is quiet, serious, and boring. Some, though, say Grover is a small, loud, goofy clown, like the character on TV's "Sesame Street."

Famous Grovers: President Grover Cleveland; jazz musician Grover Washington; Grover on TV's "Sesame Street"; baseball's Grover Cleveland Alexander

GUNTHER (Scandinavian) "battle army, warrior"

Image: Gunther is pictured as a big, strong German man with cold blue eyes who is in a position of authority — a tough military officer, perhaps.

Famous Gunthers: author John Gunther; composer Gunther ("P. D. Q. Bach") Schuller; lion tamer Gunther Gebel-Williams

GUS a short form of Gustave

Image: People think of Gus as a likable old codger — a jolly, friendly grandpa with a smile and a story for everybody.

Famous Guses: astronaut Gus Grissom; songwriter Gus ("School Days") Edwards

GUSTAVE (Scandinavian) "staff of the Goths"

Image: Gustave is pictured as a blond Swedish athlete who is somewhat arrogant or pompous.

Famous Gustaves: six Swedish kings named Gustavus; composer Gustav Mahler; novelist Gustave (*Madame Bovary*) Flaubert

GUY (French) "guide"; (Old German) "warrior"

Image: People have two different images of Guy: a dark, muscular, good-looking, blue-collar tough guy who knows where to find trouble or a short, ordinary guy who is honest, easy to talk to, and a real friend.

Famous Guys: bandleader Guy Lombardo; French writer Guy de Maupassant; hockey's Guy LaFleur; English conspirator Guy Fawkes; actors Guy ("Lost in Space") Williams, Guy ("Wild Bill Hickok") Madison; Guy Smiley on TV's "Sesame Street"

HAL a short form of Harold, Henry

Image: Hal is described as a an ordinary-looking man who is smart and unpredictable.

Famous Hals: actors Hal ("Barney Miller") Linden, Hal (*The Kidnapping of the President*) Holbrook; Prince Hal in Shakespeare's *Henry IV*; TV/filmmakers Hal March, Hal Roach; HAL 9000, the computer in the movie *2001: A Space Odyssey*

HAMILTON (Old English) "from the proud estate"

Image: From the proud estate, indeed! People usually picture Hamilton as a rich, stuffy snob.

Famous Hamiltons: former presidential advisor Hamilton Jordan; Congressman Hamilton Fish, Jr.; TV's Hamilton ("Perry Mason") Burger; actors Hamilton (*Casey at the Bat*) Camp, George (*Love At First Bite*) Hamilton

HANK a short form of Henry

Image: Hank is pictured as a hardworking, simple, and

strong manual laborer with an outgoing personality.

Famous Hanks: baseball's Hank Aaron; country singers Hank Snow, Hank Williams, Jr. and Sr.; cartoonist Hank ("Dennis the Menace") Ketcham

HANS a Scandinavian form of John

Image: People think of Hans as a blond man of German or Dutch descent who is quiet, dependable, and thoughtful.

Famous Hanses: children's story writer Hans Christian Andersen; Mary Mapes Dodge's children's story *Hans Brinker*; Dutch painter Hans Holbein

HARLAN, Harland (Old English) "from the army-land, from the hares' land"

Image: Most people say Harlan has a blue-collar, tough-guy image. Harlan is pictured as a mechanically inclined farmer or biker who is rough around the edges.

Famous Harlans: science fiction/fantasy writer Harlan Ellison; former justice Harlan Stone; fried chicken mogul Colonel Harland Sanders

HARMON an English form of Herman

Image: Harmon calls to mind a big, rugged, bearlike man with a smiling face and a heart of gold.

Famous Harmons: baseball's Harmon Killebrew; actor Mark ("St. Elsewhere") Harmon; Harmon-Kardon audio equipment

HAROLD (Scandinavian) "army-ruler"

Image: Harold is pictured as a tall, skinny, homely older man who is hardworking and likable.

Famous Harolds: perennial presidential candidate Harold Stassen; Britain's former prime minister Harold MacMillan; comic actor Harold Lloyd; novelist Harold (*The Carpet-baggers*) Robbins; Harold, Saxon king of England; the movie *Harold and Maude*

HARPER (Old English) "harp player"

Image: People describe Harper as a rich, snobby, and successful bachelor.

Famous Harpers: novelist Harper (*To Kill a Mockingbird*) Lee; *Harper's* magazine; actresses Valerie ("Rhoda") Harper, Tess (*Tender Mercies*) Harper; the city of Harper's Ferry, West Virginia; the movie *Harper*

HARRISON (Old English) "son of Harry"

Image: Harrison is pictured as a handsome, wealthy man who is either suave, daring, and arrogant or sensitive and mild mannered.

Famous Harrisons: actors Harrison (*Raiders of the Lost Ark*) Ford, Rex (*My Fair Lady*) Harrison; former Beatle George Harrison; Presidents William Henry Harrison, Benjamin Harrison; journalist Harrison E. Salisbury

HARRY (Old English) "soldier"; a short form of Harold, Harrison, Henry

Image: Most people say Harry is an older blue-collar dad who is friendly, funny, and happy-go-lucky. Some, though, see Harry as a serious businesslike man with a bad temper.

Famous Harrys: movie cop "Dirty Harry" Callahan; singer Harry ("Day O") Belafonte; actors Harry ("L.A. Law") Hamlin, Harry ("M*A*S*H") Morgan; bandleader Harry James; President Harry Truman; the movies *The Trouble with Harry*, *When Harry Met Sally*

HARVEY (Old German) "army-warrior"

Image: A warrior? Hardly! People think of Harvey as an unattractive but friendly old geezer.

Famous Harveys: assassin Lee Harvey Oswald; Harvey, the six-foot movie rabbit; actor Harvey ("The Carol Burnett Show") Korman

HECTOR (Greek) "steadfast"

Image: Hector is described as an older Hispanic family man who is plain but very masculine.

Famous Hectors: Hector, legendary Trojan War hero; composer Hector (*Symphonie Fantastique*) Berlioz; writer Hector Hugh (Saki) Munro

HENRY (Old German) "ruler of an estate"

Image: The name Henry has a number of different images: a frail, bookish nerd; an ambitious, independent entrepreneur; or a strong, easygoing farmer.

Famous Henrys: comic actors Henry ("Happy Days") Winkler, Henry ("Laugh-In") Gibson; actor Henry (*Mr. Roberts*) Fonda; many English kings named Henry; automaker Henry Ford; novelist Henry (*The Turn of the Screw*) James

HERB a short form of Herbert

Image: Herb is pictured as a fat bald man with glasses who is a classic wimp or an over-educated, dull pushover.

Famous Herbs: hockey coach Herb Brooks; bandleader Herb ("Tijuana Brass") Alpert; actor Herb ("Good Guys") Edelman; Herb Woodley in "Blondie" comics; jazz musicians Herbie Mann, Herbie Hancock; Herb, the Burger King nerd

HERBERT (Old German) "glorious soldier"

Image: People picture Herbert as a fat older man who is a well-educated, pompous loner and the hapless target of many jokes.

Famous Herberts: President Herbert Hoover; actor Herbert (*A Shot in the Dark*) Lom; conductor Herbert von Karajan; novelist Herbert George (H. G.) Wells; composer Victor (*Babes in Toyland*) Herbert

HERMAN (Latin) "high-ranking person"; (Old German) "warrior"

Image: Most people think Herman is a fat, clumsy dummy — a mousy man who is laughed at, not with.

Famous Hermans: TV's Herman ("The Munsters") Munster; the sixties band Herman's Hermits; Nazi Hermann Goering; novelists Herman (*Moby Dick*) Melville, Herman (*The Winds of War*) Wouk, Hermann (*Siddhartha*) Hesse

HERSCHEL (Hebrew) "deer"

Image: Herschel is pictured as an unattractive, old foreign man who is intelligent, down-to-earth, and quiet.

Famous Herschels: actor Herschel ("Arnie") Bernardi; English astronomer William Herschel; football's Herschel Walker

HOMER (Greek) "promise"

Image: The name Homer evokes an image of a lanky old man with a bow tie — a quiet schoolteacher, perhaps.

Famous Homers: the Greek poet Homer; "Hee Haw" comedy duo Homer and Jethro; TV's Homer ("The Simpsons") Simpson; Homer (*Cider House Rules*) Wells; children's story hero Homer (*Centerburg Tales*) Price; the city of Homer, Alaska

HORACE (Latin) "keeper of the hours"

Image: Horace is described as a highly educated, bespectacled nerd who is a real mama's boy.

Famous Horaces: the Roman poet Horace; politician Horace Greeley; educator Horace Mann; novelist Horace Walpole; jazz musician Horace Silver

HORTON (Old English) "from the gray estate"

Image: Horton strikes people as a good name for an overweight, stuffy, and very dull professor.

Famous Hortons: Dr. Seuss's Horton the elephant; singer Johnny ("Battle of New Orleans") Horton; actor Edward Everett (*The Front Page*) Horton

HOWARD (Old English) "watchman"

Image: Howard is described as either a boring middle-class man, like Howard from TV's "Happy Days," or as a rich and powerful man, like Howard Hughes.

Famous Howards: Senator Howard Baker; TV's Howard Cosell; millionaire Howard Hughes; TV's Howard ("Happy Days") Cunningham; the movie *Howard the Duck*; actor/director Ron (*Parenthood*) Howard; actors Howard (*Seven Brides for Seven Brothers*) Keel, Howard (*Kramer vs. Kramer*) Duff

HOWIE a short form of Howard

Image: People picture Howie as a grown-up Howdy Doody. Howie is described as a funny, clumsy hick or a wacky, nerdy dope.

Famous Howies: football's Howie Long; comic actor Howie ("St. Elsewhere") Mandel

HUBERT (Old German) "bright mind"

Image: Hubert is pictured two ways: knowledgeable, friendly, and talkative or small, thin, mousy, and quiet.

Famous Huberts: former vice president Hubert H. Humphrey; Flemish painter Hubert Van Eyck

HUGH (Old English) "intelligence"; a short form of Hubert

Image: People think of Hugh as a tall, thin man who is tough, smart, and rich.

Famous Hughs: TV host Hugh Downs; actor Hugh ("The Life and Legend of Wyatt Earp") O'Brian; magazine publisher Hugh (*Playboy*) Hefner; French King, Hugh Capet

HUGO a Latinized form of Hugh

Image: Most people describe Hugo as a fat man who is gentle, personable, and punctual.

Famous Hugos: musician Hugo Montenegro; French novelist Victor (*Les Miserables*) Hugo; former supreme court justice Hugo Black; Hugo science fiction awards

HUMPHREY (Old German) "peaceful Hun"

Image: The name Humphrey calls to mind "Bogie" — a ruggedly handsome, hard-boiled tough guy with a heart of gold.

Famous Humphreys: actor Humphrey (*Casablanca*) Bogart; former vice president Hubert H. Humphrey; Humphrey (*Finnegan's Wake*) Earwicker; Tobias Smollett's novel *The Expedition of Humphrey Clinker*

HUNTER (Old English) "hunter"

Image: The name Hunter drips with rugged masculinity. Hunter is seen as either a spirited adventurer or a quiet, lonely stalker.

Famous Hunters: TV's "Hunter"; actor Tab (*Damn Yankees*) Hunter; journalist Hunter S. Thompson

HYMAN (Hebrew) "life"; an English form of Chaim

Image: Hyman is described as an older Jewish man who is both a successful businessman and a gentle family man.

Famous Hymans: Admiral Hyman Rickover; Leo Rosten's novel *The Education of Hyman Kaplan*

IAN a Scottish form of John

Image: People think of Ian as a sophisticated, intellectual prankster — a Monty Python character, perhaps. Ian is pictured as a tall, thin Englishman who is likable but often labeled as a snob.

Famous Ians: Irish Protestant leader Ian Paisley; musician Ian Anderson; novelist Ian (*James Bond*) Fleming; British comic actor Ian (*I'm All Right, Jack*) Carmichael; actor Ian ("General Hospital") Buchanan

IGOR (Scandinavian) "son's army"; a Russian form of Inger

> **Image:** Igor's image comes straight from late-night horror movies. Igor is described as a short, sinister, beady-eyed man who resembles Dr. Frankenstein's hunchbacked assistant.

> **Famous Igors:** composer Igor (*The Firebird*) Stravinsky; Igor, Dr. Frankenstein's lab assistant; aeronautical engineer Igor Sikorsky; Borodin's opera *Prince Igor*

IRA (Hebrew) "watchful"

> **Image:** People describe Ira as an accountant or stockbroker who looks like an aging Woody Allen. Ira is pictured as a short Jewish man who is smart, sensitive, and an irritable complainer.

> **Famous Iras:** TV scientist Ira ("Newton's Apple") Flatow; lyricist Ira ("Embraceable You") Gershwin; novelist Ira (*The Boys from Brazil*) Levin

IRVING (Irish Gaelic) "beautiful"; (Old English) "sea friend"

> **Image:** Irving calls to mind two different images: a stuffy, stodgy, and nerdy Ivy Leaguer or a witty, talented, musical Jewish man reminiscent of Irving Berlin.

> **Famous Irvings:** composer Irving ("God Bless America") Berlin; architect Irving Schwartz; novelists Irving (*The Origin*) Stone, Irving (*The Seven Minutes*) Wallace, John (*The World According to Garp*) Irving; folktale writer Washington (*The Legend of Sleepy Hollow*) Irving

IRWIN, Erwin forms of Irving

> **Image:** Irwin is pictured as a lonely, shy, and quiet only child who collects stamps and earns grades that make his mother happy. People say Irwin will grow up to be a highly successful, hardworking businessman.

> **Famous Irwins:** novelist Irwin (*Rich Man, Poor Man*) Shaw; novelist/movie producer Irwin (*The Towering Inferno*) Allen; German Field Marshal Erwin (The Desert Fox) Rommell; financial mogul Irwin Jacobs

ISAAC (Hebrew) "he laughs"

> **Image:** People think of Isaac as a brilliant, thoughtful scholar who is either Jewish or black.

> **Famous Isaacs:** the biblical Isaac, Abraham's son; novelists Isaac (*Foundation*) Asimov, Isaac Bashevis (*Yentl, the Yeshiva Boy*) Singer; composer Isaac ("The Theme from *Shaft*") Hayes; scientist Sir Isaac Newton; violinist Isaac Stern

ISAIAH (Hebrew) "God is my helper, salvation of God"

> **Image:** Isaiah, a name with strong biblical associations, calls to mind a wise, proud, deeply religious black man who might be a farmer or basketball player. Some, though, see Isaiah as a Jewish scholar.

> **Famous Isaiahs:** the biblical Hebrew prophet Isaiah; basketball's Isiah Thomas

ISRAEL (Hebrew) "ruling with the Lord, wrestling with the Lord"

Image: People picture Israel as a tall Jewish man who is intelligent, deeply religious, and a bit odd.

Famous Israels: the nation of Israel; the name given to the biblical Jacob; author Israel (*The Mantle of Elijah*) Zangwill; playwright Israel (*The Wakefield Plays*) Horovitz; Revolutionary General Israel Putnam

IVAN a Russian form of John

Image: Most people think of Ivan as a short, balding Russian who is tough, cold, and domineering.

Famous Ivans: inside-trader Ivan Boesky; tennis's Ivan Lendl; Russian czar Ivan the Terrible; Alexander Solzhenitsyn's novel *One Day in the Life of Ivan Denisovich*; Leo Tolstoy's novella *The Death of Ivan Ilyich*; Nikolay Gogol's *The Tale of How Ivan Ivanovitch Quarreled with Ivan Nikiforovich*

JACK a form of John, Jacob; a short form of Jackson

Image: Most people think Jack is a real pistol — a macho guy who is virile, strong, cocky, and smart. Jack is also viewed as a cute, fun party animal.

Famous Jacks: President Jack Kennedy; TV's Jack ("Three's Company") Tripper; comedian Jack Benny; TV host Jack Paar; actors Jack ("Quincy") Klugman, Jack (*Batman*) Nicholson, Jack ("Dragnet") Webb; golfer Jack Nicklaus; quarterback/politician Jack Kemp

JACKSON (Old English) "son of Jack"

Image: People picture Jackson as an easygoing black man who, like Michael Jackson, is a talented musician.

Famous Jacksons: Confederate General Stonewall Jackson; President Andrew Jackson; singers Michael ("Thriller") Jackson, Jackson ("Running on Empty") Browne; presidential candidate Jesse Jackson; painter Jackson Pollock; the movie *Action Jackson*; the city of Jackson, Mississippi

JACOB (Hebrew) "supplanter"

Image: Most people think of Jacob as a highly religious man who is old-fashioned and quiet. Some, though, think he is powerful and greedy.

Famous Jacobs: the biblical Jacob, Isaac's son; former Senator Jacob Javits; Jacob (*A Christmas Carol*) Marley; fairy tale writer Jacob Grimm; scientist Jacob Bronowski

JACQUES a French form of Jacob, James

Image: The name Jacques calls to mind an adventurous Frenchman who is a bold explorer, like Jacques Cousteau, a scintillating wit, a *bon vivant*, and a great lover.

Famous Jacques: underwater explorer Jacques Cousteau; missionary/explorer Jacques Marquette; composers Jacques Offenbach, Jacques Brel; painter Jacques Louis David; hockey's Jacque Plante

JAKE a short form of Jacob

Image: Jake is described as a hardworking Jewish man who is polite, happy, and athletic.

Famous Jakes: boxer Jake (Raging Bull) La Motta; Jake (*The Sun Also Rises*) Barnes; Senator Jake Garn; TV's "Jake and the Fatman"; Jake of the Blues Brothers

JAMES an English form of Jacob

Image: James is pictured as a big, strong, handsome man who is intelligent, serious, fair, and dependable. Some, though, think of James as a rude, conceited aristocrat.

Famous James: two biblical disciples named James; James Bond, Ian Fleming's fictional superspy; soul singer James ("I Feel Good") Brown; actors James (*The Magnificent Seven*) Coburn, James (*Rebel Without a Cause*) Dean, James ("The Rockford Files") Garner, James (*Lolita*) Mason; singer James ("Sweet Baby James") Taylor; Presidents James Madison, James Buchanan, James Garfield, James Monroe, James Polk; basketball's James Worthy

JAMIE a short form of James

Image: Jamie is a unisex name that calls to mind a cute, sweet, sensual, and mischievous young man.

Famous Jamies: actor Jamie ("M*A*S*H") Farr; actress Jamie Lee ("Anything But Love") Curtis

JAN a Dutch and Slavic form of John

Image: Most people picture Jan as a big, lanky man who is helpful, pleasant, and witty. Some people, though, think of Jan as proud or stuck-up.

Famous Jans: TV host Jan Murray; actor/stuntman Jan-Michael (*Hooper*) Vincent; painters Jan Vermeer, Jan Van Eyck; football's Jan Stenerud

JARED (Hebrew) "one who rules"

Image: Jared is described as a strong, dark-haired, middle-class youth from the west.

Famous Jareds: historian Jared Sparks; actor Jared ("Dallas") Martin

JARRETT a form of Garrett

Image: Jarrett has two different images: a strong, independent romance novel hero or a young, capable, upwardly mobile professional.

Famous Jarrett: pianist Keith Jarrett

JASON (Greek) "healer"

Image: Jason is viewed as a cute, athletic, fair-haired boy. However, there is little agreement about Jason's personality. He could be personable, amusing, and popular; hardheaded, rambunctious, and naughty; or quiet, shy, and introspective.

Famous Jasons: Greek hero Jason (and the Argonauts); actors Jason (*All the President's Men*) Robards, Jason ("The Hogan Family") Bateman; Jason in *Friday the 13th* movies; TV's Jason ("Here Come the Brides") Bolt

JASPER an English form of Casper

Image: Jasper is pictured as a colorful old-timer — a scruffy old prospector or backwoods banjo picker, perhaps. Some, though, see Jasper as a meek and mild bookworm.

Famous Jaspers: painter Jasper Johns; the city of Jasper, Alberta

JAY (Old French) "blue jay"; a short form of Jacob, James, Jason

Image: People picture Jay in one of two ways: a rich man who is tall, slim, and strong or a fun-loving guy who is quick and lively, like comedian Jay Leno.

Famous Jays: TV host/ comedian Jay Leno; child actor Jay ("Dennis the Menace") North; football's Jay Schroeder

JED (Hebrew) "beloved of the Lord"; a short form of Jedediah

Image: Jed is described as a hardworking, strong, and athletic man who, like TV's Jed Clampett, is a real hillbilly.

Famous Jed: TV's Jed ("The Beverly Hillbillies") Clampett

JEFF a short form of Jefferson, Jeffrey

Image: The name Jeff evokes an image of a tall, strong, good-looking guy who is friendly and kind.

Famous Jeffs: actors Jeff (*The Fabulous Baker Boys*) Bridges, Jeff (*The Fly*) Goldblum, Jeff (*Broken Arrow*) Chandler, Jeff (*Something Wild*) Daniels; musician Jeff Lynn

JEFFERSON (Old English) "son of Jeffrey"

Image: Thanks to our third president, Jefferson is pictured as a stately leader who is tall, handsome, and highly intelligent.

Famous Jeffersons: President Thomas Jefferson; Confederate President Jefferson Davis; the rock group Jefferson Airplane/ Starship; TV's "The Jeffersons"

JEFFREY (Old French) "heavenly peace" (see also Geoffrey)

Image: Jeffrey is pictured as boyish, dark haired, and handsome. Some say Jeffrey is an intelligent know-it-all and a rich, snotty brat while others say he is an average guy who is solid, stodgy, and boring.

Famous Jeffreys: novelists Jeffery (*The Amateur Gentleman*) Farnol, Jeffrey (*Cain and Abel*) Archer; Captain Jeffrey T. (*Animal Crackers*) Spaulding; actor Jeffrey (*Amadeus*) Jones

JENO see Gino

JEREMIAH (Hebrew)
"appointed by Jehovah"

Image: Jeremiah is a biblical name that calls to mind a quiet, long-haired, sensitive hippie or a mountain man, like Jeremiah Johnson.

Famous Jeremiahs: the biblical Hebrew prophet Jeremiah; the movie *Jeremiah Johnson*; Jeremiah the bullfrog from the Three Dog Night's song "Joy to the World"

JEREMY a form of Jeremiah

Image: Jeremy is described as a tall, good-looking British lad who is either a frail, shy, naive, and sensitive child or a rich, whining, spoiled brat.

Famous Jeremys: folk singers Chad and Jeremy; British actor Jeremy ("Brideshead Revisited") Irons; chemist Jeremy Rifkin; publisher Jeremy Tarcher

JEROME (Latin) "holy name"

Image: People say Jerome is an old-fashioned name befitting a man who is funny, intelligent, and caring.

Famous Jeromes: Saint Jerome, Latin church father; composer Jerome (*Show Boat*) Kern; novelist/short story writer Jerome David (*The Catcher in the Rye*) Salinger; choreographer Jerome (*West Side Story*) Robbins; singer Jerome Hines

JERRY, Gerry short forms of Gerald, Jeremiah, Jeremy, Jerome

Image: Most people think of Jerry as a tall, friendly, fun-loving goofball with a great personality. Some think Jerry is likely to wear flashy gold chains and may come on a bit too strong.

Famous Jerrys: football's Jerry Burns, Jerry Rice; comic actors Jerry (*The Nutty Professor*) Lewis, Jerry ("Coach") Van Dyke, Jerry Canova; rock singer Jerry Lee ("Whole Lotta Shakin' Goin' On") Lewis; basketball's Jerry West; TV's "Tom and Jerry" cartoons

JESS a short form of Jesse

Image: The name Jess conjures up two different images: a tall, handsome, rich rock-and-roll star or a big, strong, freckle-faced country boy wearing blue jeans and suspenders.

Famous Jesses: TV's Jess ("Laramie") Harper; writer Jess (*I Ain't Much Baby, But I'm All I've Got*) Lair

JESSE (Hebrew) "God exists"

Image: Jesse James is the dominant image for this name — a tough, wild, free-spirited outlaw who is rotten to the core.

Famous Jesses: the biblical Jesse, David's father; presidential candidate Jesse Jackson; Senator Jesse Helms; outlaw Jesse James; TV's Jesse ("All My Children") Hubbard; track and field's Jesse Owens; Carly Simon's song "Jesse"

JESUS (Hebrew) "God will help"

Image: Jesus is pictured as a short Hispanic man who is friendly and deeply religious.

Famous Jesuses: Jesus Christ, founder of Christianity; baseball's Jesus Alou; TV's Jesus ("Hill Street Blues") Martinez

JETHRO (Hebrew) "preeminence"

Image: People describe Jethro as a character straight out of TV's "The Beverly Hillbillies" — big, tall, strong, and downright stupid.

Famous Jethros: the biblical Jethro, father-in-law of Moses; rock group Jethro Tull; TV's Jethro ("The Beverly Hillbillies") Clampett; country musicians Homer and Jethro

JIM a short form of James

Image: Jim is described as a good-looking, athletic blond who is friendly, quiet, and ordinary.

Famous Jims: comic actors Jim ("Gilligan's Island") Backus, Jim ("Gomer Pyle, U.S.M.C.") Nabors; TV evangelist/prison inmate Jim Bakker; Jim Beam liquor; TV's Jim ("The Rockford Files") Rockford; frontiersman Jim Bowie; football's Jim Brown, Jim Taylor, Jim McMahon

JIMMY a short form of James

Image: Jimmy is pictured as either a friendly, simple-minded boy or as the neighborhood tough guy.

Famous Jimmys: President Jimmy Carter; comedian Jimmy Durante; actors Jimmy (*Harvey*) Stewart, Jimmy ("L.A. Law") Smits; TV evangelist Jimmy Swaggart; sports prognosticator Jimmy (the Greek) Snyder

JOCK a short form of Jacob, John

Image: People describe Jock as a rugged athlete who is a rich, dumb wiseguy.

Famous Jocks: TV's Jock ("Dallas") Ewing; actor Jock (*Yancey Derringer*) Mahoney; Jock the dog in the movie *Lady and the Tramp*; Maine's governor John (Jock) McKernan

JODY a form of Joseph

Image: This unisex name calls to mind a cute, freckle-faced boy with a cheerful disposition, a high level of energy, and a strong interest in athletics.

Famous Jody: Jody on TV's "Family Affair"

JOE a short form of Joseph

Image: Joe is described as all-man and all-American — a strong, handsome, masculine guy who is either considerate and nice, like Joe DiMaggio, or opinionated and chauvinistic.

Famous Joes: rock singer Joe Cocker; comic actor Joe ("Saturday Night Live") Piscopo; baseball's Joe DiMaggio, Joe Garagiola, Joe Niekro; boxer Joe Louis; football's Joe Namath, Joe Montana; TV host Joe Franklin

JOEL (Hebrew) "Jehovah is the Lord"

Image: The name Joel calls to mind a small, sensitive man who is very popular and nice, though a bit conceited.

Famous Joels: the biblical Hebrew prophet Joel; entertainer Joel (*Cabaret*) Grey; singer Billy ("Piano Man") Joel; storyteller Joel Chandler (Uncle Remus) Harris

JOEY a short form of Joseph

Image: Most people picture Joey as a spoiled, bratty little troublemaker.

Famous Joeys: TV host Joey Bishop; Joey in "Dennis the Menace" comics; the musical *Pal Joey*; singer Joey Heatherton

JOHN (Hebrew) "God is gracious" (see also Jon)

Image: John, a name with strong biblical associations, calls to mind a well-groomed, intelligent man who is as solid and dependable as the Rock of Gibraltar.

Famous Johns: Saint John the Baptist; Presidents John F. Kennedy, John Adams, John Quincy Adams, John Tyler; actors John (*True Grit*) Wayne, John (*SCTV Network*) Candy, John ("Roseanne") Goodman, John (*The Paper Chase*) Houseman, John (*Dinner at Eight*) Barrymore; directors John (*The African Queen*) Huston, John (*Tarzan the Ape Man*) Derek, John (*Sixteen Candles*) Hughes; tennis's John McEnroe; football's John Elway

JOHNNY a form of John

Image: Johnny is pictured as a dark-haired, husky, boyish all-American guy who is either a quiet mama's boy or a restless troublemaker.

Famous Johnnys: TV host Johnny ("The Tonight Show") Carson; actors Johnny (*Tarzan the Ape Man*) Weissmuller, Johnny ("21 Jump Street") Depp; the legendary Johnny Appleseed; the songs "Johnny Angel," "Johnny B. Goode"; singer Johnny Cash

JON a form of John; a short form of Jonathan (see also John)

Image: Jon is thought to be a soft, cute, irresponsible phony with a roving eye.

Famous Jons: Hollywood hairdresser/movie producer Jon Peters; actors Jon (*Midnight Cowboy*) Voight, Jon ("Lassie") Provost; Jon in "Garfield" comics

JONAH (Hebrew) "dove"

Image: The name Jonah has two different images: an old-fashioned, deeply religious do-gooder or a rugged, free-spirited outdoorsman — a fisherman or birdwatcher, perhaps.

Famous Jonah: the biblical Hebrew prophet Jonah

JONATHAN (Hebrew) "Jehovah gave"

Image: The name Jonathan calls to mind a tall, thin man who is either formal and reserved, or funny like Jonathan Winters.

Famous Jonathans: the biblical Jonathan, David's friend; novelist Jonathan (*Gulliver's Travels*) Swift; comedian Jonathan Winters; General Jonathan Wainwright; Jonathan apples

JORDAN (Hebrew)
"descending"

> **Image:** Jordan is pictured as a tall, strong, dark-haired professional who is serious, industrious, and cold.

> **Famous Jordans:** basketball's Michael Jordan; actor Richard (*The Bunker*) Jordan; the country of Jordan; former presidential advisor Hamilton Jordan; actor Louis (*Gigi*) Jourdan; Jordan Marsh department stores

JOSÉ a Spanish form of Joseph

> **Image:** People say José is a dark Hispanic man who is either happy and lots of fun or streetwise and tough.

> **Famous Josés:** singer José Feliciano; actor José (*Cyrano de Bergerac*) Ferrer; baseball's José Canseco

JOSEPH (Hebrew) "he shall add"

> **Image:** The name Joseph calls to mind a strong, quiet man who is creative, considerate, and proper.

> **Famous Josephs:** the biblical Joseph, son of Jacob; the biblical Joseph, husband of Mary; actor Joseph (*Duel in the Sun*) Cotton; tycoon/patriarch Joseph Kennedy; myth scholar Joseph Campbell

JOSH a short form of Joshua

> **Image:** Josh is imagined as a cute blond who is quiet and sweet as a little boy, and nice, handsome, and active as an adult.

> **Famous Joshes:** humorist Josh Billings; TV's Josh ("Wanted — Dead or Alive") Randall

JOSHUA (Hebrew) "Jehovah saves"

> **Image:** Joshua is described as a handsome man who is shy, smart, dependable, and religious.

> **Famous Joshuas:** the biblical Joshua, successor of Moses; director Joshua (*South Pacific*) Logan; English painter Sir Joshua Reynolds; geneticist Joshua Lederberg

JUAN a Spanish form of John

> **Image:** People picture Juan as a dark Hispanic man who is either well educated and well mannered or a fiery romantic, like Don Juan.

> **Famous Juans:** Juan Valdez, advertising's Columbian coffee picker; Spanish lover Don Juan; explorer Juan Ponce de Léon; baseball's Juan Berenguer, Juan Marichal

JUDD (Hebrew) "praised"; a form of Judah

> **Image:** Most people think of Judd as a tall country boy who is fun loving but dense. Some people, though, see Judd as quiet and secretive.

> **Famous Judds:** actors Judd ("Taxi") Hirsch, Judd (*The Breakfast Club*) Nelson; Jud (*Oklahoma*) Frye; the Judds, mother-daughter singing duo

JUDE (Latin) "right in the law"

Image: The name Jude calls two different images to mind: a handsome, restless nonconformist or a nice fellow who is religious or even saintly.

Famous Judes: Saint Jude, the Apostle; Thomas Hardy's novel *Jude the Obscure*; the Beatles' song "Hey Jude"

JULES a French form of Julius

Image: Jules is pictured as a very wealthy man or a talented musician who is overweight and nice.

Famous Juleses: bandleader Jules Herman; novelist Jules (*Twenty Thousand Leagues under the Sea*) Verne; director Jules (*Never on Sunday*) Dassin; cartoonist Jules Feiffer; composer Jules Massenet; the movie *Jules and Jim*

JULIAN (Latin) "belonging or related to Julius"

Image: Julian strikes people as a suitable name for a spoiled, shy, self-centered sissy.

Famous Julians: Saint Julian, patron saint of travelers and hospitality; Roman emperor Julian; former congressman Julian Bond; singer Julian Lennon; biologist Julian Huxley; jazz saxophonist Julian ("Cannonball") Adderly

JULIUS (Greek) "youthful and downy-bearded"

Image: Julius Caesar is the dominant image for this name. People describe Julius as a regal older man who is ambitious, powerful, and domineering. Some, though, think of Julius as a tall, good-looking, popular black man, like Julius Erving.

Famous Juliuses: Roman emperor Julius Caesar; basketball's Julius (Dr. J) Erving; physicist Julius Robert Oppenheimer; singer Julius La Rosa

JUSTIN (Latin) "upright"

Image: Justin is described as a cute, brown-haired, fun-loving, mischievous brat who loves to fish and roam outdoors with his dog. People say Justin is likely to become a wealthy suburban professional who is a fair-minded, likable, solid citizen.

Famous Justins: Saint Justin, church father; horse breeder/teacher Justin Morgan; TV's Cajun chef Justin Wilson

KALEB see Caleb

KAREEM (Arabic) "noble, exalted"

Image: Not surprisingly, people picture Kareem as a tall, black, religious basketball star, like Kareem Abdul Jabbar.

Famous Kareem: basketball's Kareem Abdul Jabbar

KARL see Carl

KEITH (Old Welsh) "from the forest"; (Scotch Gaelic) "from the battle place"

>   **Image:** The name Keith calls to mind a tall, thin, handsome blond who is quiet, friendly, and nice.

>   **Famous Keiths:** actors Keith (*Choose Me*) Carradine, Brian ("Family Affair") Keith; guitarist Keith Richards of the Rolling Stones

KEN a short form of names containing "ken"

>   **Image:** Ken is pictured as a tall, handsome blond who is popular and fun, but shallow.

>   **Famous Kens:** actors Ken ("Mayberry, R.F.D.") Berry, Ken ("Wiseguy") Wahl; Barbie and Ken dolls; novelist Ken (*One Flew over the Cuckoo's Nest*) Kesey

KENDALL (Old English) "from the bright valley"

>   **Image:** People view Kendall as well dressed, good-looking, and intelligent. Kendall might be a shy student, an eccentric writer, or a rich, stodgy doctor.

>   **Famous Kendall:** basketball's Kendall Gill

KENNETH (Irish Gaelic) "handsome"; (Old English) "royal oath"

>   **Image:** Kenneth is described as an ideal advisor — intelligent, friendly, straight, and proper. Some, though, see Kenneth as old-fashioned, stubborn, and stingy.

>   **Famous Kenneths:** actor Kenneth (*The Producers*) Mars; literary critic Kenneth Burke; poet Kenneth Koch; English politician/writer Kenneth Clarke; children's novelist Kenneth (*The Wind and the Willows*) Grahame

KENNY a short form of Kenneth

>   **Image:** People see Kenny as an all-American boy who is a football hero in his youth and a kindhearted, devoted family man as an adult.

>   **Famous Kennys:** singers Kenny Loggins, Kenny ("The Gambler") Rogers; football's Kenny (The Snake) Stabler; Kenny on TV's "The Cosby Show"; musician Kenny G.

KENT (Welsh) "white, bright"; a short form of Kenton

>   **Image:** The name Kent has two different images: a smart, strong, and blunt all-American or a conservative, proper British aristocrat.

>   **Famous Kents:** England's Earl of Kent; superhero Clark ("Superman") Kent; actor Kent ("Adam-12") McCord; baseball's Kent Hrbek, Kent Tekulve; Kent cigarettes

KERMIT (Irish Gaelic) "free man"

>   **Image:** Kermit is an unusual name that reminds people of a short, fat, fashion-conscious older man with a unique character.

>   **Famous Kermits:** muppet Kermit the Frog; Kermit ("Mr. Blooper") Schafer

KERRY (Irish) "dark, dark-haired"; (see also Cary)

> **Image:** Dark-haired? Most people do not think so. They describe Kerry as a good-looking, athletic blond who is warm and popular.

KEVIN (Irish Gaelic) "gentle, lovable"

> **Image:** Kevin is pictured as a young, athletic all-American boy who is friendly and kind, though a bit stubborn.
>
> **Famous Kevins:** Saint Kevin of Ireland; actors Kevin ("Knots Landing") Dobson, Kevin (*A Fish Called Wanda*) Kline; basketball's Kevin McHale

KIM (Old English) "chief, ruler"

> **Image:** Kim is a unisex name that calls to mind a slim, long-haired, cute Oriental man who is very nice. Some people, though, see Kim as loud and brassy.
>
> **Famous Kims:** North Korean leader Kim Il Sung; double agent Kim Philby; Rudyard Kipling's novel *Kim*; actresses Kim (*True Grit*) Darby, Kim (*Vertigo*) Novak

KIPP (Old English) "from the pointed hill"

> **Image:** Kipp is viewed as a cute blond preppy who is rich, well dressed, and thoroughly spoiled.
>
> **Famous Kip:** comedian Kip Addotta

KIRBY (Scandinavian) "from the church village"

> **Image:** Kirby has two distinct images: a short, pudgy athlete who is friendly and popular, like baseball's Kirby Puckett, or a curly-haired, bespectacled, studious scholar.
>
> **Famous Kirbys:** baseball's Kirby Puckett; TV host Durward Kirby

KIRK (Scandinavian) "from the church"

> **Image:** Kirk is viewed as a take-charge kind of guy — a tall, handsome man with a good-natured personality and a great deal of strength.
>
> **Famous Kirks:** actors Kirk ("Growing Pains") Cameron, Kirk (*Along the Great Divide*) Douglas; TV's Captain James T. ("Star Trek") Kirk; Kirk on TV's "Dear John"

KNUTE (Scandinavian) "knot"; a Danish form of Canute

> **Image:** Knute is pictured as a big, burly Swedish man who is as tough as nails and as smart as a rock.
>
> **Famous Knutes:** football's Knute Rockne; Danish/English King Canute

KURT a German form of Conrad (see also Curt)

> **Image:** Kurt is described as a strong, tough, macho German man who is aloof and hard to get to know.
>
> **Famous Kurts:** actor Kurt (*Silkwood*) Russell; Austria's President Kurt Waldheim; novelist Kurt (*Slaughterhouse Five*) Vonnegut; composer Kurt (*The Threepenny Opera*) Weill; psychologist Kurt Lewin

KYLE (Irish Gaelic) "handsome, from the strait"

Image: Kyle is described as a cute, baby-faced blond who is quiet, conceited, and self-centered.

Famous Kyles: football's Kyle Rote; novelist Kyle (*Falconhurst Fancy*) Onstott

LAMAR (Old German) "famous throughout the land"

Image: People think of Lamar as a good-looking black man who is either a nerdy mama's boy or a talented performer or athlete.

Famous Lamars: actress Hedy Lamarr; football's Lamar Hunt

LAMONT (Scandinavian) "lawyer"

Image: Lamont is pictured as a black man with two opposing images: a tall, handsome, suave, and debonair social climber or a lazy, bad-tempered bully.

Famous Lamonts: Lamont ("The Shadow") Cranston; the Lamont Cranston Band; TV's Lamont ("Sanford and Son") Sanford

LANCE (Old German) "land"

Image: Lance is described as a romance novel hero — a handsome, virile, rich, and dynamic playboy.

Famous Lances: actor Lance ("James at 16") Kerwin; football's Lance Rentzel, Lance Alworth; banker Bert Lance; TV's Lance ("Falcon Crest") Cumsen

LANE (Middle English) "from the narrow road"

Image: Most people think of Lane as a tall, dark, and handsome sophisticate who is a self-centered, trendy social climber. Some, though, think Lane is fat, friendly, and easygoing.

Famous Lanes: Teamsters head Lane Kirkland; football's Bobby Layne, Richard (Night Train) Lane; basketball's Jerome Lane

LANNY a short form of Orland, Roland

Image: The name Lanny has two very different images: a jolly, overweight guy with a superficial style or an introverted, lightweight guy with a nerdy whine.

Famous Lannys: golfer Lanny Wadkins; hockey's Lanny McDonald

LARRY a short form of Lawrence

Image: Most people think of Larry as easygoing and friendly — a barrel of laughs every time he goes bowling. Others think Larry is evil, like TV's business tycoon, J. R. Ewing.

Famous Larrys: actor Larry ("Dallas") Hagman; comic actors Larry ("F Troop") Storch, Larry ("The Three Stooges") Fine; harmonica player Larry

Adler; basketball's Larry Bird,
Larry Nance; boxer Larry
Holmes; football's Larry
Csonka; radio/TV host
Larry King

LARS a Scandinavian form of
Lawrence

Image: The name Lars calls to
mind a tall, robust, Scandinavian blond who might be
either a quiet farmer or an
aloof aristocrat.

Famous Lars: Phyllis's husband Lars on TV's "The Mary
Tyler Moore Show"

LAWRENCE, Laurence (Latin)
"from Laurentium, laurel-crowned"

Image: Lawrence is viewed as
a tall, thin, stately aristocrat
who is talented, social, and
proper and has great strength
of character, like Sir Laurence
Olivier and Lawrence of Arabia
all rolled up into one.

Famous Lawrences: the
movie *Lawrence of Arabia*;
actor Sir Laurence Olivier;
bandleader Lawrence Welk;
football's Lawrence Taylor;
novelists Laurence (*Tristram
Shandy*) Sterne, D. H. (*Lady
Chatterley's Lover*) Lawrence

LEE (Old English) "from the
meadow"

Image: The name Lee conjures
up two different images: a
strong, masculine, self-
confident cowboy or a quiet,
conservative sophisticate.

Famous Lees: actors Lee
("The Six Million Dollar Man")
Majors, Lee (*Gorky Park*)
Marvin; assassin Lee Harvey
Oswald; lawyer F. Lee Bailey;

General Robert E. Lee; Lee
jeans

LEIF (Old Norse) "beloved"

Image: Leif is described as a
tall, rugged Scandinavian with
blond hair, piercing blue eyes,
and a beard.

Famous Leifs: explorer Leif
Erickson; pop singer Leif
Garrett

LENNY a short form of Leonard

Image: Lenny is pictured in
several different ways: a big,
slow, clumsy simpleton, like the
character in John Steinbeck's
novel *Of Mice and Men*; a
sleazy, conniving weasel with
underworld connections; a
mischievous prankster with a
sense of humor; or a blue-
collar nerd, like the character
on TV's "Laverne and Shirley."

Famous Lennys: comic Lenny
Bruce; TV's Lenny ("Laverne
and Shirley") Kosnowski;
Lennie (*Of Mice and Men*)
Small; football's Lenny
Dawson, Lenny Moore;
basketball's Lenny Wilkens

LEO (Latin) "lion"; a short form
of Leander, Leonard, Leopold

Image: Most people think of
Leo as strong but gentle. He is
described as a fiery rebel who
expresses himself as an artist
or a peace marcher.

Famous Leos: thirteen popes
named Leo; author Leo (*Living,
Loving, and Learning*)
Buscaglia; guitarist Leo Kottke;
novelist Leo (*War and Peace*)
Tolstoy; baseball's Leo
Durocher; Leo the astrological
sign

LEON (French) "lion, lionlike"; a French form of Leo; a short form of Leonard, Napoleon

Image: Leon is often pictured as a big black man with a blue-collar job and a strong-willed, outgoing personality.

Famous Leons: boxer Leon Spinks; musicians Leon Redbone, Leon Russell

LEONARD (Old German) "bold lion"

Image: Most people think of Leonard as a strange, nerdy bookworm, but some see Leonard as an unintelligent, lower-class tough.

Famous Leonards: the movie *Leonard Part VI*; conductor Leonard Bernstein; actor/director Leonard ("Star Trek") Nimoy; the Lynyrd Skynyrd band; inventor/artist Leonardo da Vinci; boxer Sugar Ray Leonard; TV's Dr. Leonard ("Star Trek") McCoy

LEOPOLD (Old German) "bold for the people"

Image: People describe Leopold as a nerdy, bespectacled scholar or a sneaky, egotistical criminal.

Famous Leopolds: Belgian Kings Leopold I, II, III; conductor Leopold Stokowski; Leopold (*Ulysses*) Bloom; writer/naturalist Aldo Leopold

LEROY (Old French) "king"

Image: People describe Leroy as a black or Hispanic man who is unattractive but has a heart of gold.

Famous Leroys: Jim Croce's song "Leroy Brown"; Leroy in the movie *Fame*; football's Leroy Kelly; musician Leroy Van Dyke; baseball's Leroy (Satchel) Paige; auto racer Lee Roy Yarborough

LES a short form of Leslie, Lester

Image: Les is described as a short, athletic, bespectacled man who might be a sneaky car salesman or a crook.

Famous Leses: bandleader Les Brown; guitarist Les Paul; TV's Les ("WKRP in Cincinnati") Nessman

LESLIE (Scottish Gaelic) "from the gray fortress"

Image: Leslie is a unisex name with two different images: an intelligent older man who is quiet, serious, and snobby or a sweet, friendly sprite reminiscent of Leslie Caron.

Famous Leslies: actors Leslie (*Gone with the Wind*) Howard, Leslie (*Airplane*) Nielsen; novelist Leslie (*The Saint*) Charteris; conductor Leslie Fiedler; actress Leslie (*Gigi*) Caron; singer Lesley ("It's My Party") Gore

LESTER (Latin) "from the chosen camp"; (Old English) "from Leicester"

Image: Lester is pictured as an awkward, quiet man who is a real bookworm — a hard-working accountant, scientist, or computer geek, perhaps.

Famous Lesters: musician Lester Flatt; politician Lester B. Pearson; jazz musician Lester Young; football's Lester Hayes;

Lester, ventriloquist Willie Tyler's dummy; comedian Jerry Lester

LEVI (Hebrew) "joined in harmony"

Image: Like the jeans that bear this name, Levi is regarded as a rugged, down-to-earth, and masculine cowboy or westerner.

Famous Levis: the biblical Levi, Jacob and Leah's son; Levi Strauss jeans; Israel's Prime Minister Levi Eshkol; former vice president Levi Morton; singer Levi Stubbs of the Four Tops

LEWIS (Welsh) "lionlike"; a short form of Llewellyn (see also Louis)

Image: The name Lewis calls to mind a stocky, intelligent man who is thoughtful and shy.

Famous Lewises: children's story writer Lewis (*Alice's Adventures in Wonderland*) Carroll; novelist Sinclair (*Babbitt*) Lewis; former justice Lewis F. Powell; Louisiana Purchase explorer Meriwether Lewis; rock singer Huey Lewis

LINCOLN (Old English) "from the settlement by the pool"

Image: Lincoln is pictured as a tall, dark, distinguished, and stern leader who is scrupulously honest and fair, like President Lincoln.

Famous Lincolns: President Abraham Lincoln; North Pole explorer Lincoln Ellsworth; journalist Lincoln Steffens

LINUS (Greek) "flaxen-haired"

Image: People say Linus is a cute, sensitive little kid, like the "Peanuts" comics character, who will grow up to be an introverted scholar, like Linus Pauling.

Famous Linuses: Linus ("Peanuts") Van Pelt; the biblical Linus, Paul's companion; physicist Linus Pauling; Linus (*Sabrina*) Larrabee

LIONEL (Old French) "lion cub"

Image: Thanks to Lionel Richie, most people think of Lionel as a handsome, talented black man who is soft and caring. Some, though, see Lionel as a stern aristocrat.

Famous Lionels: actor Lionel (*It's a Wonderful Life*) Barrymore; singer Lionel ("All Night Long") Richie; jazzman Lionel Hampton; TV's Lionel ("The Jeffersons") Jefferson; Lionel trains; English poet Lionel Johnson

LLOYD (Welsh) "gray-haired"

Image: The name Lloyd calls to mind an old, upper-class professional who is smart, straitlaced, and stuffy — a financier or architect, perhaps.

Famous Lloyds: vice-presidential candidate Lloyd Bentsen; architect Frank Lloyd Wright; Lloyd's of London insurance company; actors Christopher (*Back to the Future*) Lloyd, Lloyd (*Airplane*) Bridges

LON a short form of Alonzo, Lawrence

Image: The name Lon has two very different images: a blue-collar country boy or a mysterious, foreboding foreigner reminiscent of a Lon Chaney character.

Famous Lon: actor Lon Chaney

LONNIE a short form of Alonzo, Lawrence

Image: The name Lonnie has three different images: a quiet, scrawny, effeminate kid; a popular, sexy party animal; or an ignorant rebel without a cause.

Famous Lonnies: actress Loni ("WKRP in Cincinnati") Anderson; baseball's Lonnie Smith

LORENZO a form of Lawrence

Image: The name Lorenzo calls to mind a tall, dark, and handsome European man who is charming, suave, and daring.

Famous Lorenzos: actor Lorenzo ("Falcon Crest") Lamas; Florentine statesman Lorenzo de Medici; lyricist Lorenz ("Blue Moon") Hart; Renaissance sculptor Lorenzo Ghiberti; Lorenzo Music, voice of TV's "Garfield the Cat"

LORNE a form of Lawrence

Image: Lorne's image comes straight from TV's "Bonanza" and actor Lorne Greene. Lorne is described as a big, broad-shouldered, outdoorsy, and dependable family man.

Famous Lornes: actor Lorne ("Bonanza") Greene; producer Lorne ("Saturday Night Live") Michaels

LOU a short form of Louis

Image: Lou is pictured as a big, husky, blue-collar man who is a hardworker and a friendly neighbor.

Famous Lous: baseball's Lou Brock, Lou Gehrig, Lou Piniella; comedian Lou Costello; strongman Lou ("The Incredible Hulk") Ferrigno; singer Lou Rawls; TV's "Lou Grant"; football coach Lou Little; football's Lou (The Toe) Groza

LOUIS (Old German) "renowned warrior" (see also Lewis)

Image: Most people picture Louis as a cute blond who is strong, playful, and good-natured. Some, though, see Louis as rich and snobby.

Famous Louises: many French kings named Louis; musician Louis Armstrong; chemist Louis Pasteur; naturalist Louis Agassiz; Louis Braille, teacher of the blind; boxer Joe Louis; architects Louis Skidmore, Louis Sullivan; actor Louis (*Gigi*) Jourdan; Western novelist Louis (*How the West Was Won*) L'Amour

LOWELL (Old French) "little wolf"

Image: Lowell is described as a thin, feminine-looking, older man who is quiet, old-fashioned, and distinguished.

Famous Lowells: journalist/announcer Lowell Thomas;

former senator Lowell Weicker; poets Amy Lowell, James Russell Lowell

LUCAS a Danish, Dutch, German, or Irish form of Lucius, Luke

Image: Lucas is pictured as a strong, handsome young man who is creative, determined, and mighty tough.

Famous Lucases: movie director George (*Star Wars*) Lucas; the movie *Lucas*; TV's Lucas ("The Rifleman") McCain; actor Lukas (*Witness*) Haas

LUDWIG a German form of Louis

Image: The name Ludwig has a "mad professor" image. Ludwig is described as a serious German scholar who is decidedly eccentric.

Famous Ludwigs: composer Ludwig van Beethoven; architect Ludwig Mies van der Rohe; philosopher Ludwig Wittgenstein; Ludwig, mad king of Bavaria

LUIS a Spanish form of Louis

Image: Most people imagine Luis as a swarthy, rotund Hispanic man who is an energetic, freewheeling adventurer.

Famous Luises: atomic physicist Luis Alvarez; director Luis Buñuel; baseball's Luis Aparicio; Luis on TV's "Sesame Street"

LUKE (Greek) "from Lucania"; a form of Lucius

Image: Luke is pictured as either strong, wiry, loyal, and

dumb or fun, friendly, and rowdy.

Famous Lukes: the biblical Luke, physician and New Testament writer; Luke (*Star Wars*) Skywalker; the movie *Cool Hand Luke*; TV's Luke ("The Dukes of Hazzard") Duke

LUTHER (Old German) "famous warrior"

Image: The name Luther is strongly associated with both Martin Luther and Dr. Martin Luther King, Jr. People describe Luther as a strong, energetic, outspoken, and deeply religious leader.

Famous Luthers: Protestant reformer Martin Luther; civil rights leader Dr. Martin Luther King, Jr.; horticulturalist Luther Burbank; Lex Luthor, Superman's foe

LYLE (Old French) "from the island"

Image: The name Lyle has two very different images: a tall, thin, rich, and well-educated wimp or a big, slow, hard-working, and kind-hearted guy.

Famous Lyles: football's Lyle Alzado; actor Lyle ("Wonder Woman") Waggoner; baseball's Sparky Lyle; musician Lyle Lovett

LYNDON (Old English) "from the linden tree hill"

Image: Lyndon Johnson is the dominant image for this name. Lyndon is pictured as a distinguished, older political leader who is polite but ruthless.

Famous Lyndons: President Lyndon Baines Johnson; political extremist Lyndon LaRouche; William Thackeray's novel *Barry Lyndon*

LYNN (Old English) "waterfall, pool below a fall"

Image: Lynn is a unisex name that calls to mind a tall, thin, confident, intelligent athlete, like wide-receiver Lynn Swann, who might be either sweet and friendly or bossy and abrasive.

Famous Lynns: football's Lynn Swann, Mike Lynn; auto executive Lynn Townshend; cartoonist Lynn ("For Better or For Worse") Johnston

MAC (Scottish Gaelic) "son of"; a short form of names beginning with "mac," "max," "mc"

Image: The name Mac calls to mind two very different images: a rigid, determined banker type or a rough but fun-loving truck driver.

Famous Macs: singer Mac Davis; director Mack Sennett; TV's Mac ("Knots Landing") McKenzie; Mack trucks; the song "Mack the Knife"

MALCOLM (Scottish Gaelic) "follower of Saint Columba

Image: Malcolm is pictured as a commanding figure who is either a well-bred, wealthy, distinguished business leader, like Malcolm Forbes, or a strong-willed rebel, like Malcolm X.

Famous Malcolms: magazine publisher Malcolm Forbes; the Black Muslims's Malcolm X; actors Malcolm (*A Clockwork Orange*) McDowell, Malcolm-Jamal ("The Cosby Show") Warner; Australia's Prime Minister Malcolm Fraser; former secretary of commerce Malcolm Baldridge; King Malcolm of Scotland

MANUEL a short form of Emmanuel

Image: Most people think of Manuel as a quiet and hard-working Hispanic man. Some, though, see Manuel as wild and irresponsible.

Famous Manuels: Panama's General Manuel Noriega; composer Manuel (*The Three-Cornered Hat*) de Falla; tennis's Manuel Orantes

MARC see Mark

MARCEL (Latin) "little and warlike"

Image: People see Marcel as a mustachioed Frenchman who is either an effeminate wimp or a good-looking womanizer.

Famous Marcels: mime Marcel Marceau; painter Marcel Duchamp; novelist Marcel Proust

MARCO a form of Mark

Image: Marco is described as a Hispanic or Italian man who is tall, dark, strong, and very masculine.

Famous Marcos: explorer Marco Polo; TV's Marco ("One Life to Live") Dane

MARCUS a form of Mark

Image: The name Marcus calls to mind either a big, strong, handsome athlete or a simple, boring businessman.

Famous Marcuses: football's Marcus Allen; Roman emperor Marcus Aurelius Antoninus; TV's "Marcus Welby, M.D."; black nationalist Marcus Garvey

MARIO an Italian form of Mark

Image: Mario is pictured as a dark, handsome Italian ladies' man who is romantic and fun.

Famous Marios: auto racer Mario Andretti; politician Mario Cuomo; opera singer Mario Lanza; novelist Mario (*The Godfather*) Puzo; hockey's Mario Lemieux; Nintendo's Mario Brothers

MARK, Marc (Latin) "warlike"

Image: Warlike? Hardly! People say Mark is an athletic, extremely good-looking guy, a fun-loving free spirit, and a sensitive friend.

Famous Marks: the biblical Mark, evangelist and Gospel writer; Roman general Marc Antony; actor Mark ("St. Elsewhere") Harmon; novelist/ humorist Mark Twain; painter Marc Chagall; General Mark Clark; hockey's Mark Messier; basketball's Mark Price; football's Mark Gastineau

MARLON, Marlin (Old French) "little falcon"

Image: Marlon is viewed as either a rugged, muscular, moody, intense tough guy or a blond, happy-go-lucky clown.

Famous Marlons: actor Marlon (*The Godfather*) Brando; TV naturalist Marlin ("Wild Kingdom") Perkins

MARSHALL (Old French) "steward, horse-keeper"

Image: Most people think of Marshall as a proud, masculine man who would be at home as either a western lawman or a wealthy professional. Some, though, think of Marshall as a quiet homebody.

Famous Marshalls: singer Marshall Crenshaw; actor E. G. ("The Defenders") Marshall; media theorist Marshall McLuhan; General George Marshall; the Marshall Tucker Band; Marshall Field's department stores

MARTIN (Latin) "warlike"

Image: The name Martin has two different images: an effeminate blond male cheerleader or a straitlaced, older businessman.

Famous Martins: actors Martin ("Kennedy") Sheen, Martin (*Innerspace*) Short, Martin ("Mission: Impossible") Landau, Martin ("Fernwood 2-Night") Mull; Protestant reformer Martin Luther; President Martin Van Buren; Saint Martin of Tours; aerospace company Martin-Marietta; theologian Martin (*I and Thou*) Buber; civil rights leader Dr. Martin Luther King, Jr.

MARTY a short form of Martin

Image: Most people say Marty is the life of the party — a small guy who is wild, crazy, and full of life. Some, though, say Marty is a messed-up, nerdy kid.

Famous Martys: comic actor Marty (*Young Frankenstein*) Feldman; country singer Marty ("A White Sport Coat") Robbins; cartoon producer Marty Krofft; Spin and Marty on TV's "The Mickey Mouse Club"; Marty (*Back to the Future*) McFly

MARVIN (Old English) "lover of the sea"

Image: Most people picture Marvin as a pleasant, middle-aged, skinny, bespectacled musician, like Marvin Hamlisch. Some, though, picture Marvin as a strong, nasty tough guy, like actor Lee Marvin.

Famous Marvins: actor Lee (*Cat Ballou*) Marvin; Motown singer Marvin ("I Heard It Through the Grapevine") Gaye; composer Marvin Hamlisch; lawyer Marvin Mitchelson; "Marvin" comics

MASON (Old French) "stoneworker"

Image: Mason is viewed as a hard-boiled, tight-lipped businessman or professional.

Famous Masons: child actors Mason Reese, James (*Lolita*) Mason; composer Mason Williams; TV's "Perry Mason"

MATT a short form of Matthew

Image: The name Matt calls to mind the rough and tough action/adventure movie hero Matt Helm. People say Matt would be at home on horseback or a motorcycle.

Famous Matts: actor Matt (*The Outsiders*) Dillon; TV's Marshal Matt ("Gunsmoke") Dillon; detective Matt Helm

MATTHEW (Hebrew) "gift of the Lord"

Image: The name Matthew has two distinct images: an outgoing young individualist who is cute, strong, and mischievous or a hardworking, reserved, traditional family man.

Famous Matthews: the biblical Matthew, disciple and Gospel writer; actors Matthew (*Ferris Bueller's Day Off*) Broderick, Matthew (*Birdy*) Modine; Commodore Matthew Perry; poets Matthew Prior, Matthew Arnold

MAURICE (Latin) "dark-skinned"

Image: People describe Maurice as either a wealthy, ambitious banker type or as a thin, talented Frenchman who might be an extravagant interior decorator or a ladies' man.

Famous Maurices: French entertainer Maurice (*Gigi*) Chevalier; singer Maurice Gibb of the Bee Gees; composer Maurice (*Bolero*) Ravel; painter Maurice Utrillo; children's book illustrator Maurice Sendak; the movie *Maurice*

MAX a short form of Maximilian, Maxwell

Image: The name Max has two very different images: a tough

184

guy who is intelligent, cocky, and strong or an older man who is easygoing, well liked, and loyal.

Famous Maxes: boxer Max Baer; jazz musician Max Roach; the movie *Mad Max*; Miracle Max in the movie *The Princess Bride*; painters Max Ernst, Max Parrish; physicist Max Planck; actor Max (*The Virgin Spring*) von Sydow; Coca-Cola's Max Headroom

MAXWELL (Old English) "from the influential man's well"

Image: Maxwell strikes most people as a name for either a wealthy, quiet, older gentleman or a bungling, overconfident detective, like TV's Maxwell Smart.

Famous Maxwells: actor Maxwell Caulfield; TV's Maxwell ("Get Smart") Smart, Maxwell Q. ("M*A*S*H") Klinger; dramatist Maxwell (*The Masque of Queens*) Anderson; General Maxwell Taylor; the Beatles' song "Maxwell's Silver Hammer"; editor Maxwell Perkins

MAYNARD (Old German) "powerful, brave"

Image: The name Maynard reminds people of TV's Dobie Gillis's buddy Maynard G. Krebs — an unkempt, awkward, bookish geek with big ears, a pocket protector, and a comic book collection.

Famous Maynards: TV's Maynard G. ("Dobie Gillis") Krebs; Mayor Maynard Jackson; jazz musician Maynard Ferguson

MEL a short form of Melvin

Image: Mel is described three different ways: a huge, bald, middle-aged, sarcastic tough guy, like Mel on TV's "Alice"; a tall, thin, attractive singer; or a charming, humorous artist.

Famous Mels: cartoon voice Mel ("Bugs Bunny") Blanc; actor Mel (*The Year of Living Dangerously*) Gibson; singers Mel Tillis, Mel Torme; Mel on TV's "Alice"; basketball's Mel Turpin; director Mel (*Young Frankenstein*) Brooks

MELVIN (Irish Gaelic) "polished chief"

Image: A polished chief? Not according to most people. Melvin is pictured as either a thin, shy, intelligent nerd or a heavy, friendly, hardworking farmhand or gardener.

Famous Melvins: lawyer Melvin Belli; former secretary of defense Melvin Laird; English novelist Melvyn (*Kingdom Come*) Bragg

MERLIN (Middle English) "falcon"

Image: Most people visualize Merlin as a tall, old, highly intelligent magician, like the wizard of Arthurian legend. Some, though, see Merlin as a big, dumb farmer.

Famous Merlins: Merlin of Arthurian legend; football's Merlin Olsen

MERV a short form of Mervin

Image: Most people imagine Merv as a sleazy, low-class guy with big bucks — a game show host, drug dealer, or car salesman, perhaps. Some, though, think of Merv as intelligent, sophisticated, and well read.

Famous Merv: TV host Merv Griffin

MERVIN, Mervyn forms of Marvin

Image: People picture Mervin as either a grumpy old man or a quiet, studious nerd.

Famous Mervins: director Mervyn (*Quo Vadis*) LeRoy; Mervyn's department stores

MICAH a Hebrew form of Michael

Image: The name Micah calls to mind the biblical prophet. Micah is thought to be a tall, strong Jewish man who is quiet, gentle, and highly religious.

Famous Micahs: the biblical Hebrew prophet Micah; Sheriff Micah ("The Rifleman") Torrance

MICHAEL (Hebrew) "who is like the Lord"

Image: Michael is described as a strong, handsome man who is both a smart, successful hardworker and an easygoing, lighthearted family man.

Famous Michaels: singer Michael ("Thriller") Jackson; actors Michael (*Educating Rita*) Caine, Michael J. ("Family Ties") Fox, Michael ("Little House on the Prairie") Landon, Sir Michael Redgrave; Massachusetts governor Michael Dukakis; Saint Michael

the Archangel; basketball's Michael (Air) Jordan

MICKEY a short form of Michael

Image: Mickey is a unisex name with a comical image that comes straight from Mickey Mouse. People say Mickey is a cute kid who is silly, lighthearted, and lots of fun.

Famous Mickeys: actors Mickey (*National Velvet*) Rooney, Mickey (*Diner*) Rourke; singer Mickey Dolenz of the Monkees; country singer Mickey Gilley; baseball's Mickey Mantle; mystery writer Mickey (*Mike Hammer*) Spillane; Walt Disney's Mickey Mouse

MIKE a short form of Michael

Image: Mike is pictured as a strong, masculine guy who is either friendly and easygoing or tough and bullying.

Famous Mikes: TV host Mike Douglas; TV reporter Mike Wallace; Massachusetts governor Mike Dukakis; TV detectives Mike Hammer, Mike Mannix; rock group Mike and the Mechanics

MILES (Latin) "soldier"; (Old German) "merciful"

Image: The name Miles has two images: a rich, smart, sexy, powerful man — an oil tycoon, explorer, or movie star, perhaps — or a plain, serious, straitlaced klutz.

Famous Mileses: jazz musician Miles Davis; Pilgrim Miles Standish; Miles (*The Maltese Falcon*) Archer

MILO a German form of Miles

Image: Most people picture Milo as a skinny, unpopular, and insecure nerd.

Famous Milos: the sculpture Venus de Milo; Milo in "Bloom County" comics; Milo in the movie *Escape from the Planet of the Apes*; Milo (*Catch-22*) Minderbender

MILTON (Old English) "from the mill town"

Image: The name Milton calls to mind either a skinny, timid bookworm or a funny, dumpy family man.

Famous Miltons: poet John (*Paradise Lost*) Milton; comedian Milton Berle; artist Milton Avery; economist Milton Friedman; the Milton-Bradley game company

MITCH a short form of Mitchell

Image: Mitch is described as a big, husky, freckled man who is either tough and aggressive or jovial and down-to-earth.

Famous Mitches: gymnast Mitch Gaylord; chorus leader Mitch Miller; singer Mitch Ryder; Senator Mitch McConnell; basketball's Mitch Richmond

MITCHELL a Middle English form of Michael

Image: Mitchell is pictured as a masculine, handsome, rich young man who is intelligent, thoughtful, and right at home in a Porsche.

Famous Mitchells: Watergate's John and Martha Mitchell; novelist Margaret (*Gone with the Wind*) Mitchell

MOHAMMED see Muhammad

MONTE, Monty (Latin) "mountain"; short forms of names containing "mont"

Image: Monty is described as a loud, corny, obnoxious, fast-talking comedian or insincere game show host.

Famous Montys: TV host Monty ("Let's Make a Deal") Hall; comic actor Monty Woolley; TV's "Monty Python's Flying Circus"; the city of Monte Carlo, Monaco; Alexandre Dumas's novel *The Count of Monte Cristo*

MONTGOMERY (Old English) "from the rich man's mountain"

Image: From the rich man's mountain, indeed! Montgomery is perceived as a sexy, wealthy aristocrat.

Famous Montgomerys: actor Montgomery Clift; actress Elizabeth ("Bewitched") Montgomery; British field marshal Bernard Montgomery

MONTY see Monte

MOREY, Morrie short forms of Maurice, Morris, Morse, Seymour

Image: People say Morey is either a short, funny man who enjoys life or a smart, ambitious hardworker.

Famous Morey: comic actor Morey ("The Dick Van Dyke Show") Amsterdam

MORGAN (Scottish Gaelic) "from the edge of the sea"

Image: This unisex name calls to mind a smart, successful, tough-minded businessman, like banker J. P. Morgan.

Famous Morgans: banker J. P. Morgan; actress Morgan Fairchild

MORRIE see Morey

MORRIS an English form of Maurice

Image: Most people picture Morris as an overweight, bespectacled lawyer. Some, though, see him as plump, lazy, funny, and very finicky like Morris the Nine Lives cat.

Famous Morrises: singer Morris ("Jungle Love") Day; TV's Morris the Nine Lives cat; former senator Morris Udall

MORT a short form of Mordecai, Mortimer

Image: Two main impressions of Mort emerge: an opinion- ated, obnoxious troublemaker, like Mort Downey, Jr., or a skinny, awkward dummy.

Famous Morts: cartoonist Mort ("Beetle Bailey") Walker; TV host Mort Downey, Jr.

MORTIMER (Old French) "still water"

Image: Mortimer is viewed as inept and strange, like "dum- my" Mortimer Snerd, or as a self-centered troublemaker.

Famous Mortimers: Edgar Bergen's dummy Mortimer Snerd; Walt Disney's Mortimer Mouse (later Mickey); philosopher Mortimer Adler; Mortimer (*Arsenic and Old Lace*) Brewster

MORTON (Old English) "from the town near the moor"

Image: People picture Morton as a mature older man who is strong and silent.

Famous Mortons: TV host Morton Downey, Jr.; orchestra leader Morton Gould; football's Morten Anderson; Morton salt

MOSES (Hebrew) "saved"

Image: Moses is a name with strong biblical associations. People describe Moses as a white-haired old ruler who is honest, righteous, and wise.

Famous Moseses: the biblical Moses, Hebrew leader and lawgiver; basketball's Moses Malone; painter Grandma Moses

MUHAMMAD, Mohammed (Arabic) "praised"

Image: People describe Muhammad as a strong black boxer who likes to boast, like Muhammad Ali. Some, though, describe Muhammad as a dark-skinned foreigner who is very religious.

Famous Muhammads: Mohammed, the founder of Islam; boxer Muhammad Ali; religious leader Elijah Muham- mad; Iran's Shah Mohammad Reza Pahlavi

MURRAY (Scottish Gaelic) "sailor"

Image: Murray is pictured as a big, slow man who is quiet, kind, and always there when you need him.

Famous Murrays: actors Bill (*Stripes*) Murray, F. Murray (*Amadeus*) Abraham; physicist Murray Gell-Mann; TV's Murray

("The Mary Tyler Moore Show")
Slaughter

MYRON (Greek) "fragrant
ointment"

Image: Myron is pictured as
a likable "superbrain" who will
probably become an
accountant.

Famous Myrons: comedian
Myron Cohen; musician Myron
("The Lawrence Welk Show")
Floren; actor Myron (*No Time
for Sergeants*) McCormick

NAPOLEON (Greek) "lion of the
woodland dell"; (Italian) "from
Naples"

Image: Thanks to Napolean
Bonaparte, people describe
Napolean as a short, handsome leader who is strong
willed, cunning, and arrogant.

Famous Napoleons: France's
Emperor Napoleon Bonaparte;
TV's Napoleon ("The Man from
U.N.C.L.E.") Solo; baseball's
Napoleon Lajoie

NAT a short form of Nathan,
Nathaniel

Image: Nat is pictured as a
big, musical man who is
friendly and dependable.

Famous Nats: singer Nat King
Cole; insurrectionist Nat
Turner; TV producer Nat
("Sergeant Bilko") Hiken; critic
Nat Hentoff

NATE a short form of Nathan,
Nathaniel

Image: Two different images of
Nate come to mind: a homely,
gawky hick or a cute athlete
who is neat, clean, and
precise.

Famous Nates: basketball's
Nate Thurmond, Nate
Archibald

NATHAN (Hebrew) "gift"; a short
form of Nathaniel

Image: Nathan is described as
either a quiet, capable, and
trustworthy man or a sneaky
gangster who wears a plaid
suit, like Nathan Detroit in the
musical *Guys and Dolls*.

Famous Nathans: the biblical
Nathan, Hebrew prophet;
Revolutionary hero Nathan
Hale; Confederate General
Nathan Forrest; Nathan (*Guys
and Dolls*) Detroit

NATHANIEL (Hebrew)
"gift of God"

Image: The name Nathaniel
has two very different images:
an outgoing, lighthearted
mischief-maker or a quiet,
conservative, dignified
man — a minister, perhaps.

Famous Nathaniels: the
biblical disciple Nathaniel
(Bartholomew); novelists
Nathaniel (*The Scarlet Letter*)
Hawthorne, Nathaniel (*Miss
Lonelyhearts*) West

NEAL see Neil

NED a short form of names
beginning with "Ed"

Image: People picture Ned as
a tall older man who is quiet,

hardworking, and highly intelligent.

Famous Neds: actors Ned (*Superman*) Beatty, Ned (*The Last of the Mohicans*) Romero; Ned (*Twenty Thousand Leagues under the Sea*) Land; Ned Nickerson, boyfriend of fictional detective Nancy Drew

NEIL, Neal (Irish Gaelic) "champion"

Image: Most people view Neil as a smart, talented man who is a high achiever with a good personality. Some, though, perceive Neil as spoiled and stubborn.

Famous Neils: astronaut Neil Armstrong; singers Neil ("Sweet Caroline") Diamond, Neil ("Breaking Up Is Hard to Do") Sedaka, Neil ("Heart of Gold") Young; playwright Neil (*Brighton Beach Memoirs*) Simon

NELSON (English) "son of Neil"

Image: The name Nelson calls to mind a prim, wimpy, bespectacled scholar or a successful man who is wealthy, intelligent, and classy.

Famous Nelsons: bandleader Nelson Riddle; singer Ricky ("Garden Party") Nelson; comedian Charles Nelson ("The Hollywood Squares") Reilly; singer/actor Nelson ("Indian Love Call") Eddy; South Africa's black leader Nelson Mandela; former vice president Nelson Rockefeller; British admiral Lord Nelson

NEVILLE (Old French) "from the new town"

Image: Most people picture Neville as an Englishman who is either a rich, suave sophisticate or a quiet, absent-minded professor.

Famous Nevilles: British statesman Neville Chamberlain; actor Neville ("Laredo") Brand; novelist Nevil (*On the Beach*) Shute; conductor Neville Marriner

NICHOLAS (Greek) "victory of the people"

Image: Thanks to Saint Nicholas, most people think of Nicholas as cute, fat, jolly, and generous. Some, though, think of Nicholas as a spoiled, tempermental devil.

Famous Nicholases: actor Nicholas (*Moonstruck*) Cage; Charles Dickens's novel *Nicholas Nickleby;* Saint Nicholas, the original Santa Claus; Russia's Czar Nicholas; astronomer Nicolaus Copernicus

NICK a short form of Nicholas

Image: Most people picture Nick as a strong, swarthy gangster. Some, though, see Nick as a clever, suave good guy, like Nick Charles.

Famous Nicks: actor Nick (*Cannery Row*) Nolte; Nick ("The Thin Man") Charles; Nick (*The Great Gatsby*) Carraway; football's Nick Buoniconti; TV's Nick ("Family Ties") Moore

NIGEL (Latin) "black"

Image: Nigel is described as a thin British intellectual who is capable, clever, and suave.

Famous Nigel: actor Nigel (Sherlock Holmes's sidekick, Dr. Watson) Bruce

NOAH (Hebrew) "wandering, rest"

Image: Noah is pictured as an old, bearded, homely man who is very courageous, like the biblical Noah.

Famous Noahs: the biblical ark-builder Noah; radio personality Noah Adams; lexicographer Noah Webster; actors Noah (*The Mark of Zorro*) Beery, Sr., Noah (*Sergeant York*) Beery, Jr.

NOEL (French) "the Nativity, born at Christmas"

Image: Noel is increasingly viewed as a unisex name. A boy with this name is seen as cheerful, bookish, and sophisticated, like playwright Noel Coward. The name also has a wimpy or effeminate connotation.

Famous Noel: playwright Sir Noel Coward

NOLAN, Noland (Irish Gaelic) "famous, noble"

Image: Most people describe Nolan as a handsome, strong athlete who is a fickle heartbreaker. Some, though, describe Nolan as a high-class stuffed shirt.

Famous Nolans: baseball's Nolan Ryan; actor Lloyd Nolan

NORBERT (Scandinavian) "brilliant hero"

Image: Norbert is pictured as an odd-looking, bespectacled, stuffy nerd.

Famous Norberts: cybernetics expert Norbert Wiener; Saint Norbert

NORMAN (Old French) "Norseman"

Image: Most people imagine Norman as a big, fat nerd who is quiet and smart. Some, though, see Norman as a masculine, powerful leader.

Famous Normans: actor Norman ("Three's Company") Fell; novelist Norman (*The Naked and the Dead*) Mailer; religious leader Norman Vincent Peale; artist Norman Rockwell; Norman (*Psycho*) Bates; football's Norm Van Brocklin; TV producer Norman ("All in the Family") Lear

OGDEN (Old English) "from the oak valley or hill"

Image: Ogden strikes people as an appropriate name for an upper-class Englishman who is quiet, boring, and snobby; or a dry, literary wit, like poet Ogden Nash.

Famous Ogdens: poet Ogden Nash; actor David Ogden ("M*A*S*H") Stiers; the city of Ogden, Utah

191

OLAF, Olav (Scandinavian) "ancestral talisman"

> **Image:** Olaf is described as a large, blond Scandinavian who is not very bright.
>
> **Famous Olafs:** several Norwegian kings named Olaf

OLIVER (Latin) "olive tree"; (Scandinavian) "kind, affectionate"

> **Image:** The name Oliver calls to mind several different images: a dirty, carefree, and mischievous boy, like Oliver Twist; a curious, perceptive bookworm; a loving, devoted man; or a silly, funny comic, like Oliver Hardy.
>
> **Famous Olivers:** the musical *Oliver;* Charles Dickens's novel *Oliver Twist;* actors Oliver Reed, Oliver Hardy; Lieutenant Colonel Oliver North; director Oliver (*Platoon*) Stone; jurist Oliver Wendell Holmes; TV's Oliver Wendell ("Green Acres") Douglas

OMAR (Arabic) "first son, highest, follower of the Prophet"

> **Image:** The name Omar has two images: an elderly Arab leader who is wealthy, obese, and lethargic or a dark, handsome actor who is suave and romantic, like Omar Sharif.
>
> **Famous Omars:** actor Omar (*Doctor Zhivago*) Sharif; Edward Fitzgerald's poem *The Rubáiyát of Omar Khayyám*

ORLANDO (Old English) "from the pointed land"

> **Image:** Orlando is described as a dark, attractive Hispanic man who is flashy or even tasteless.
>
> **Famous Orlandos:** baseball's Orlando Cepeda; Ariosto's epic poem *Orlando Furioso*; Orlando in Shakespeare's play *As You Like It;* the city of Orlando, Florida; singer Tony Orlando

ORSON (Latin) "bearlike"

> **Image:** Two different images of Orson come to mind: a fat, deep-voiced, creative genius, like Orson Welles, or a funny, happy guy.
>
> **Famous Orsons:** comedian Orson ("I've Got a Secret") Bean; actor/director Orson (*Citizen Kane*) Welles

ORVILLE (Old French) "from the golden estate"

> **Image:** Most people think of Orville as a down-home, fun-loving country boy who just stepped off the farm. Some, though, see Orville as a frail, old-fashioned nerd.
>
> **Famous Orvilles:** popcorn magnate Orville Redenbacher; aviator Orville Wright; former secretary of agriculture Orville Freeman

OSCAR (Scandinavian) "divine spearman"

> **Image:** People imagine Oscar as either a funny, lazy, carefree slob or a nasty, stubborn grouch.
>
> **Famous Oscars:** TV's Oscar ("The Odd Couple") Madison; Oscar the Grouch on TV's "Sesame Street"; novelist/playwright Oscar (*The Importance of Being Earnest*) Wilde; Oscar

Mayer meats; designer Oscar de la Renta; pianist Oscar Peterson; Oscar, the Academy Awards statuette; actor Oskar (*Jules and Jim*) Werner; pianist/comedian Oscar Levant; basketball's Oscar Robertson

OSWALD (Old English) "having power from God"

Image: Lee Harvey Oswald, President Kennedy's assassin, gave Oswald a bad name. People say Oswald is a sneaky, deceitful, and deranged killer.

Famous Oswalds: assassin Lee Harvey Oswald; Oswald the Rabbit, Walt Disney's first cartoon character; historian Oswald (*The Decline of the West*) Spengler

OTIS (Old English) "son of Otto"; (Greek) "keen of hearing"

Image: Otis is described as a black man who is either energetic, friendly, and fun or fat, clumsy, and wimpy.

Famous Otises: singers Otis Day, Otis ("Sitting on the Dock of the Bay") Redding; Otis elevators; Otis B. (*A Night at the Opera*) Driftwood; football's Ottis Anderson; basketball's Otis Smith; Otis the town drunk on TV's "The Andy Griffith Show"

OTTO (Old German) "rich"

Image: Otto is pictured as a traditional, rich German who is stiff, stern, and rather strange.

Famous Ottos: director Otto (*Exodus*) Preminger; German conductor Otto Klemperer; librettist/songwriter Otto Harbach; Roman emperor Otto I; German Prince Otto von Bismarck; Otto the dog in "Beetle Bailey" comics

OWEN a form of Evan

Image: Owen is pictured as a tall, gray-haired, attractive sophisticate who is either friendly and dependable or phony and snobbish.

Famous Owens: TV's "Owen Marshall, Counselor at Law"; physicists Sir Owen Richardson, Owen Chamberlain; novelist Owen (*The Virginian*) Wister; Owen in the movie *Throw Momma from the Train*; radio host Owen Spann

OZZIE a short form of names beginning with "Os"

Image: Ozzie's image comes straight from "Ozzie and Harriet." People picture Ozzie as a friendly, middle-class family man who is bumbling and lots of fun.

Famous Ozzies: actor Ozzie ("The Adventures of Ozzie and Harriet") Nelson; singer Ozzy Osborne; baseball's Ozzie Smith; football's Ozzie Newsome; actor Ossie Davis

PABLO a Spanish form of Paul

Image: Thanks to Pablo Picasso and Pablo Casals, people describe Pablo as a creative, talented, and intellectual artist.

Famous Pablos: cellist Pablo Casals; painter Pablo (*Guernica*) Picasso; poet Pablo Neruda

PADDY an Irish short form of Patrick

Image: People picture Paddy as a chubby, outgoing Irishman who can sing and tell stories until the bar closes.

Famous Paddys: writer Paddy (*Network*) Chayefsky; Paddy (*The Thorn Birds*) Cleary

PARKER (Middle English) "guardian of the park"

Image: Most people say Parker is a distinguished businessman who is clean-cut, conservative, and calm. Some, though, think Parker is an outrageous, unpredictable California boy.

Famous Parkers: actors Parker ("The Hardy Boys") Stevenson, Fess ("Davy Crockett") Parker; "Judge Parker" comics; Parker Brothers' pens; Agatha Christie's detective Parker Pyne; Peter ("Spiderman") Parker

PAT a short form of names containing "pat"

Image: Pat is described as an ordinary man who is funny, talkative, and outgoing.

Famous Pats: singer Pat Boone; comedian/vintner Pat Paulsen; First Lady Pat Nixon; cartoonist Pat Oliphant; TV host Pat ("Wheel of Fortune") Sajak; hockey's Pat La Fontaine

PATRICK (Latin) "nobleman"

Image: People picture Patrick as an athletic Irishman who is happy, popular, and sensitive.

Famous Patricks: Saint Patrick, patron saint of Ireland; actors Patrick ("Dallas") Duffy, Patrick (*Dirty Dancing*) Swayze, Patrick ("The Prisoner") McGoohan; patriot Patrick Henry; basketball's Patrick Ewing

PAUL (Latin) "small"

Image: Most people think of Paul as dignified, steady, and firm, but others think he is charismatic, creative, and kind.

Famous Pauls: the biblical Apostle Paul; Pope John Paul II; Revolutionary war hero Paul Revere; singers Paul ("Having My Baby") Anka, former Beatle Paul ("Yesterday") McCartney, Paul ("Bridge Over Troubled Water") Simon, Paul Stookey of Peter, Paul, and Mary; French painter Paul Cezanne; composer Paul Williams; actors Paul (*The Hustler*) Newman, Paul (*Crocodile Dundee*) Hogan; comic actor Paul ("Bewitched") Lynde

PEDRO a Spanish form of Peter

Image: People picture Pedro as a poor dark Hispanic man who is simple, religious, and hardworking.

Famous Pedros: Spanish soldier Pedro de Alvarado; Brazil's Emperors Pedro I, II; Chile's conqueror Pedro de Valdivia

PERCIVAL (Old French) "pierce-the-valley"

Image: Percival is described as a stuffy, prim, snobby, and proper British highbrow.

Famous Percivals: Sir Percival of Arthurian legend; astronomer Percival Lowell; novelist Percival C. (*Beau Geste*) Wren

PERCY (French) "from Percy"; a short form of Percival

Image: Thanks to Percy Blakeney, the Scarlet Pimpernel, Percy is pictured as a prim-and-proper man (black or British) who is rich, fussy, and secretive.

Famous Percys: musician Percy Faith; millionaire columnist Percy Ross; poet Percy Bysshe Shelley; novelist Walker (*The Moviegoer*) Percy; Sir Percy (*The Scarlet Pimpernel*) Blakeney; Ernie Kovacs's character "Percy Dovetonsils"; singer Percy ("When a Man Loves a Woman") Sledge

PERRY (Middle English) "pear tree"; (Old French) "little Peter"

Image: Thanks to Perry Mason, Perry is viewed as an adept, well-dressed attorney who is smart, inquisitive, and refined. Out of the courtroom, Perry is pictured as a quiet, laid-back family man.

Famous Perrys: TV's "Perry Mason"; singer Perry Como; designer Perry Ellis; Commodore Matthew Perry; TV's Perry ("The Adventures of Superman") White

PETER (Greek) "rock"

Image: Most people describe Peter as unpretentious, honest, and open. Some, though, think Peter is ambitious and compulsive.

Famous Peters: the biblical disciple Peter; actors Peter ("Columbo") Falk, Peter (*Easy Rider*) Fonda, Peter (*Oceans Eleven*) Lawford, Peter (*Lawrence of Arabia*) O'Toole, Peter (*The Pink Panther*) Sellers, Peter (*The Maltese Falcon*) Lorre; singers Peter Yarrow of Peter, Paul, and Mary, Peter Frampton; rock musician Peter Spero; basketball's Pete Maravich, Pete Anderson; children's story hero Peter Pan; comic book hero Peter ("Spiderman") Parker; the nursery rhymes "Peter, Peter Pumpkin Eater," "Peter Piper"

PHIL a short form of Filbert, Filmore, Philip

Image: Phil is pictured as an ordinary guy, who is easygoing, likable, and honest.

Famous Phils: TV host Phil Donahue; comic actor Phil Silvers; baseball's Phil Rizzuto, Phil Niekro; record producer Phil Spector; skier Phil Mahre;

singer Phil ("Against All Odds") Collins; hockey's Phil Esposito, Phil Housely

PHILIP, Phillip (Greek) "lover of horses"

Image: The name Philip has several different images: a dashing military man; a stuck-up prince; a wealthy business-man; or a brainy introvert.

Famous Philips: the biblical disciple Philip; Britain's Prince Phillip; several French and Spanish kings named Philip; detective Philip Marlowe; novelist Philip (*Goodbye, Columbus*) Roth

PHILLIPE a form of Philip

Image: People think Phillipe is a wealthy, dark-haired French-man who is either a gentle, loving romantic or a sly and daring playboy.

Famous Phillipe: the Phillipe Pattels watch

PHINEAS (Hebrew) "oracle"

Image: Thanks to Phineas T. Barnum, people picture Phineas as an unconventional showman and entrepreneur.

Famous Phineases: circus promoter Phineas T. Barnum; TV's Mayor Phineas T. ("The Howdy Doody Show") Bluster, Phineas J. ("Tennessee Tuxedo") Whoopee; Phineas (*Around the World in Eighty Days*) Fogg

PIERRE a French form of Peter

Image: Pierre is described as a dark Frenchman who is romantic, charming, suave,

and flamboyant — perhaps effeminate. Pierre is also a popular name for a poodle.

Famous Pierres: designer Pierre Cardin; former press secretary Pierre Salinger; Canada's former prime minister Pierre Trudeau; chemist Pierre Curie; conductor Pierre Boulez; hockey's Pierre Turgeon, Pierre Pilote; French folk hero "Lucky Pierre"

PRESCOTT (Old English) "from the priest's cottage"

Image: People think of Prescott as a wealthy, sophisticated, and snobby banker.

Famous Prescotts: historian William Prescott; former senator Prescott Bush; the city of Prescott, Arizona

QUENTIN (Latin) "fifth, fifth child"

Image: Quentin is pictured as a wealthy, upper-class sophis-ticate who is strange and mysterious.

Famous Quentins: basketball's Quentin Dailey; San Quentin prison; actor/writer Quentin (*How to Become a Virgin*) Crisp; Sir Walter Scott's novel *Quentin Durward*; senator Quentin Burdick; Quentin on TV's "Dark Shadows"

QUINCY (Old French) "from the fifth son's estate"

Image: Quincy is described as either an intelligent detective or a distinguished black musician, like Quincy Jones.

Famous Quincys: jazz musician Quincy Jones; President John Quincy Adams; TV's "Quincy"; Professor Quincey Adams (*Horsefeathers*) Wagstaff

RALPH (Old English) "wolf-counselor"

Image: People picture Ralph as a short, easygoing, working-class guy who spends more time drinking than thinking.

Famous Ralphs: poet Ralph Waldo Emerson; TV's Ralph ("The Honeymooners") Kramden; the Reverend Dr. Ralph David Abernathy; early comedy *Ralph Roister Doister*; baseball's Ralph Branca, Ralph Kiner; consumer advocate Ralph Nader

RÁMON a Spanish form of Raymond

Image: Rámon is described as a dark, handsome ladies' man who is smart and disciplined but may be operating on the wrong side of the law.

Famous Rámons: actors Rámon (Martin Sheen) Estevez; actor Rámon (the first *Ben-Hur*)

Novarro; baseball's Rámon Martinez

RAMSEY (Old English) "from the ram's island, from the raven's island"

Image: Ramsey is described as an older gentleman who is funny, sexy, and unconventional.

Famous Ramseys: public official Ramsey Clark; jazz pianist Ramsey Lewis; British statesman Ramsey MacDonald

RANDALL a form of Randolph

Image: Most people think of Randall as an effeminate mama's boy who is nice but boring.

Famous Randalls: poet Randall Jarrell; actor Tony ("The Odd Couple") Randall

RANDOLPH (Old English) "shield-wolf"

Image: The name Randolph calls to mind a rich sophisticate who is strong, handsome, and stuffy.

Famous Randolphs: actor Randolph Scott; newspaper publisher William Randolph Hearst; Randolph Churchill, father of Winston Churchill

RANDY a short form of Randall, Randolph

Image: Randy is pictured as a tall, thin, likable guy who is either a quiet, intelligent hard-worker or an athletic, fun-loving country boy with a great sense of humor.

Famous Randys: Randy Bush, President Bush's son; singer Randy ("Short People")

Newman; country singers Randy Scruggs, Randy Travis; basketball's Randy Breuer; football's Randy White

RAY (Old French) "kingly, king's title"; a short form of names beginning with "Ray"

Image: People think of Ray as a short dark-haired man who is strong and hardworking — a logger or cowboy, perhaps.

Famous Rays: dancer/actor Ray (*The Wizard of Oz*) Bolger; singer Ray ("Georgia") Charles; bandleader Ray Coniff; TV's Ray ("Dallas") Krebs; boxer Sugar Ray Leonard; actor Ray (*Dial M for Murder*) Milland; novelist Ray (*Fahrenheit 451*) Bradbury

RAYMOND (Old English) "mighty or wise protector"

Image: Mighty or wise protector, indeed! Thanks to Raymond Burr, most people picture Raymond as a big, heavy older man who is intelligent, nice, and as steady as a rock.

Famous Raymonds: actors Raymond ("Perry Mason") Burr, Raymond Massey; mystery writer Raymond (*The Big Sleep*) Chandler; writer/poet Raymond Carver

REED (Old English) "red-haired"

Image: Reed strikes many people as a good name for a preppy, rich, and self-confident snob who is almost plastic.

Famous Reeds: surgeon Walter Reed; business executive Thomas Reed; musician Jerry Reed; actor Robert ("The Brady Bunch") Reed; hockey's Reed Larson; basketball's Willis Reed; film critic Rex Reed

REGGIE a short form of Reginald

Image: Thanks to Reggie Jackson, Reggie is pictured as an arrogant, conceited, athletic smart aleck. And, thanks to Archie's comic strip pal, Reggie is also pictured as a rich, snooty snob with slicked-down black hair and a turned-up nose.

Famous Reggies: baseball's Reggie Jackson; Reggie in "Archie" comics; football's Reggie Rucker; basketball's Reggie Miller

REGINALD (Old English) "powerful and mighty"

Image: Reginald Van Gleason seems to have captured the spirit of this name as a snooty British blue blood and elegant fop.

Famous Reginalds: TV's "The Fall and Rise of Reginald Perrin"; painter Reginald Marsh; playwright Reginald ("Studio One") Rose; Jackie Gleason's character Reginald Van Gleason III

REMINGTON (Old English) "from the raven estate"

Image: Remington is described as a tall, dark, and handsome British man who is either a rich, distinguished, and boring sculptor or a dashing, sexy detective.

Famous Remingtons: TV's "Remington Steele"; painter/sculptor Frederic Remington; the Remington rifle

RENÉ (French) "reborn"; a French short form of Reginald (through Renault)

    Image: People think of René as a cute, sweet, redheaded French homosexual.

    Famous Renés: philosopher René Descartes; painter René Magritte; bacteriologist René Jules Dubois

REUBEN (Hebrew) "behold, a son"

    Image: Most people picture Reuben as a quiet, old Jewish intellectual who is likely to be a loner.

    Famous Reubens: the biblical Reuben, son of Jacob; boxer Rubin (Hurricane) Carter; Reuben sandwiches; football's Reuben Mays; Flemish painter Peter Paul Rubens; the songs "Reuben, Reuben, I've Been Thinking," and "Reuben James"; Panamanian singer Ruben Blades

REX (Latin) "king"

    Image: Thanks to Rex Harrison's portrayal of Professor Henry Higgins, Rex is pictured as a strong, regal man who is nice in his own way, but quite abrupt. Some, though, see Rex as a tough loner — a pilot or thief, perhaps. Rex is also a popular name for a dog.

    Famous Rexes: actor Rex (*My Fair Lady*) Harrison; film critic Rex Reed; Sophocles's play *Oedipus Rex*; mystery writer Rex Stout; country singer Rex Allen

RHETT (Welsh) "enthusiastic"; a Welsh form of Reese

    Image: Rhett's image comes straight from Rhett Butler. Rhett is described as a big, handsome, old-fashioned southern man with an eye for the ladies and a mind of his own.

    Famous Rhetts: Rhett (*Gone with the Wind*) Butler; football's Rhett Dawson

RICARDO a form of Richard

    Image: Ricardo is described as a tall, dark, handsome Cuban man who has a distinguished appearance and a confident, kind manner.

    Famous Ricardos: actor Ricardo ("Fantasy Island") Montalban; TV's Ricky ("I Love Lucy") Ricardo; conductor Riccardo Muti

RICH a short form of Richard

    Image: The name Rich calls to mind a good-looking, dark-haired, clean-cut all-American boy who is levelheaded and sure of himself.

    Famous Riches: comedians Rich Little, Rich Hall; drummer Buddy Rich; baseball's Rich Allen; TV's "Richie Rich" cartoons; singer Lionel Richie; TV's Richie ("Happy Days") Cunningham

RICHARD (Old German) "powerful ruler"

    Image: The name Richard has two images: a handsome, strong, and athletic all-American boy or an honest, serious, and dedicated corporate man.

Famous Richards: actors Richard (*Who's Afraid of Virginia Woolf?*) Burton, Richard (*Shogun*) Chamberlain, Richard (*Jaws*) Dreyfuss, Richard (*Goodbye, Columbus*) Benjamin, Richard (*An Officer and a Gentleman*) Gere; President Richard Nixon; composer Richard (*Oklahoma*) Rodgers; English Kings Richard I-III

RICK a short form of Richard

Image: Thanks to Rick Nelson, Rick is pictured as a tall, dark, handsome, and athletic singer who likes to have fun. Some also picture Rick as a loyal friend reminiscent of Rick Blaine in the movie *Casablanca.*

Famous Ricks: singer Rick ("Hello Mary Lou") Nelson; actors Rick (*Honey, I Shrunk the Kids*) Moranis, Ricky Schroeder; Rick (*Casablanca*) Blaine; pop singer Rick Springfield; TV's Ricky ("I Love Lucy") Ricardo; basketball's Rick Barry, Rick Mahorn

RICO a form of Richard

Image: People say Rico is an ignorant, macho high-school drop-out who likes gang warfare and girl chasing.

Famous Ricos: baseball's Rico Carty; TV's Rico ("Miami Vice") Tubbs; Rico in the movie *Little Caesar*

RINGO (Old English) "ring"; a form of Ring

Image: Ringo is described as a thin, unkempt, creative musician with a crazy look in his eye, like Ringo Starr.

Famous Ringos: former Beatle Ringo Starr; the song "Johnny Ringo"

ROB a short form of Robert

Image: Rob is pictured as one heck of a nice guy — chubby, good-natured, and very friendly.

Famous Robs: Rob Roy, Scotland's Robin Hood; actor Rob (*About Last Night*) Lowe; comic actor/director Rob (*The Princess Bride*) Reiner; TV's Rob ("The Dick Van Dyke Show") Petrie

ROBERT (Old English) "bright fame"

Image: The name Robert has two different images: a good-looking, strong athlete who is funny and outgoing or a stocky, average man who is quiet and conservative.

Famous Roberts: actors Robert (*Butch Cassidy and the Sundance Kid*) Redford, Robert ("It Takes a Thief") Wagner, Robert (*The Music Man*) Preston, Robert (*The Big Sleep*) Mitchum, Robert ("Marcus Welby, M.D.") Young, Robert ("The Wild, Wild West") Conrad, Robert (*Ivanhoe*) Taylor, Robert ("Spenser: For Hire") Urich; former senator Robert F. Kennedy; poet Robert ("Stopping by Woods on a Snowy Evening") Frost; King Robert the Bruce of Scotland

ROBIN a form of Robert; a short form of Robinson

Image: The name Robin has two different images: a quiet, studious hardworker or an energetic, outgoing comedian, like Robin Williams.

Famous Robins: Robin Hood of English legend; Robin, Batman's sidekick; comic actor Robin (*Good Morning, Vietnam*) Williams; singer Robin Gibb of the Bee Gees; TV host Robin ("Lifestyles of the Rich and Famous") Leach

ROCHESTER (Old English) "from the stone camp"

Image: The name Rochester calls to mind a stuffy rich man or an older black man who is very funny, like Jack Benny's butler Rochester.

Famous Rochesters: Rochester, Jack Benny's butler; the cities of Rochester, New York, and Rochester, Minnesota; Edward (*Jane Eyre*) Rochester

ROCK (Old English) "from the rock" a short form of Rochester, Rockwell

Image: Rock is described as all brawn and no brains — a big, muscular athlete who is tough, bullheaded, and as solid as a rock.

Famous Rock: actor Rock (*Giant*) Hudson

ROCKY a short form of Rochester, Rockwell

Image: Rocky's image comes straight from the movies — a tough, muscle-bound man who prefers fighting over thinking.

Famous Rockys: Rocky (*Rocky*) Balboa; boxers Rocky Marciano, Rocky Graciano;

Rocky the flying squirrel on TV's "The Bullwinkle Show"; the Beatles' song "Rocky Raccoon"; the movie *The Rocky Horror Picture Show*; Rocky in the movie *Mask*

ROD a short form of names beginning with "Rod"

Image: Rod is pictured as a tall, handsome man who is either athletic and popular or strange and mysterious, like Rod Serling on the TV's "The Twilight Zone."

Famous Rods: singer Rod ("Maggie May") Stewart; TV science fiction writer/host Rod ("The Twilight Zone") Serling; actors Rod (*The Birds*) Taylor, Rod (*On the Waterfront*) Steiger; tennis's Rod Laver; basketball's (Hot) Rod Hundley

RODERICK (Old German) "famous ruler"

Image: Roderick is imagined as a handsome, wealthy British man who is intelligent and stuffy.

Famous Rodericks: Roderick (*The Fall of the House of Usher*) Usher; Henry James's novel *Roderick Hudson*

RODNEY (Old English) "from the island clearing"

Image: People think of Rodney as a heavy guy who is friendly, carefree, and very funny, like Rodney Dangerfield.

Famous Rodneys: comic actors Rodney (*Back to School*) Dangerfield, Rodney Allen Rippy

ROGER (Old German) "famous spearman"

Image: Roger is viewed as a good-looking man who is friendly, likable, and lots of fun.

Famous Rogers: newscasters Roger Chaffee, Roger Mudd; baseball's Roger Maris; singer Roger ("King of the Road") Miller; actor Roger ("James Bond") Moore

ROLAND (Old German) "from the famous land"

Image: Most people think of Roland as a bearded, overweight man who is an easygoing, fun sports car driver — a popular professor or writer, perhaps.

Famous Rolands: the medieval epic *Song of Roland*; Canada's Governor General Roland Michener; actor Gilbert (*Captain Kidd*) Roland; French writer Romain Rolland

ROLF (Old German) "famous wolf"; a German form of Ralph; a short form of Rudolph

Image: Rolf is pictured as a German man who is either rigid, rough, and hardheaded or soft-spoken, warm, and goofy. Some people also think Rolf is a good name for a dog.

Famous Rolfs: John Rolfe, Pocahontas's husband; Rolf in the movie *The Sound of Music*; Rowlf the muppet dog

ROMAN (Latin) "from Rome"

Image: People think of Roman as a handsome, sexy Italian man who is strong, reliable, and romantic.

Famous Romans: football's Roman Gabriel; director Roman (*Chinatown*) Polanski; TV's Roman ("Days of Our Lives") Brady

ROMEO (Italian) "pilgrim to Rome"

Image: Thanks to the famous star-crossed lovers, people picture Romeo as a handsome Italian lover who is terribly romantic.

Famous Romeos: Shakespeare's play *Romeo and Juliet*; Alfa Romeo automobiles

RON a short form of Ronald, Aaron

Image: Ron is described as a short, heavy, and average man who is easygoing, trustworthy, hardworking, and nice.

Famous Rons: actor/director Ron ("Happy Days") Howard; baseball's Ron Santo, Ron Guidry; hockey's Ron Francis

RONALD a Scottish form of Reginald

Image: The name Ronald has several images: trustworthy, open-minded, and fair; old-fashioned, formal, stuffy, and strong-willed; or bumbling, forgetful, and dumb.

Famous Ronalds: President Ronald Reagan; clown Ronald McDonald; actor Ronald (*Lost Horizon*) Colman

RONNIE a short form of Ronald

Image: Ronnie is a unisex name that calls to mind a little boy who is either good-natured and fun or whiny and wimpy.

Famous Ronnies: country singer Ronnie Milsap; singer Ronnie Spector of the Ronettes; football's Ronnie Lott; actor Ronny (*Robocop*) Cox

ROOSEVELT (Old Dutch) "from the rose field"

Image: Roosevelt's image comes from the presidents of the same name. Roosevelt is desribed as a distinguished leader who is rich, powerful, and strong willed. The name is also associated with powerful black football players.

Famous Roosevelts: Presidents Franklin D. Roosevelt, Theodore Roosevelt; football's Roosevelt Grier, Roosevelt Brown; TV's Roosevelt ("Sesame Street") Franklin

RORY (Irish Gaelic) "red king"; an Irish form of Roderick

Image: People think of Rory as a cute, dark, stocky guy who is happy and adventurous.

Famous Rorys: actor Rory Calhoun; Irish rebel chief Rory O'Moore

ROSCOE (Scandinavian) "from the deer forest"

Image: Roscoe is pictured as either a heavy, strong, dim-witted, and funny hillbilly or as a quiet, clean-cut preppy, like tennis star Roscoe Tanner.

Famous Roscoes: actor Roscoe Lee Brown; tennis's Roscoe Tanner; TV's Roscoe P. ("The Dukes of Hazzard") Coltrane

ROSS (Old French) "red"; (Scottish Gaelic) "headland"; a short form of Roscoe

Image: Most people picture Ross as a prototypical nice guy — tall, handsome, friendly, easygoing, sensitive, and caring.

Famous Rosses: TV's Ross ("All My Children") Chandler; novelist Ross MacDonald

ROY (Old French) "king"; a short form of Royal, Royce

Image: Roy is described as a big country boy who is an entertaining, compassionate cowboy, like Roy Rogers.

Famous Roys: singing cowboy Roy Rogers; singers Roy ("Only the Lonely") Orbison, Roy Acuff; baseball's Roy Smalley, Roy Campanella; boxer Roy Harris; artist Roy Lichtenstein; hockey's Patrick Roy

RUDOLPH (Old German) "famous wolf"

Image: Most people think of Rudolph as an Italian lover who is dramatic, romantic, and suave. To some, though, Rudolph is helpful, quiet, and restrained.

Famous Rudolphs: dancer Rudolf Nureyev; actor Rudolph (*The Sheik*) Valentino; the song "Rudolph the Red-Nosed Reindeer"; Nazi leader Rudolf Hess; engineer Rudolf Diesel; Rudolf, crown prince of Austria

RUDY a short form of names beginning with "Rud"

Image: Most people picture Rudy as a round, red-faced kid who is happy and lots of fun.

Famous Rudys: designer Rudi (topless bathing suit) Gernreich; singer Rudy Vallee; Rudy (*Rich Man, Poor Man*) Jordache; former senator Rudy Boschwitz; Minnesota's former governor Rudy Perpich; TV's Rudy ("The Cosby Show") Huxtable

RUFUS (Latin) "red-haired"

Image: People think of Rufus as a tempermental grouch who is a wild and crazy oddball.

Famous Rufuses: politician Rufus King; Revolutionary general Rufus Putnam; musician Rufus of Chaka Khan and Rufus; Rufus T. (*Duck Soup*) Firefly

RUPERT an Italian and Spanish form of Robert

Image: Rupert is thought of as a rich, stuffy tycoon, like Rupert Murdoch, or a sensitive poet, like Rupert Brooke.

Famous Ruperts: media tycoon Rupert Murdoch; Bavaria's Prince Rupert; poet Rupert Brooke; singer Rupert ("The Piña Colada Song") Holmes

RUSS a short form of Cyrus, Ruskin, Russell

Image: Russ is pictured as a fun, spritely, friendly, and easygoing guy with a sparkling wit and curly red hair.

Famous Russ: actor/dancer Russ (*Tom Thumb*) Tamblyn

RUSSELL (French) "red-haired, fox-colored"

Image: Most people describe Russell as a self-centered, spoiled brat who is hyper and unreliable. Some, though, describe Russell as quiet, honest, and considerate.

Famous Russells: columnist Russell Baker; playwright Russel (*The Sound of Music*) Crouse

RUSTY (French) "redhead"; a short form of Russell

Image: A redhead? You bet! Rusty is pictured as a red-headed, freckle-faced young country boy who is happy, loyal, and a bit mischievous. Rusty is also pictured as a happy, loyal, and mischievous Irish setter.

Famous Rustys: Rusty Jones rustproofing; Rusty on TV's "The Adventures of Rin-Tin-Tin"

RYAN (Irish Gaelic) "little king"

Image: Ryan is described as a strong, active man who is extremely good-looking, though shy, like Ryan O'Neal.

Famous Ryans: actors Ryan (*Love Story*) O'Neal, Robert (*Billy Budd*) Ryan; baseball's Nolan Ryan

SAL a short form of Salvatore

Image: The name Sal has two different images: a short, curly-haired, dark Italian kid who is a greasy, street-smart tough or a big, stocky blue-collar man who is fun loving and easygoing.

Famous Sals: actors Sal (*Rebel Without a Cause*) Mineo, Sal ("Soap") Viscuso; baseball's Sal Bando, Sal (The Barber) Maglie; the song "My Gal Sal"

SALVATORE, Salvador
(Italian) "savior"

Image: Most people think of Salvatore as a good-looking, dark-haired Italian man who is talented, charming, kind, strong, and family oriented.

Famous Salvatores: painters Salvator Rosa, Salvador Dali; Chile's former President Salvador Allende

SAM a short form of Samson, Samuel

Image: Sam is described as strong, gentle, loyal, down-to-earth, and one heck of a good friend.

Famous Sams: Uncle Sam; newscaster Sam Donaldson; fictional detective Sam Spade; TV's Sam ("Cheers") Malone; actor/playwright Sam (*Fool for Love*) Shepard; comedian Sam

Levenson; former senator Sam Rayburn; the "Son of Sam" murders; golfer Sam Snead

SAMMY a short form of Samson, Samuel

Image: Sammy's image comes straight from Sammy Davis, Jr. People imagine Sammy as a thin black entertainer who is funny and versatile.

Famous Sammys: entertainer Sammy Davis, Jr.; TV's Sammy Jo ("Dynasty") Carrington; Budd Schulberg's novel *What Makes Sammy Run?*; football's Sammy Baugh

SAMSON (Hebrew) "like the sun"

Image: Samson is described as a lovable, long-haired strongman with a weakness for women, like the biblical hero of the same name.

Famous Samson: the biblical Samson, betrayed by Delilah

SAMUEL (Hebrew) "heard or asked of God"

Image: Samuel is pictured as a strong, capable, intelligent man who is rather withdrawn.

Famous Samuels: the biblical prophet Samuel; novelist/humorist Samuel (Mark Twain) Clemens; movie mogul Samuel (M.G.M.) Goldwyn; Revolutionary leader Samuel Adams; composer Samuel Barber; labor leader Samuel Gompers

SANFORD (Old English) "from the sandy river crossing"

Image: Thanks to TV's Fred Sanford, people picture Sanford as an older black man who is poor, easygoing, and very funny.

Famous Sanford: TV's "Sanford and Son"

SAUL (Hebrew) "asked for"

Image: Thanks to the biblical Saul, people describe Saul as an earnest, religious man who would make a poor ruler.

Famous Sauls: the biblical Saul, King of Israel; novelist Saul (*Seize the Day*) Bellow; artist Saul Steinberg; urban activist Saul Alinsky

SCOTT (Old English) "Scotsman"

Image: Most people picture Scott as a good guy who is tall, good-looking, bright, easygoing, friendly, and nice. Some, though, think Scott is a conceited brat.

Famous Scotts: actors George C. (*Patton*) Scott, Scott ("Charles in Charge") Baio, Scott (*Return to Horror High*) Jacoby; astronaut Scott Carpenter; composer Scott (*The Entertainer*) Joplin; novelists F. Scott (*The Great Gatsby*) Fitzgerald, Sir Walter (*Ivanhoe*) Scott; nineteenth-century slave Dred Scott

SEAN an Irish form of John
(see also Shaun)

Image: People think of Sean as either a small, moody loner, like Sean Penn, or a good-looking, adventurous, upper-class British sophisticate, like Sean Connery.

Famous Seans: actors Sean (*James Bond*) Connery, Sean (*Fast Times at Ridgemont High*) Penn; actress Sean (*Wall Street*) Young; Irish diplomat Sean MacBride

SEBASTIAN (Latin) "venerated, majestic"

Image: People picture Sebastian as a big, highly intelligent man who is polite and trustworthy.

Famous Sebastians: Saint Sebastian, third-century martyr; actor Sebastian ("Family Affair") Cabot; English runner Sebastian Coe; Sebastian in Shakespeare's plays *Twelfth Night*, *The Tempest*; Sebastian (*Brideshead Revisited*) Flyte

SETH (Hebrew)
"substitute, appointed"

Image: Seth is viewed as a strong, quiet farm boy or outdoorsman who is intelligent, hardworking, and reliable.

Famous Seths: the biblical Seth, Adam and Eve's son; clockmaker Seth Thomas; inventor Seth Boyden; TV's Major Seth ("Wagon Train") Adams

SEYMOUR (Old French) "from Saint Maur"

Image: Seymour is pictured as an unconventional genius or artist who is quiet, shy, and outlandish.

Famous Seymours: computer designer Seymour Cray; actress Jane (*The Four Feathers*) Seymour

SHANE an Irish form of John
(through Sean)

Image: Thanks to the novel *Shane*, people describe Shane as a handsome, quiet, manly cowboy who prefers to go it alone.

Famous Shanes: Jack Schaefer's novel *Shane*; actor Shane ("High Mountain Rangers") Conrad

SHAUN, Shawn Irish forms of John; forms of Sean (see also Sean)

Image: Shawn is pictured as a good-looking young man who is playful, popular, and nice.

Famous Shauns: singer/actor Shaun ("The Hardy Boys") Cassidy; Shaun the Postman in James Joyce's novel *Finnegan's Wake*; choreographer Ted Shawn; basketball's Shawn Kemp; comic actor Dick (*The Producers*) Shawn

SHELDON (Old English) "from the farm on the ledge"

Image: Sheldon strikes many people as a good name for an awkward, introverted, bright nerd who is a good-looking, overdressed mama's boy.

Famous Sheldons: novelist Sidney (*The Other Side of Midnight*) Sheldon; TV producer Sheldon ("The Andy Griffith Show") Leonard

SHERLOCK (Old English) "fair-haired"

Image: Sherlock's image comes straight from the world's most famous detective. Sherlock is pictured as a tall, thin man who is curious, perceptive, intelligent, and confident.

Famous Sherlocks: fictional detective Sherlock Holmes; TV's Sherlock ("Sesame Street") Hemlock

SHERMAN (Old English) "shearer"

Image: Most people describe Sherman as an elderly, pudgy, bespectacled man who is smart but lacks common sense. Some, though, say Sherman is a tough fighter and stern authoritarian, like General William Tecumseh Sherman.

Famous Shermans: TV's Colonel Sherman ("M*A*S*H") Potter; General William Tecumseh Sherman; Sherman tanks; actor Sherman ("The Jeffersons") Hemsley

SHERWIN (Middle English) "swift runner"

Image: People consider Sherwin as a name for a great military leader — powerful, wealthy, and heroic.

Famous Sherwin: Sherwin-Williams paint

SHERWOOD (Old English) "from the bright forest"

Image: Sherwood is pictured as either a strong, tall, bold, and dashing man of action, like Robin Hood, or as a conceited British stuffed shirt.

Famous Sherwood: novelist Sherwood (*Winesburg, Ohio*) Anderson

SID a short form of Sidney

Image: Sid is described as lovable and funny, like comedian Sid Caeser.

Famous Sids: entertainer Sid ("Your Show of Shows") Caesar; punk rocker Sid Vicious of the Sex Pistols; TV producer Sid ("Donny and Marie") Krofft

SIDNEY (Old French) "from Saint Denis"

Image: The name Sidney calls to mind a capable professional who is handsome and good hearted. Some, though, think Sidney is unconventional or unpredictable.

Famous Sidneys: actors Sydney (*The Maltese Falcon*) Greenstreet, Sidney (*Guess Who's Coming to Dinner*) Poitier; directors Sydney (*Tootsie*) Pollack, Sidney (*Serpico*) Lumet; novelist Sidney (*The Other Side of Midnight*) Sheldon; the city of Sydney, Australia; poet Sir Philip Sidney; TV's Dr. Sidney ("M*A*S*H") Freedman; Sydney Biddle (The Mayflower Madam) Barrows

SIEGFRIED (Old German) "victorious peace"

Image: Siegfried is pictured as a wiry, old German composer, psychologist, or scientist who is intelligent, introverted, and eccentric. Siegfried is also imagined as a German Shepherd.

Famous Siegfrieds: Siegfried in the German epic *Nibelungenlied*; German novelist Siegfried (*The Survivor*) Lenz; poet Siegfried Sassoon; TV's Conrad ("Get Smart") Siegfried; Siegfried (*All Creatures Great and Small*) Farnon; Wagner's opera *Siegfried*

SIGMUND (Old German) "victorious protector"

Image: Thanks to Sigmund Freud, Sigmund is pictured as a gray-haired, highly intelligent psychoanalist.

Famous Sigmunds: psychoanalyst Sigmund Freud; composer Sigmund ("The Student Prince") Romberg; TV's "Sigmund and the Sea Monsters"

SILAS (Latin) "Silvanus (the forest god)"

Image: People say Silas is an old farmer who is quiet, hardworking, old-fashioned, and miserly.

Famous Silases: George Eliot's novel *Silas Marner*; William Dean Howells's novel *The Rise of Silas Lapham*; basketball's Paul Silas

SIMON (Hebrew) "he who hears"

Image: Simon is described as a strong, well-built man who is either quiet and simple, like Simple Simon, or intelligent and creative, like Paul Simon or Neil Simon.

Famous Simons: the biblical disciple Simon; Simon (*Uncle Tom's Cabin*) Legree; playwright Neil (*Plaza Suite*) Simon; musician Paul ("Bridge Over Troubled Water") Simon; TV's "Simon & Simon"; the nursery rhyme "Simple Simon"; the game Simon Says; TV's Simon ("The Saint") Templar

SINCLAIR (Old French) "from Saint Clair"

Image: Most people picture Sinclair as a small-town writer who is sensitive, warm, and entertaining.

Famous Sinclairs: novelists Sinclair (*Arrowsmith*) Lewis, Upton (*The Jungle*) Sinclair; Sinclair gas stations

SKIP (Scandinavian) "shipmaster"

Image: People describe Skip as either a young kid who is happy and likable or a rich prep-school snob.

SOL a short form of Solomon

Image: Sol is pictured as a chubby Jewish man who is either a quiet, balding accountant or a greasy-haired car salesman.

Famous Sols: the mythological sun god Sol; promoter Sol Hurok

SOLOMON (Hebrew) "peaceful"

Image: The name Solomon calls to mind a short, bald rabbi or prophet who is strong, gentle, and wise.

Famous Solomons: the biblical Solomon, king of Israel; the nursery rhyme "Solomon Grundy"; football's Jesse Solomon, Fred Solomon; investment bankers Salomon Brothers

SONNY (American) "son"

Image: People think of Sonny as a short, street-smart, airheaded singer who will never grow up.

Famous Sonnys: singer Sonny Bono; jazz saxophonist Sonny Rollins; TV's Sonny ("Miami Vice") Crockett; boxer Sonny Liston; football's Sonny Jurgensen; country musician Sonny Osbourne

SPARKY (American) "sparkling"

Image: Sparky is described as full of energy — quick, spunky, and lots of fun.

Famous Sparkys: baseball's Sparky Anderson, Sparky Lyle; former senator Spark Matsunaga

SPENCER (Middle English) "dispenser of provisions"

Image: Spencer's image comes primarily from Spencer Tracy. People imagine Spencer as a gray-hairer older man who has a great sense of humor.

Famous Spencers: actor Spencer (*Inherit the Wind*) Tracy; basketball's Spencer Haywood; TV's "Spenser: For Hire"; poet Edmund (*The Faerie Queene*) Spenser

SPIKE (Middle English) "a long, heavy nail"

Image: Spike is pictured as an independent, dirty, street-wise tough who might be a bully or a boxer. Some people also think Spike is a great name for a dog.

Famous Spikes: drummer Spike Jones; actor/director Spike (*Do the Right Thing*) Lee

STAN a short form of names containing "stan"

Image: The name Stan has two clear images: a big, strong, steady blue-collar guy, like Stan Musial, or a short, thin, wimpy comedian, like Stan Laurel.

Famous Stans: comic actor Stan Laurel; baseball's Stan (The Man) Musial; tennis's Stan Smith; hockey's Stan Mikita

STANFORD (Old English) "from the rocky ford"

Image: The name Stanford is associated with education because of Stanford University. People think Stanford is a wealthy, collegiate, formal, upper-class intellectual.

Famous Stanfords: Stanford University; biochemist Stanford Moore

STANLEY (Old English) "from the rocky meadow"

Image: The name Stanley has two different images: a quiet, older blue-collar laborer or a skinny, goofy nerd.

Famous Stanleys: explorer Stanley Livingston; wrestling commissioner Stanley Blackburn; Stanley (*A Streetcar Named Desire*) Kowalski; TV's Stanley ("Three's Company") Roper; the Stanley steamer car

STEFAN, Stephane forms of Stephen

Image: Thanks to tennis star Stefan Edberg, people picture Stefan as a strong, great-looking Scandinavian man who is wealthy and cool.

Famous Stefans: tennis's Stefan Edberg; jazz violinist Stephane Grapelli

STEPHEN (Greek) "crown" (see also Steven)

Image: Most people think of Stephen as a strong, active professional who is wealthy, devoted, and proper. Some, though, think Stephen is a tall, thin writer.

Famous Stephens: novelists Stephen (*Carrie*) King, Stephen (*The Red Badge of Courage*) Crane; actor Stephen (*Jumbo*) Boyd; politician Stephen Douglas; composers Stephen (*West Side Story*) Sondheim, Stephen ("Old Folks at Home") Foster; Saint Stephen, patron saint of Hungary

STERLING (Old English) "valuable"

Image: Sterling strikes people as a good name for a silver-haired, dapper old aristocrat who is wealthy, stuffy, mannerly, and a little strange.

Famous Sterlings: actors Sterling ("The Lone Ranger") Hayden, Sterling (*My Fair Lady*) Holloway; sterling silver; auto racer Sterling Moss

STEVE a short form of Stephen, Steven

Image: People think of Steve as a good guy who is strong, good-looking, humorous, friendly, and lots of fun.

Famous Steves: comic actor Steve (*All of Me*) Martin; TV host Steve Allen; baseball's Steve Carlton, Steve Garvey, Steve Lombardozzi; singer Steve Lawrence; actor Steve (*Bullitt*) McQueen; hockey's Steve Yzerman; football's Steve Largent; rock musician Steve Winwood

STEVEN a form of Stephen (see also Stephen)

Image: Steven is described as a tall, muscular, good-looking man who is quiet, mild mannered, and nice.

Famous Stevens: director Steven (*E.T. — The Extra-Terrestrial*) Spielberg; TV's Steven ("Family Ties") Keaton

STEVIE a short form of Stephen, Steven

    Image: Stevie is pictured as either a cute, outgoing tomboy or a young mama's boy who is shy and withdrawn.

    Famous Stevies: singers Stevie ("Don't You Worry 'Bout a Thing") Wonder, Stevie Nicks of Fleetwood Mac, Stevie Ray Vaughan

STEWART, Stuart (Old English) "caretaker, steward"

    Image: The name Stewart has two very different images: a cool, virile hotshot or an intelligent, articulate, well-bred snob.

    Famous Stewarts: actors Stewart (*The Prisoner of Zenda*) Granger, Jimmy (*It's a Wonderful Life*) Stewart, Stuart (*Those Magnificent Men in Their Flying Machines*) Whitman; former Justice Potter Stewart; singer Rod ("Maggie May") Stewart; auto racer Jackie Stuart

STU a short form of Stuart

    Image: Stu is described as a short, dumpy, out-of-shape wimp who is worldly but boring.

    Famous Stu: football's Stu Voight

STUART see Stewart

SVEN (Scandinavian) "youth"

    Image: Sven is pictured as a big, muscular, blond-haired, blue-eyed Scandinavian man with a good sense of humor.

    Famous Svens: basketball's Sven Nater; badminton's Sven Anderson

SYLVESTER (Latin) "from the woods"

    Image: Most people think of Sylvester as one of Sylvester Stallone's characters: good-looking, muscular, spirited, and dumb. Some, though, think of Sylvester as a pampered prince.

    Famous Sylvesters: actor Sylvester (*Rocky*) Stallone; Sylvester the cartoon cat

TAB (Middle English) "drummer"

    Image: People think of Tab as a handsome blond who is an intelligent outdoorsman.

    Famous Tabs: actor Tab Hunter; Tab soda

TAD a Polish short form of Thaddeus (through Taddeusz)

    Image: The name Tad has two different images: a tall, stuck-up brat right out of a soap opera or a small boy who is quiet, well mannered, and intelligent.

    Famous Tads: playwright Tad Mosel; Tad Lincoln, Abraham Lincoln's son; Tad on TV's "All My Children"

TED a short form of names beginning with "Ed" or "Ted"

    Image: Ted is described as a businesslike man of medium build who is charming and good-natured.

    Famous Teds: cable TV tycoon Ted Turner; actors Ted ("Cheers") Danson, Ted ("The Mary Tyler Moore Show") Knight; newscaster Ted Koppel; executed murderer Ted Bundy; Senator Ted Kennedy; baseball's Ted Williams

TEDDY a form of Ted

    Image: The name Teddy has two distinct images: a tough, strong outdoorsman, like Teddy Roosevelt, or a cute, pudgy, and very cuddly bear.

    Famous Teddys: President Teddy Roosevelt; Senator Teddy Kennedy; singer Teddy Pendergrass; teddy bears

TERENCE (Latin) "smooth"

    Image: The name Terence calls to mind either a lively, thin, tall black man or a dark-haired, mild-mannered wimp.

    Famous Terences: the Roman playwright Terence; singer Terence Trent D'Arby; actor Terence (*Billy Budd*) Stamp

TERRY a short form of Terence

    Image: Terry is pictured as a fun-loving guy who is athletic, friendly, and lots of laughs.

    Famous Terrys: football's Terry Bradshaw; Terry Moore, Doris Day's son; actor Terry (*I'm All Right, Jack*) Thomas;

humor writer Terry (*Candy*) Southern; "Terry and the Pirates" comics

THAD a short form of Thaddeus

    Image: People picture Thad as either a big-boned, strong, handsome college student or as a clumsy, scatter-brained wimp.

    Famous Thads: jazz cornetist Thad Jones; Senator Thad Cochran

THADDEUS (Greek) "courageous"; (Latin) "pleasure"

    Image: People describe Thaddeus as a handsome, preppy, and distinguished tycoon-in-training with a pretentious three-piece suit and gold Rolex.

    Famous Thaddeuses: the biblical disciple Thaddeus; politician Thaddeus Stevens

THEO a short form of names beginning with "Theo"

    Image: Most people picture Theo as TV's Theo Huxtable — a good-looking black man. Some, though, see Theo as a small, quiet bookworm.

    Famous Theos: TV's Theo ("The Cosby Show") Huxtable, Theo ("Kojak") Kojak

THEODORE (Greek) "gift of God"

    Image: The name Theodore has two radically different images: a strong presidential man who is hardheaded and honest, like Theodore Roosevelt, or a chubby, funny little kid, like Theodore Cleaver.

Famous Theodores: TV's Theodore ("Leave It to Beaver") Cleaver; children's story writer Theodore (Dr. Seuss) Geisel; President Theodore Roosevelt; folk singer/actor Theodore (*The African Queen*) Bikel; novelist Theodore (*Sister Carrie*) Dreiser

THOMAS (Aramaic-Hebrew) "twin"

Image: Thomas is described as an intelligent, reliable, well-educated man with a quiet wit.

Famous Thomases: the biblical disciple "Doubting" Thomas; inventor Thomas Edison; President Thomas Jefferson; novelists Thomas (*Death in Venice*) Mann, Thomas (*The Return of the Native*) Hardy; Archbishop of Canterbury Saint Thomas à Becket; theologian Saint Thomas (*Summa Theologia*) Aquinas; TV's Thomas ("Magnum, P.I.") Magnum

THOR (Scandinavian) "thunder"

Image: Thor is regarded as the ultimate Viking — a strong, muscular man who is either hurling thunderbolts or acting as a ruthless, ambitious executive.

Famous Thors: the mythological Thor, Norse god of thunder; adventurer Thor (*Kontiki*) Heyerdahl; Thor in "Marvel Family" comics

THORNTON (Old English) "from the thorny farm"

Image: People picture Thornton as a British businessman, attorney, or writer who is pompous, upstanding, and dull.

Famous Thornton: playwright Thornton (*Our Town*) Wilder

TIM a short form of Timothy

Image: People describe Tim as a small, thin man who is intelligent, easygoing, and funny.

Famous Tims: actors Tim ("McHale's Navy") Conway, Tim (*Bull Durham*) Robbins; singer Tiny ("Tiptoe through the Tulips") Tim; Tiny (*A Christmas Carol*) Tim; football's Tim Brown; hockey's Tim Kerr

TIMMY a short form of Tim

Image: People think of Timmy as an unpleasant little boy who is either a sneaky, spoiled brat or a skinny sissy.

Famous Timmy: TV's Timmy ("Lassie") Martin

TIMOTHY (Greek) "honoring God"

Image: Most people imagine Timothy as a cute little kid who is shy and sweet. Some are reminded of Timothy Leary — intelligent, weird, and lost in a drug-induced haze.

Famous Timothys: drug guru Timothy Leary; the biblical Timothy, Paul's friend; actors Timothy (*East of Eden*) Bottoms, Timothy (*Ordinary People*) Hutton

TOBY (Hebrew) "the Lord is good"; a short form of Tobias

Image: Toby is pictured as an innocent young boy with shaggy blond hair and blue eyes.

Famous Tobys: the Walt Disney movie *Toby Tyler*; Sir Toby (*Twelfth Night*) Belch; Uncle (*Tristram Shandy*) Toby; Toby on TV's "Mayberry, R.F.D."

TODD (Middle English) "fox"

Image: Todd is perceived as a regular guy who is big, easygoing, hardworking, and nice.

Famous Todds: singer Todd Rundgren; actor Todd ("Diff'rent Strokes") Bridges; TV's Tod ("Route 66") Stiles; producer Mike Todd

TOM a short form of Thomas

Image: Tom is viewed as an all-American, average guy who can fit in anywhere: confident, likable, and down-to-earth.

Famous Toms: actors Tom (*Top Gun*) Cruise, Tom (*Big*) Hanks, Tom (*The Big Chill*) Berenger, Tom ("Magnum, P.I.") Selleck; the nursery rhyme "Tom, Tom, the Piper's Son"; the children's story of Tom Thumb; Harriet Beecher Stowe's novel *Uncle Tom's Cabin*; Mark Twain's novel *The Adventures of Tom Sawyer*; basketball's Tom Chambers; singer Tom ("What's New, Pussycat?") Jones; radio talk show host Tom Snyder

TOMMY a short form of Thomas

Image: Tommy is viewed as the boy-next-door — a good-looking, little blond mama's boy.

Famous Tommys: bandleader Tommy Dorsey; comedian Tommy Smothers; choreographer Tommy Tune; The Who's rock opera *Tommy*; baseball's Tommy Lasorda; football's Tommy Kramer

TONY a short form of Anthony

Image: People think of Tony as a friendly, well-built athlete who is levelheaded and able to take care of himself.

Famous Tonys: actors Tony (*Gentlemen Prefer Blondes*) Curtis, Tony ("Who's the Boss?") Danza; Tony the Frosted Flakes Tiger; the Tony awards; football's Tony Dorsett; skier Toni Sailer; boxer Tony Zale

TRAVIS (Old French) "at the crossroads"

Image: Travis is described as a good-looking cowboy or drifter who cannot be trusted.

Famous Travises: country singer Randy Travis; fictional detective Travis McGee; TV's Andy ("WKRP in Cincinnati") Travis

TRENT (Latin) "torrent"

Image: Trent is described as either a proud, upper-crust Ivy League school graduate or a straight-shooting athlete.

Famous Trents: basketball's Trent Tucker; singer Terence Trent D'Arby; Senator Trent Lott

TREVOR (Irish Gaelic) "prudent"

Image: People picture Trevor as a British man who is either a strong, dependable, middle-of-the-road bloke or a tall, thin, wealthy, upper-crust snob.

Famous Trevors: actor Trevor (*Brief Encounter*) Howard; boxer Trevor Berbick

TROY (Irish Gaelic) "foot soldier"

Image: Troy is described as either a short, muscular, inner-city bully or a tall, cool blond who is outgoing and fun.

Famous Troys: actor Troy (*Seizure*) Donahue; the ancient city of Troy

TRUMAN (Old English) "faithful man"

Image: People think of Truman as a small, heavyset man who is principled and distinguished — a writer or wealthy professional, perhaps.

Famous Trumans: President Harry S Truman; novelist Truman (*Breakfast at Tiffany's*) Capote; football's Trumaine Johnson

TY a short form of names beginning with "Ty"

Image: Ty is pictured as either a daring, old-fashioned baseball player or a sexy ladies' man.

Famous Tys: baseball's Ty Cobb; actor Ty ("Bronco") Hardin

TYLER (Old English) "maker of tiles"

Image: The name Tyler has two images: a wealthy, arrogant preppy or a fat, friendly, carefree outdoorsman.

Famous Tylers: President John Tyler; the Walt Disney movie *Toby Tyler*; football's Wendell Tyler

TYRONE (Greek) "sovereign"; (Irish Gaelic) "land of Owen"

Image: People picture Tyrone as a strong, good-looking black man who is confident, energetic, and proper.

Famous Tyrones: actor Tyrone (*Witness for the Prosecution*) Power; theater director Tyrone Guthrie

ULYSSES (Latin-Greek) "Odysseus, wrathful"

Image: Thanks to President Ulysses S. Grant, people think of Ulysses as a strong, brave military man who is a powerful leader.

Famous Ulysses: Ulysses in Homer's epic *The Odyssey*; President Ulysses S. Grant; James Joyce's novel *Ulysses*

VAN (Dutch) "of noble descent"; a short form of many Dutch surnames

Image: Of noble descent, indeed! People picture Van as a tall, strong blond who is outgoing, self-assured, and decidedly upper-class.

Famous Vans: pianist Van Cliburn; actors Van (*Madame Bovary*) Heflin, Van (*The Caine Mutiny*) Johnson; rock singer Van ("Moondance") Morrison

VANCE (Middle English) "thresher"

Image: Vance is described as a handsome, tanned blond who is freewheeling and rich.

Famous Vances: author Vance (*The Hidden Persuaders*) Packard; diplomat Cyrus Vance

VAUGHN, Vaughan (Welsh) "small"

Image: Vaughn is viewed as a tall, suave, wealthy, and sophisticated man — an entertainer or spy, perhaps.

Famous Vaughns: singers Vaughn Monroe, Stevie Ray Vaughan, Sarah Vaughan; actor Robert ("The Man from U.N.C.L.E.") Vaughn; composer Ralph Vaughn Williams

VERN a short form of Vernon

Image: The name Vern has two different images: a dull, unattractive, nerdy older man or a handsome, dark-haired man who is bold, aggressive, and overwhelming.

Famous Verns: novelist Jules (*Twenty Thousand Leagues Under the Sea*) Verne; Vern of "Hey Vern" TV commercial/movie fame; basketball's Vern Fleming

VERNON (Latin) "springlike, youthful"

Image: The name Vernon calls to mind either a cute, happy, and outgoing guy or a dull, weird nerd.

Famous Vernons: Mount Vernon, George Washington's home; dancer Vernon Castle; baseball's Mickey Vernon

VIC a short form of Victor

Image: Vic is described as a sneaky, bespectacled old greaseball with underworld connections — a drug dealer or Hell's Angel, perhaps.

Famous Vics: singer Vic Damone; actor Vic ("Alice") Tayback

VICTOR (Latin) "conqueror"

Image: Victor is pictured as a real charmer — a handsome, dark-haired gentleman who is talented, sexy, and smooth.

Famous Victors: musical comedian Victor Borge; actor Victor (*Samson and Delilah*) Mature; novelist Victor (*Les*

Miserables) Hugo; composer
Victor ("Naughty Marietta")
Herbert; TV's Victor ("L.A.
Law") Sifuentes

VINCENT (Latin) "conquering"

Image: Most people think of
Vincent as a quiet, artistic man
who is serious and under-
standing. Some, though, see
Vincent as sinister and evil, like
a Vincent Price character.

Famous Vincents: actors
Vincent (*Moonstruck*)
Gardenia, Vincent (*The Pit
and the Pendulum*) Price,
Jan-Michael (*Hooper*) Vincent;
painter Vincent Van Gogh;
Saint Vincent de Paul

VINNY, Vinnie short forms of Vincent

Image: Vinny is described as a
short, dark-haired Italian man
who, like TV's Vinnie Barbarino,
is cocky and very funny.

Famous Vinnys: football's
Vinny Testaverde; TV's Vinnie
("Welcome Back, Kotter")
Barbarino, Vinnie ("Wiseguy")
Terranova

VIRGIL (Latin) "rod or staff bearer"

Image: The name Virgil has
two different images: a wimpy,
redheaded mama's boy or an
elder statesman or executive
who is easygoing and
intelligent.

Famous Virgils: the Roman
poet, Virgil; composer Virgil
Thomson; astronaut Virgil
(Gus) Grissom; Virgil Earp,
Wyatt's brother

VITO (Latin) "alive"

Image: Vito is viewed as the
ultimate Godfather — a
heavyset Italian gangster who
is powerful, tough, and mean.

Famous Vito: syndicate leader
Vito Genovese; Vito (*The
Godfather*) Corleone

VLADIMIR (Slavic) "powerful prince"

Image: Most people picture
Vladimir as a serious Russian
man who is a dancer, scientist,
or musician, perhaps. To
some, though, Vladimir is
the Russian equivalent of
the common American
name "Joe."

Famous Vladimirs: pianists
Vladimir Horowitz, Vladimir
Ashkenazy; novelist Vladimir
(*Lolita*) Nabokov; Russia's
ruler Vladimir the Great

WADE (Old English) "advancer, from the river crossing"

Image: Wade is described
as one cool dude — a cute,
strong all-American who
walks on the wild side.

Famous Wades: baseball's
Wade Boggs; football's Wade
Wilson; actor Wayde ("Colt
.45") Preston

WALDO (Old German) "ruler";
a short form of Oswald, Waldemer

Image: The name Waldo has two different images: a big, ham-handed, neighborly buffoon or a quiet, studious nerd.

Famous Waldos: the movie *The Great Waldo Pepper*; philosopher/poet Ralph Waldo Emerson; the French heretic Waldo; *Where's Waldo?* children's books

WALKER (Old English) "thickener of cloth, fuller"

Image: Walker is described as either a serious, wise, and proper older businessman or a sneaky spy.

Famous Walkers: actor Robert (*Batman*) Walker; novelist Walker (*The Moviegoer*) Percy; photographer Walker Evans; football's Herschel Walker; Johnny Walker scotch; Hiram Walker whiskey; John Walker, double agent for the Soviets

WALLACE (Old English) "Welshman"

Image: Wallace is pictured as a big elderly man who is either mild mannered and boring or headstrong and boisterous.

Famous Wallaces: actors Wallace (*Treasure Island*) Beery, Wallace (*My Dinner with André*) Shawn; poet Wallace Stevens; novelists Irving (*The Seven Minutes*) Wallace, Lew (*Ben-Hur*) Wallace; Wallis Warfield Simpson, Duchess of Windsor; Scottish patriot William Wallace; TV reporter Mike Wallace; architect Wallace K. Harrison

WALLY a short form of names beginning with "Wal"

Image: Two different descriptions of Wally come to mind: a clean-cut teenager who is friendly and very jovial, like Wally Cleaver, or a mild-mannered, henpecked, timid mouse, like Wally Cox.

Famous Wallys: TV's Wally ("Leave It to Beaver") Cleaver; actor Wally ("Mr. Peepers") Cox

WALT a short form of Walter

Image: Walt is described as a nice older gentleman who is creative and thoughtful.

Famous Walts: cartoon/movie director/mogul Walt Disney; poet Walt ("Song of Myself") Whitman; cartoonist Walt ("Pogo") Kelly; artist Walt Kuhn; basketball's Walt Bellamy

WALTER (Old German) "powerful warrior"

Image: People think of Walter as a tall, smart man who is serious, authoritative, and solid, like Walter Cronkite.

Famous Walters: newscasters Walter Cronkite, Walter Winchell; actors Walter ("The Real McCoys") Brennan, Walter (*The Odd Couple*) Matthau; former vice president Walter Mondale; football's Walter Payton; baseball's Walter Johnson; navigator Sir Walter Raleigh; economist Walter Heller; poet Walter de la Mare

WARD (Old English) "guardian"

Image: TV dad Ward Cleaver is the dominant image for this name — a tall, fatherly man who is easygoing, caring, and wise.

Famous Wards: TV's Ward ("Leave It to Beaver") Cleaver; actor Ward ("Wagon Train") Bond; poet Julia Ward Howe

WARREN (Old German) "defender"

Image: The name Warren has two different images: a handsome, shifty tough guy who is always in trouble or a hardworking accountant who is bright and boring.

Famous Warrens: actor Warren (*Bonnie and Clyde*) Beatty; President Warren G. Harding; football's Warren Moon; former Chief Justice Warren Burger; rock musician Warren Zevon

WAYLAND, Waylon
(Old English) "from the land by the road"

Image: Most people picture Wayland as an old-fashioned farmer who likes to sing, fish, and tell jokes. Some people also think Wayland is stubborn or annoying.

Famous Waylands: Wayland, the invisible blacksmith of English legend; country singer Waylon Jennings; ventriloquist Wayland Flowers

WAYNE (Old English) "wagoner"; a short form of Wainwright

Image: Most people picture Wayne as a big, rugged cow-poke who is outgoing and outdoorsy, like John Wayne. Some, though, think Wayne is a weird, whiny nerd.

Famous Waynes: hockey's Wayne Gretzky; singer Wayne Newton; actors John (*Big Jake*) Wayne, Wayne ("M*A*S*H") Rogers; crime-fighter Bruce ("Batman") Wayne

WENDELL (Old German) "wanderer"

Image: People picture Wendell as either a smart, wimpy nerd or a rich, ostentatious snob.

Famous Wendells: lawyer Oliver Wendell Holmes; former vice president Wendell Wilkie; former senators Wendell Anderson, Wendell Ford; football's Wendell Tyler

WERNER (Old German) "armed defender"; a German form of Warner

Image: Werner is described as a yuppie of German descent who is wealthy, poised, and self-important.

Famous Werners: comic actor Werner ("Hogan's Heroes") Klemperer; rocket scientist Wernher Von Braun; est guru Werner Erhard

WES a short form of names beginning with "Wes"

Image: People think of Wes as an athletic cowboy who is a friendly, easygoing practical joker.

Famous Weses: jazz guitarist Wes Montgomery; basketball's Wes Unseld

WESLEY (Old English) "from the western meadow"

Image: The name Wesley has two different images: a wimpy, spoiled, sweet, snobby sissy or a clever, young professional with a mischievous streak.

Famous Wesleys: John Wesley, founder of Methodism; football's Wesley Walker; TV's Wesley ("Star Trek: The Next Generation") Crusher; Wesley in the movie *The Princess Bride*

WHITNEY (Old English) "from the white island, from fair water"

Image: People picture Whitney as a rich, conservative, southern gentleman who is a well-dressed snob.

Famous Whitneys: civil-rights leader Whitney Young; singer Whitney Houston; inventor Eli Whitney

WILBUR a German form of Gilbert

Image: Wilbur is described as a nerdy introvert who is curious, but a bit slow.

Famous Wilburs: aviator Wilbur Wright; Wilbur the Pig in E.B. White's children's story *Charlotte's Web*; TV's Wilbur ("Mr. Ed") Post; former secretary of Health, Education, and Welfare Wilbur Cohen

WILFRED, Wilford (Old German) "resolute and peaceful"

Image: People think of Wilfred as a gray-haired, bespectacled older man who is either a clumsy wallflower; a stuffy, distinguished gentleman; or a helpful butler.

Famous Wilfreds: Saint Wilfrid, patron saint of bakers; actors Wilfrid (*Let's Make Love*) Hyde White, Wilford (*Cocoon*) Brimley

WILL a short form of names beginning with "Will"

Image: Will is described as a thin, good-looking young blond who is shy, nice, and articulate — a writer, perhaps. Some, though, see Will as a kindly grandfather.

Famous Wills: humorist Will Rogers; columnist George Will; Robin Hood's companion Will Scarlet; TV's Will ("Lost in Space") Robinson; actor Will ("The Waltons") Geer

WILLARD (Old German) "resolutely brave"

Image: Most people picture Willard as an overweight, balding farmer or weatherman who is an honest hardworker. Willard reminds some people of rats, thanks to the movie *Willard*.

Famous Willards: TV weatherman Willard ("The Today Show") Scott; the movie *Willard*; chemist Willard Libby

WILLIAM (Old German) "determined guardian"

Image: William is pictured as a tall, distinguished professional who is conservative, intelligent, serious, and very boring.

Famous Williams: William the Conqueror; Prince William of Orange; actors William ("Cannon") Conrad, William ("My Three Sons") Demerest, William (*Stalag 17*) Holden, William (*Body Heat*) Hurt, William ("Star Trek") Shatner; playwright William Shakespeare; Presidents William Taft, William Henry Harrison; legendary archer William Tell

WILLIE, Willy short forms of names beginning with "Will"

Image: People describe Willie as a short, skinny country boy who is friendly, good-natured, and musical, but also very dull.

Famous Willies: singer Willie ("On the Road Again") Nelson; the movie *Willy Wonka and the Chocolate Factory*; baseball's Willie Mays; track and field's Willie Davenport; football's Willie Gault

WINSLOW (Old English) "from the friend's hill"

Image: Most people think of Winslow as a wealthy older English aristocrat or professional who is either thoughtful and generous or naughty.

Famous Winslows: painter Winslow Homer; football's Kellen Winslow

WINSTON (Old English) "from the friendly town"

Image: The name Winston brings the commanding image of Sir Winston Churchill immediately to mind — a strong, serious, cigar-smoking British statesman.

Famous Winstons: Britain's former prime minister Sir Winston Churchill; jazz pianist George Winston; novelist Winston (*The Poldark Saga*) Graham

WINTHROP (Old English) "from the wine village"

Image: Winthrop is perceived as a stuffy, snobby, rich old Englishman.

Famous Winthrops: plutocrat Winthrop Rockefeller; Puritan John Winthrop

WOLFGANG (Old German) "advancing wolf"

Image: People describe Wolfgang as a brilliant German composer who is strong willed, emotional, and unhappy, like Wolfgang Amadeus Mozart.

Famous Wolfgangs: composer Wolfgang Amadeus Mozart; physicist Wolfgang Pauli

WOODROW (Old English) "from the passage in the woods"

Image: The name Woodrow has several different images: a poor black farmer with holes in his clothes; a frontiersman; or an uptight, three-piece-suited snob.

Famous Woodrow: President Woodrow Wilson

WOODY a short form of names containing "wood"

Image: Woody is described as shy, moody, and funny, like Woody Allen.

Famous Woodys: actor/director Woody (*Bananas*) Allen; football's Woody Hayes; comic actor Woody ("Cheers") Harrelson; folk singer Woody Guthrie; bandleader Woody Herman; "Woody Woodpecker" cartoons

WYATT (Old French)
"little warrior"

>**Image:** The name Wyatt calls to mind an old-fashioned cowboy or gunslinger, like Wyatt Earp.

>**Famous Wyatts:** Sheriff Wyatt Earp; Wyatt in the movie *Easy Rider*

YALE (Old English) "from the corner of the land"

>**Image:** Yale is described as a smart, preppy, collegiate, and handsome rich boy who would be right at home at the university that bears his name.

>**Famous Yales:** Yale University; Yale locks

YVES (Scandinavian) "archer"; a French form of Ivar

>**Image:** Most people picture Yves as rich, suave, continental, and debonair — a designer or playboy, perhaps.

>**Famous Yves:** actor Yves (*Let's Make Love*) Montand; designer Yves Saint Laurent; artist Yves Tanguy

ZACHARY (Hebrew) "Jehovah hath remembered"

>**Image:** Zachary is an old-fashioned name that calls to mind either a strong, rugged, resourceful explorer or a rich, self-centered, spoiled kid.

>**Famous Zacharys:** President Zachary Taylor; Zachary, son of comic actor Robin Williams; TV's Zachary ("Lost in Space") Smith

ZACK a short form of Zachariah, Zachary

>**Image:** Most people think of Zack as a young country boy who will grow up to be either a funny-looking hillbilly or a rugged mountain man.

ZANE an English form of John

>**Image:** Zane is described as either a rugged cowboy or a quiet man who writes macho Western novels, like Zane Grey.

>**Famous Zane:** Western novelist Zane Grey

ZEKE a short form of Ezekiel, Zachary

>**Image:** Zeke is described as a hairy hillbilly who is dirty, smelly, and dumb.

>**Famous Zeke:** football's Zeke Bratkowski